Somer Brodribb teaches feminist theory/politics and women's social and political thought at the University of Victoria, British Columbia. She has worked with the Yukon Indian Women's Association to establish an emergency shelter for Native and non-Native women, and as a Canadian contact for the Feminist International Network in Resistance to Reproductive and Genetic Engineering (FINRRAGE). She studied in the Feminist focus of the Ontario Institute for Studies in Education, University of Toronto where she was active in the Centre for Women's Studies. For nine years she has been associated with the journal, *Resources for Feminist Research*.

NOTHING MAT(T)ERS:

A Feminist Critique of Postmodernism

Somer Brodribb

Spinifex Press Pty Ltd,
504 Queensberry Street,
North Melbourne, Vic. 3051
Australia

First published by Spinifex Press, 1992

Typeset in 11/14 pt Times
        by Lorna Hendry, Melbourne
Production by Sylvana Scannapiego,
        Island Graphics, Melbourne
Made and Printed in Australia by Impact Pty
        Ltd.
Cover design: Liz Nicholson, Design BITE

National Library of Australia
Cataloguing-in-Publication entry:
CIP
  Brodribb, Somer, 1954–
  Nothing mat(t)ers: a feminist critique of
  postmodernism

  ISBN 1 875559 07 8

  1. Feminist criticism. 2. Postmodernism.
  3. Feminist theory. I Title.

305.4201

Contents

Acknowledgements

Many friends and colleagues contributed to this book through their support and encouragement. In particular, I would like to thank Suzanne Blaise, Pippa Brewster, Peggy Bristow, Gail Buckland, Annette Burfoot, Frieda Forman, Heather Guylar, Daphne Johnston, Julie Lee, Cath McNaughton, Heather McPherson, and everyone at *Resources for Feminist Research/Documentation sur la recherche féministe*.

This book began as a dissertation at the University of Toronto, and its genesis would not have been possible without the presence of Mary O'Brien and her words of substance. Warm thanks also to my committee of Madeline Grumet, Alkis Kontos, Angela Miles, Dorothy Smith and Jeri Wine.

Doctoral fellowships granted by the Social Sciences and Humanities Research Council of Canada are also gratefully acknowledged. I also want to acknowledge the support of the University of Victoria, British Columbia, and acknowledge its genuine support for this writing project. Thanks to Doris Lam and Laurel Barnes in particular.

Special thanks to Karen Ogden, Acting Dean, Faculty of Arts, University of Manitoba, and Keith Louise Fulton, Joint Chair of Women's Studies for the Prairies and Northwest Territories, who both saw me through interesting times at a university under investigation by the Manitoba Human Rights Commission for systemic discrimination against women. The Winnipeg S.D.B. Feminist Co-op provided an ideal research environment, and the Prairie fire and feminism of Chris Clark, Terry Gray, Margaret Clark and Simone Clark sustained me on an everyday basis. Thanks also to the students in my French Feminist Thought seminar.

Special thanks to Cindy Mallin of Added Touch for her skilful word-processing. Jane Rhodes of the Art Gallery of Ontario found the Greek vase at the right moment. Sylvia Bardon of the Department of Political Science, University of Victoria, provided valuable assistance with the index. I am grateful to Angela Miles for her comments on a preliminary version of the introduction, and to Jennifer Waelti-Walters who graciously helped with some of the translations.

For their fierce commitment to feminist writing I am grateful to Renate Klein, Janice Raymond, Gloria Bowles and Susan Hawthorne. Without their support, this book would not have been brought to light.

And I owe much to my family for their strength and resilience: Gwendoline Morgan, Mae Lamothe, Heather Mackey, Ann Brodribb, Meghan Athena McCusker. To my mother, Hilda Mackey, I owe the most.

Preface

"Postmodernism has become an unavoidable issue for feminists" pronounced a recent issue of *The Women's Review of Books* (Ebert: 1991, p. 24). So unavoidable, in fact, that it is impossible to be for or against it, according to Michèle Barrett (in Ebert: 1991, p. 24). So postmodernism is ideology in action? Interrupting the contemporary romance, I insist that although postmodernism does seem to dominate contemporary theorizing, it is not beyond critique. Indeed, it is very possible to reject postmodernism for feminism. In fact, Valerie Solanas was probably the first to make the gesture in a non-scholarly way, targeting pop-misogynist Andy Warhol.

Feminism/Postmodernism (1990) edited by Linda Nicholson, *Gender and Knowledge, Elements of a Postmodern Feminism* (1990) by Susan Hekman, and Jane Flax's *Thinking Fragments, Psychoanalysis, Feminism and Postmodernism in the Contemporary West* (1990), among others, seem to indicate that the writers known as poststructuralists by Linda Alcoff (1988) and Chris Weedon (1987) are increasingly discussed as postmodernists. Perhaps one must sympathize with the French who do not know how they will be received, how they will be recognized, when they land in America. As Foucault remarked, "What is postmodernism? I'm not up to date" (Raulet: 1983, p. 204).[1]

This book focuses on the masculinity of postmodernist/poststructuralist theory and the texts considered central in its debates. Feminist postmodernism offers little support to a critical analysis of masculine ideology. Feminist postmodernists consider their work a reading and representation of Foucault, Derrida, Lacan, even Nietzsche and Freud. It is impossible to understand feminist postmodernism without reference to the writing it has nominated as central: masculine texts. These texts deserve critique, and familiarity with them is required even in order to engage feminist postmodernism over

---

1. Michel Foucault is one of Hekman's preferred "postmodern feminists" (1990, p. 155). Douglas Kellner (1989b) refers to Foucault's *The Order of Things* and *The Archaeology of Knowledge* as postmodern texts. My discussion of terminology is found in Chapter One, pp. 4-13 and 19-20.

questions of strategy and subjectivity. My argument is that these texts have not been understood as masculine sex/sects; their misogyny is not peripheral – misogyny is not peripheral – and a great deal of thought about *that* is required.

It is possible to avoid the fate of Ariadne and the love-death[2] ritual with Dionysian irrationality, binary twin of Apollonian logos. The princess of Crete enabled Theseus to enter the labyrinth and slay the Minotaur, said to be the child of her mother's lust. They sailed away but Ariadne was abandoned by Theseus on Naxos, where she grieved until she was rescued by the god of love and forgetfulness and disappeared; seduced, abandoned, abducted, absent. Titian displays a desolated Ariadne standing at the cliff, and the god of rapture approaches. Testart, the Father of immaterial reproduction, sighs "I gave the little eggs names" (in Breen: 1982) and imagines the gratitude of Amandine at puberty.[3] From Theseus to Testart, the art and science of taking women out of their bodies, senses, minds – times; cutting the cords between women, masculine metamorphoses and fantasies of the feminine. From the discord of the labyrinth which enables the Matador to slay the Minotaur, to the laboratory which ruptures material connection; always the extrauterine ecstasy of Dionysus, who had no mother that bore him. *Les Immatériaux*: this is the postmodern dream.

The Labyrinth introduces the phenomenon of the postmodern Lord-become-woman, and raises critical questions about the politics of feminist work which is fascinated by the Master discourse. This section also briefly highlights diverse feminist works which raise various critical questions, from specific locations, about the oppressive practices of postmodernism.

Chapter 1 charts the personal and political context of the "prophets of prick and prattle"[4] through the accounts by their contemporaries, anti-fascist writers Simone de Beauvoir and Maria-Antonietta Macciocchi. A history of definitions and categories presents structuralism, poststructuralism, deconstruction and postmodernism. The central mood of *fin-de-siècle* crisis and melancholy is considered in terms of a relegitimation of masculine dominance and *indifference*. Dematerialization of creativity and the disconnection of community are raised in relation to female sacrifice.

Chapter 2 considers feminist encounters with structuralism. The potency of absence in the work of Lévi-Strauss and Sartre is discussed in terms of masculine orientations

---

2. My analysis of the cult of Dionysus as the murder of the (M)other is in contrast to the essentialist and male-supremacist orientation of Paglia (1990). She bases her work on de Sade and takes the view that rape and domination are "natural". It is the ordinary approach of the "glorious" penis and the rude vulva/mean uterus: "An erection is architectural, sky-pointing... In the war for human identity, male tumescence is an instrument, female tumescence an obstruction. The fatty female body is a sponge" (1990, p. 91). A heterosexist dualism: dynamic Dionysus adds energy (masculinity) to mere, swampy matter. An important feminist text on woman and the domination of nature is Patricia Mills, *Woman, Nature and Psyche*, New Haven: Yale University Press (1987).
3. See Brodribb (1988b) for a discussion of women and the culture of the new reproductive technologies; and Chapter 6 for a discussion of Lyotard's *Les Immatériaux*.
4. Mary O'Brien, personal discussion, 1982.

to form and content, subjectivity and substance. The centrality of nothing, nothingness and neutrality springs from masculine temporality and temporizing.

Chapter 3 introduces Foucault's rejection of Sartre's dialectical and historical formulations and concern with authenticity. The originality of Foucault's contributions, and feminist responses to his work, are evaluated. Foucault's epistemology of annihilation as the order of things is related to Nietzsche's work on chaos, space and the masculine feminine.

In Chapter 4, Derrida and Foucault warn of the shame of origin, and their debate on madness, anteriority and reason is posed in this context. Derrida's fixation with dissemination and de/meaning versus conception and new embodiment is a central theme; the penis as artful dodger.

Chapter 5 contrasts the work of Lacan and Irigaray on ethics in terms of the absence and presence of the Other. Lacan's morbid phallic lack is repudiated by Irigaray's divine, mystic healing of sexual difference through an amorous birth. The flaws in Irigaray's position are elucidated. Current Anglo-American feminist psychoanalytic criticism, and the strategies of the bearded woman are critiqued.

Chapter 6 points to the postmodern genesis of immateriality, and argues that Dionysian delirium is another mask of masculinist reason. The articulation of creativity and murder in de Sade and Lacan is central to postmodern possession. A discussion of de Beauvoir, O'Brien and other feminist work attempts to illuminate the feminist potential to make sense.

Paris, July 14, 1985

Dear Mary,

Just saw an exhibition showing in Paris right now called Les Immatériaux *(the immaterials); appropriate name for its abstract tyranny: the talking heads of Lacanian structuralism are finally disembodied. In fact, the exhibition leads through a birth tunnel and then spills you out into a theatre of the non-body for a period of Sartrean anguish and nothingness, and the appropriation of the birth process for death by means of slides and voices from genetic experimentation. A screen shows a huge pregnant belly (no other parts of the woman are visible) and a wall traces the various kinds of paternal, nuclear affiliation the new reproductive materials afford. So that you enter the Theatre of the Non-Body and end up in the Labyrinth of Language: Theseus enters the womb and kills mat(t)er!* Les Immatériaux *is curated by Lyotard (the author of* The Postmodern Condition*); it is really tied to an ideology of modernization begun by de Sade and culminating in the growing opinion that these new technologies will finally liberate "us" from the dirty animality of the maternal body. And after the emergency conference last week in Sweden! (We changed the name to the Feminist International Network for Resistance to Reproductive and Genetic Engineering).* Les Immatériaux *is really about* The Mother Machine *and a total mining of the local female body as raw material. It was sort of a lecherous hymn to Amandine, the first French "test-tube" baby: in fact, the "Father" of IVF here recently told a men's magazine how he fantasized about Amandine and how she would be at puberty: would she ever understand what she owed him? He also dreams of pregnancy for men, in the oral cavity: patriarchal genesis at last! Je n'y crois pas.*

Amitiés,

Somer

Introduction

THE LABYRINTH

Dionysus, the "gentle-man", merry mind-poisoner, kills women
softly. Male Approval Desire, under his direction, lacks a sense of
distance from The Possessor. The Dionysian M-A-D-woman
desires the approval of her god because she loves him as herself.
She and he, after all, are two in one flesh. She and he are of one
mind. She has lost her Self in his house of mirrors, and she does
not know whose face she sees in her beatific visions.
Thus Dionysus drives women mad with his femininity, which
appears to be a relief from the stern masculinity of Apollo (Daly:
1978, p. 69).

XIII

we are unworthy your beauty,
you are near beauty the sun,

you are that Lord become woman.
                                        (H.D., "The Master")

In her poem, "The Master" (1981) written between 1934-35, H.D. evokes
her relationship to Sigmund Freud, as patient and friend. Hilda Doolittle's *Tribute to
Freud* (1956) expands upon her respect, admiration, indeed adoration of Freud. The
poem refers to "The Master's" revelation of the origin and significance of H.D.'s
bisexuality, and her gratitude. What H.D. wishes then is that "the old man" will be
rewarded by becoming woman, which he must have been close to being: how else
could he possibly *know*. Or, as Mary Daly says, "she loves him as herself" (1978,
p. 69). In "The Master," Freud/God gives the poet her self-understanding, "explaining"
her bisexuality. But he forbids her "infantile" desires to prophesy and to meet the
Mother. In some sense, she tries to satisfy this desire by turning him into the Mother:
Freud becomes the Goddess, the Lord becomes woman. Thus, H.D. attempts to master
some part of her exploitation. Rachel Blau DuPlessis in "Romantic Thralldom in

H.D." finds she "was vulnerable to the power of what she termed the 'héros fatal', a man whom she saw as her spiritual similar, an artist, a healer, a psychic. Again and again this figure that she conspired to create betrayed her; again and again she was reduced to fragments from which her identity had once more to be painfully reconstructed" (1979, p. 179). H.D. was a key figure in the Modernist school, and I am charging that the "romantic thralldom" she suffered is replicated in feminist encounters with postmodernism, poststructuralism, and deconstruction. H.D. tried to turn the Lord Freud into a woman, but not even her magic could pull that off. Pull off the phallus.[1]

Postmodernism is an addition to the masculinist repertoire of psychotic mind/body splitting and the peculiar arrangement of reality as Idea: timeless essence and universal form. When women appear in French philosophy as Sartrean holes and slime (Collins and Pierce: 1976) or Deleuzian bodies without organs (Guattari and Deleuze: 1983), the mind – and the matter – is masculine. Plato answered the question of Being by awarding true reality to the realm of ideas; the sensible world possesses only the appearance of reality. Postmodernism is no less metaphysical: here, too, the idea absorbs and denies all presence in the world. This particular trend in patriarchal thinking is neither new nor original: the Collège de France and the Freud school which created it have respectable traditions in Cartesian politics. Julia Penelope has uncovered the "patriarchal linguistic agenda" (1990, p. 17) of the Académie Française, founded by Cardinal Richelieu in 1635 with the purpose of creating a grammar that would correct women. The institutions as well as the texts which were patrons to postmodernism excluded and expelled women, including Simone de Beauvoir and Luce Irigaray. The rule is that only man may appear as woman. Derrida creates Veronica – "true image" in medieval Latin – woman as representation of the transparency of meaning. Then he deconstructs her while denouncing feminists for defining her: Veronica must be his and must be appearance only. She must be his (appearance) only. She may be summoned to appear, but shall not summon the Collège, to account; to politics, responsibility, justice. In any case, once at court, the jester Lacan rules that the law is the phallus and woman cannot speak; Lacan will speak in her place, however, since only man may represent woman.

Once satisfied to control her body and her movements, once pleased to create images of her and then order her body to conform, the Master of Discourse now aspires to the most divine of tasks: to create her in his image, which is ultimately to annihilate her. This is his narcissistic solution to his problem of the Other. But to do this, to create her in his image, he must be able to take her image, educating her to sameness and deference. Taking her body, taking her mind, and now taking her image. But the task of taking women's image is ill-advised. In his narcissistic dreaming, he

---

1. Some of the best H.D. scholarship is represented by the works of Rachel Blau DuPlessis (1979; 1986; 1981); Susan Stanford Friedman (1981; 1985; 1990); Deborah Kelly Kloepfer (1984) and Friedman and DuPlessis (1990).

hallucinates, and even if we are called an illusion, he must ask: Where did the illusion of woman come from? What evil genius placed the idea of woman in man? In short, the New Age masculinity of self-deluded alchemists and shape-shifters is not going to be a successful strategy. There is something irreducible about Veronica after all, as they always suspected. She informs herself that women matter.

Foucault would have written on hysterical women, Lacan tried to write as an hysteric (Clément: 1983; Derrida: 1978a; and Deleuze and Guattari: 1988), write of becoming-woman. In the section, "Memories of a Sorcerer, III" Deleuze and Guattari write "becoming-woman, more than any other becoming, possesses a special introductory power; it is not so much that women are witches, but that sorcery proceeds by way of this becoming-woman" (1988, p. 248). Is this male apprenticeship some sort of talisman to frighten contemporary feminists (previously known as "hysterics")?[2] Related to this is the curious omission of the sorceress in Foucault's history of sexuality, his intriguing point of departure. The *scientia sexualis* ignores, but begins directly after, the witch hunts. Yet is was the new printing press that enabled the dissemination of precise symptoms for inquisitors to extort as confessions. *The Malleus Maleficarum*, the first postmodern text, standardized patriarchal hysteria about female sources.[3]

What is the meaning of this particular ideology of masculine domination? Strange timing: the subject is now annulled by ungenerous and disingenuous white western wizards while women's, Black and Third World liberation movements are claiming their voices (Hooks: 1991; Hartsock: 1990; Christian: 1988; Barry: 1990; de Lauretis: 1989; Lazreg: 1988). Gallop (1988, p. 100) argues that postmodernism "dephallicizes modernism so men can claim to be current. If modernism...is itself a defense against feminism and the rise of women writers, postmodernism is a more subtle defense, erected when modernism would no longer hold."

We know we are in a world where politics is the separation of the public and the private, and man's,[4] Western man's, image is everywhere. He is fascinated by this image and at the same time bored by it. His images, of himself and us, are before our eyes: this noxious narcissist has placed his body of knowledge across our desire to

---

2. One of the most studied of Freud's "cases" of hysteria was Anna O., who in reality was the Jewish feminist Bertha Pappenheimer. Her experiences with male dominance and women's rights organizations are chronicled in a preliminary way by Marion A. Kaplan (1979), in Chapter 2 of *The Jewish Feminist Movement in Germany*. See also Dianne Hunter (1985) "Hysteria, Psychoanalysis and Feminism: The Case of Anna O.," in *The (M)other Tongue*, edited by Shirley Nelson Garner et al.

3. Catherine Clément's sexist history of the sorceress in *The Newly Born Woman* (Cixous and Clément: 1975/1986) turns the persecution into a co-dependency relationship, a dysfunctional familial encounter. She hints at sado-masochism: "The hysteric must 'quit the show'" and be "done with the couple: perversion and hysteria, inquisitor and sorceress" (1975/1986, p. 56).

4. A note on usage: I use the masculine form only as I argue that it is precisely the masculine which is meant by and in postmodern texts. Their positions and arguments cannot be uncritically extended to women – to do so would render women's experiences invisible. This book studies masculine ideology, and it points to the masculine referentiality of these concepts. *He, his* and *man* are therefore appropriate.

know. I reach for my body, but this "male-stream" (O'Brien: 1981, p. 5) corpus has imposed itself between my experience and my reflection. The access to formal knowledge is mediated by the Master (Le Doeuff: 1989, pp. 100-128; Lorde: 1981). The way to myself and other women is blocked by this male icon as a point of reference, for reverence. And I have to make arguments which sound extravagant to my ears, that women exist. That women are sensible. Only knowledge of the male body and male thought is considered essential, the female is unessential, the female is essentialist. And to contradict this, to speak against masculine culture, is so un-cultured. The Masters of discourse have also said that it requires a great deal of sophistication to speak like a woman, clearly it's best left to men. Their texts play with and parade a hysterical femininity, in our best interests of course, to help us transcend the category of woman we somehow got into, and the neurotic idea that we can tell the truth. Or that we know when they're lying. Talking, writing, telling stories out of school: this is what we are forbidden. The Master wants to keep the narrative to himself, and he's willing to explode the whole structure of discourse if we start to talk. They don't want to hear our stories: listening to women's stories of incest and rape almost cost Sigmund Freud his career before he decided that these were simply female fantasies of desire for the father. He probed women's unconscious and denied our reality: his theory of human psyche and sexuality is an act of fear and betrayal. And he told us: it didn't happen, you made it up, you wanted it, you brought it on yourself. What is the Master Narrative? That we can't tell the truth, we can't tell the difference, between our rights and their wrongs. We can't tell.

The assertion that only sex is power and the arrogation of creativity to the mas-culine sex and the rendering of all creativity as sexual – this is patriarchal aesthetics.[5] Patriarchal passion sees violent sex as the essential creative act, even aesthetically, through a sort of metaphysical transubstantiation. This is their romantic belief that sex with the Master can produce the artistic spirit in the student. Male creativity is thus born in another, her work is given depth through the violent transgression of her boundaries. The Maestro's magic wand, the charismatic penis, is the conductor of true art. Great works of art can only be produced after a journey through violent and sordid sex which reveals and brings into being the true nature of the other: degradation. One can only create from pain, and sex. The superior Master, of course, creates pain in another, makes his mark by leaving marks. What is central to the rape artist's ideology is that matter is worthless and must be given form. His. Matter must be recreated by man. Mother must be recreated by, and as, the masculine. Mother is dissociated from creativity and communication. Flesh is created by the word of god, not by the body of woman. Creation requires destruction, one is posed only in being opposed to another, consciousness is hostile to all others. Men are hostile and creative, women are sometimes good material.

---

5. Fortunately, we have Audre Lorde's (1984) vision of the uses of the erotic for connection and community, work and joy.

For us then, to speak is difficult, and it seems we must shift from amnesia to aphasia as parts of our consciousness appear unreal to us. Loss of memory, loss of speech: it is as though we cannot speak and cannot remember at the same time. Being fully conscious is dangerous. Women's memory, women's language, women's body and sexuality have been annulled in the patriarchal tradition which has feared the female sex. What we are permitted, encouraged, coerced into, and rewarded for, is loving the male sex and male sex: the bad girls are the ones who don't, and who thereby risk men's rage and women's fear. As bell hooks writes: "[m]ale supremacist ideology encourages women to believe we are valueless and obtain value only by relating to or bonding with men. We are taught that our relationships with one another diminish rather than enrich our experience. We are taught that women are 'natural' enemies, that solidarity will never exist between us because we cannot, should not, and do not bond with one another" (1991b, p. 29).

Postmodernism exults female oblivion and disconnection; it has no model for the acquisition of knowledge, for making connections, for communication, or for becoming global, which feminism has done and will continue to do.[6] You have to remember to be present for another, to be just, to create sense. But "the demon lover" will not do this. Robin Morgan recognizes why:

If I had to name one quality as the genius of patriarchy, it would be compartmentalization, the capacity for institutionalizing disconnection. Intellect severed from emotion. Thought separated from action. Science split from art. The earth itself divided; national borders. Human beings categorized: by sex, age, race, ethnicity, sexual preference, height, weight, class, religion, physical ability, *ad nauseam*. The personal isolated from the political. Sex divorced from love. The material ruptured from the spiritual. The past parted from the present disjoined from the future. Law detached from justice. Vision dissociated from reality (1989, p. 51).

Feminists like Anne-Marie Dardigna (1981) and Andrea Nye (1988) have disclosed how psychoanalytic theory refuses to acknowledge the anguish of women's lives and stories of brutality which threaten the son's reconciliation with the Father necessary to his inheritance of privilege. As Nye argues, "the imaginary male self is threatened not by fusional maternal animality, but by the always-present possibility of renewed accusations from abused women, not by the nothingness of the intersubjective, but by an empathy that will make him vulnerable to others' experiences" (1988, p. 161). The refusal to feel for or with women, the rejection of solidarity with women, assures the son's access to the Father's power. In fact, the Master from Vienna located the voice of the conscience in the Other – in the voice of the murdered father who becomes, with difficulty, the external internal voice – so that the ego is one's own but the conscience is founded only from an external threat of retaliation for murder (Freud: 1913). Indeed, ego and conscience are not connected here!

---

6. This was the case in Nairobi, 1985. See Charlotte Bunch (1987), *Passionate Politics*, Section Five, "Global Feminism", pp. 269-362.

According to Dardigna,[7] it is really the fascination for the all-powerful father that is at the centre of masculine desire (1981, p. 188). To desire a woman is in some sense to recognize her, and this threatens a loss of control over the divisions he has made in his life between his mind and his body, his reason and his emotion; between the women he uses for sex and the women he talks with about postmodernism. And the women writers he criticizes, not daring to confront the Father. As Wendy Holloway (1984) has shown, he withholds, withdraws, and does not meet her social, sexual, emotional, political desires: too demanding, he will not satisfy her. Denying women's desire, politically or sexually, is a male power play. Andrea Nye's (1988) rewriting of the Freud creation story tells of male fears of the Father's revenge and disinheritance from patriarchal powers: getting close to women means losing economic and political power.

Once there was a family headed by a brutal authoritarian father who in secret had a tendency to abuse his wife, his daughters and any women who came under his power. Sometimes he even abused his sons. His sons were uneasy about their father and about other men but they were men themselves. Therefore, they knew they were supposed to respect their father and learn to be like him. One son, however, listened to his mother, his nurse, and the talk of other women. He became very uneasy. The women told him of crimes that his father and other fathers had committed against women and about their suffering. But this son was also a man. He knew that he too had to become a father. Then he made his discovery. There was only one solution. The women were lying, they were in love with the father and wanted to be seduced. They had only fantasized the father's mistreatment. Now the son knew that he had been guilty also; he had suspected his father out of jealousy. And he repented. Now all the sons could come together, celebrating the father's memory and rejoicing that the father had committed no faults. Now they could follow in the father's footsteps and if accusations were made by the women or by any younger sons who happened to listen to women, the men would know what to say (1988, p. 159).

In this way, Freud felt he penetrated the mystery of female anguish: mysterious because women were unreal to him. Lacanian psychoanalysis also says we mean yes when we say no: "the tension of desire hidden in the most professed horror of incest" (1953, p. 12). In fact, the Freudian Oedipal myth warns men of the risks of loving the mother: death as a Father, death of the King.

Suzanne Blaise has argued that the current oppression of women would not have been possible without the death, the murder, of the mother. In *Le rapt des origines ou le meurtre de la mère, De la communication entre femmes*, Blaise (1988) shows how the

---

7. In her interpretation of the myth of Adam and Eve in the garden, Anne-Marie Dardigna recalls Eve's gesture of subversion: Eve senses the presence of the Tree of Knowledge, she tastes the fruit, and introduces new values of pleasure and perception. When she disrupts the pact of Father and Son, she is punished by male domination of her desire: "Thy desire shall be thy husband, and he shall rule over thee." In Genesis, the Father-Son alliance is reasserted: "the Father and the Son are reconciled by denying the desire of Eve as subject and transforming her into an object of their desire" (1981, p. 179). Men remain fearful of the dangers: knowing women, and knowing a woman threaten the Law of the Fathers.

male murder of the mother and the massacre of the value of the female and the maternal is continually reenacted among women. Drawing from forty years of experience in the women's movement in France, she shows how the original murder of the mother by the sons has had serious repercussions for communication between women politically and personally. She reconsiders the current divisions, impasses, betrayals and violent denunciations among women in this light. Clearly, our relationship to other women, to our sex, symbolically and politically, is full of consequences for our sexuality. Blaise asks what it would mean for the personal and collective body of women to recognize that sexual politics is also the politics of matricide (1988, p. 11): "To possess the mother, man destroyed the woman; to possess the daughter, he destroyed the mother" (1988, p. 10).

Feminists have begun to think through the effects for female sexuality of the wounding of the mother/daughter relationship. The mothers were also daughters, and this question has to be considered in generational as well as psychical time, as Luce Irigaray (1981, p. 65) shows:

But have I ever known you otherwise than gone? And the home of your disappearance was not in me…I received from you only your obliviousness of self, while my presence allowed you to forget this oblivion. So that with my tangible appearance I redoubled the lack of your presence.

But forgetfulness remembers itself when its memorial disappears. And here you are, this very evening, facing a mourning with no remembrance. Invested with an emptiness that evokes no memories. That screams at its own rebounding echo. A materiality occupying a void that escapes its grasp.

Irigaray also argues that sameness and differences among women must be named. But we have to overcome our aphasia and our amnesia to *speak* our *minds* and live our time. Temporally, sex is *momentous*, while procreation is *duration*. Remedying aphasia, Irigaray (1985d) wrote "When our lips speak together." Remembering birth, Mary O'Brien (1981) showed how biological reproduction is the substructure of human history, the unity of natural and cyclical time. Identifying blackness and whiteness, bell hooks recharges circuits of community, "homeplace" (1990, pp. 33-50), spaces of resistance.

But such critiques of the misogyny of masculinist theory have been interrupted, arrested. Julia Kristeva, the self-styled "father of semiotics" has brought us the phallic mother: the phallus becomes the mother of us all in Kristeva's magical replacement of male supremacy. Her work is tied to the Lacanian formula of desire and/for female aphasia:

On a deeper level, however, a woman cannot "be"; it is something which does not even belong in the order of *being*. It follows that a feminist practice can only be negative, at odds with what already exists so that we may say "that's not it" and "that's still not it". In "woman" I see something that cannot be represented, something that is not said, something above and beyond nomenclatures and ideologies. There are certain "men" who are familiar with this phenomenon; it is what some modern texts never stop signifying: testing the limits of language and sociality – the law and its transgression, mastery and (sexual) pleasure – without reserving one for males and the other for females, on the condition that it is never mentioned. (Kristeva: 1974/1981, p. 137, 138)

According to Kristeva, "women exist" is an essentialist statement, but nothing *is*, negation *is*, and is a higher form of being than woman.[8] More mundanely, this is the ideological practice of the organization of consent and deconstruction of dissent, necessary for professional practice. For Kristeva, woman is an attitude, not a sexual or political subject. As Ann Rosalind Jones (1981, p. 249) remarks, "'woman' to Kristeva represents not so much a sex as an attitude, any resistance to conventional culture and language; men, too, have access to the *jouissance* that opposes phallogocentrism." Woman represents the semiotic – an oceanic bliss/swamp of the mother-child dyad, a communication of rhythm, preverbal sound. "She" is an attitude best held by men: for Kristeva, it is in the work of male authors Joyce, Artaud, Mallarmé, etc. that this semiotic state of union with the maternal is best elaborated. This, I suspect, is why Kristeva forbids women to mention the game, to *move* to subjectivity: it would block men's access to the primal maternal source of their verbal creativity, it would profane men's ancestral memories of Mother. If women claim and proclaim this matrix, it would be horrid. Then there would be real chaos. So women must be still and think of the linguistic empire. In Kristeva's view, "woman" or "women" by women is a bad attitude.

Let's be realistic, say some women. Do you really think that you can start from scratch and just leave theory out entirely, just because it's male? Don't you see that you can pick and choose from it all in order to make feminist theory? Or, as Elizabeth Grosz[9] puts it in introducing feminists to Jacques Lacan, "feminists may be able to subvert and/or harness strategically what is useful without being committed to its more problematic ontological, political and moral commitments" (1990, p. 7). This is based on her understanding of psychoanalysis as "a method of reading and interpreting (where questions of truth, bias and verification are not relevant)" (1990, p. 21). That rational – or irrational – science is pure methodology is an old ideology which feminist critiques of science have exposed (Keller: 1985; Harding, et. al: 1983; Lloyd: 1984). These recent feminist analyses of masculine rationality show how subjective it is, how it masks and develops masculine domination. Such epistemological critiques warn against a dangerous and superficial neutrality.

The objection to "starting from scratch" denies women's social and political thought and its suppression. First of all, women, who try to use unprocessed ingredients in their

---

8. For an examination of critical approaches to Kristeva's work, see Eleanor Kuykendall (1989) who illustrates how Kristeva endorses Freudian paradigms and "leaves no place for a feminine conception of agency" (1989, p. 181). Gayatri Spivak is quite clear: "I'm repelled by Kristeva's politics: what seems to me to be her reliance on the sort of banal historical narrative to produce 'women's time': what seems to me Christianizing psychoanalysis; what seems to me to be her sort of ferocious western Europeanism: and what seems to me to be her long-standing implicit sort of positivism: naturalizing of the chora, naturalizing of the pre-semiotic, etcetera" (1989, p. 145).

9. Grosz displays more inadvertent masculine supremacy with the statement: "Given the mother's (up to now) indispensable role in bearing children..." (1990, p. 146). Artificial wombs and placentas are still a fantasy. Even if Grosz is referring to "contract mothers", this negation of them as mothers participates in the patriarchal ideology which privileges genetic genealogy over birth (Brodribb: 1989a).

recipes in order to avoid preserving masculine categories and implications, are punished. As anyone who has ever done it knows, confronting patriarchy or critiquing "male-stream" (O'Brien: 1981, p. 5) knowledge is not "easy": it involves risk and there are consequences. There is so little support for radically feminist work; its costs are exorbitant politically, personally, economically, intimately, as Dale Spender's *Women of Ideas and What Men Have Done to Them* (1983) attests. All feminist work faces a reality of exceptional hostility masked by a self-satisfied ideology of acceptance by sexist institutions, some of which currently consume Women's Studies like a prestige item. Radical work is perceived as dangerous, and discomfits those who have made more stable arrangements within patriarchal systems. Rather than forbidding originality then, let us remember the *scratching out* of women's writing as a historical and political process. Our derision should be directed towards male-stream thought and the processes which exclude, distort and suppress women's writing and history. As Virginia Woolf demonstrates, we must continually interrogate this "civilization" and ask: "[w]here in short is it leading us, the procession of the sons of educated men?" (1947, p. 115).

As for the idea that feminists should be ragpickers in the bins of male ideas, we are not as naked as that. The notion that we need to salvage for this junk suggests that it is not immediately available everywhere at all times. The very up-to-date products of male culture are abundant and cheap; it is one of life's truly affordable things. In fact, we can't pay not to get it, it's so free. So what we have is a difficulty in refusing, of *not* choosing masculine theoretical products.

The second difficulty here is the relationship of theory to action implicit in the notion that feminist theory must be an arrangement of and selection from male theory, not a knowledge that considers female experiences. Underneath this notion lies the historically specific dualism of intellect vs act, theory vs practice, a masculine methodology and ideology which has trained and constrained us all. Even to the point where now some suggest (Weedon: 1987; Nicholson: 1990; Hekman: 1990) that male theory should be the vanguard for feminist practice, again reflecting a sense of inferiority and belief that all feminist thought will be and should be derivative of masculine texts not women's practice. Also, this approach does not recognize other feminists and other feminisms as alternatives to the male text. Are not the works of women and feminists: Black, lesbian, Jewish, working-class, Third World, Native – a more significant source for understanding difference and otherness than the writings of white, western men?

Barbara Christian's excellent article points to how womanist prose is being neglected. This new white western male [10] theory is a language that "mystifies rather

---

10. See Hooks (1990, 1991a) for a critical consideration of differences on race, sex and difference. Barry (1990, p. 100) criticizes the racism of some feminist postmodernism. Contrary to its claimed superiority on this issue, *Feminism/Postmodernism*, for example, contains no substantial engagement with the issue as Modleski points out (1991, p. 18). In her forthcoming Chapter 9, "Postmodern Reductionisms: Diversity versus Specificity," Angela Miles argues that the "integrative politics of
cont. next page

than clarifies" the condition of Blacks and women (1988, p. 17). Related to the theory/action obfuscations of postmodernism, is the question of experience and what Hartsock (1983) and others have called a "standpoint". Responding to the charges that political feminism is "essentialist", Modleski points out: "But surely for many women the phrase 'women's experience' is shorthand for 'women's experience of political oppression', and it is around this experience that they have organized and out of this experience that they have developed a sense of solidarity, commonality and community" (1991, p. 17). Indeed, the writing of bell hooks is a profound examination of the obstacles to, but potentials for, female solidarity. It is grounded in black, female experience. Hooks illuminates race differences and racist processes, and reconceptualizes female community and solidarity. She charges that essentialism is perpetuated by white hetero-patriarchy, while marginalized groups beginning from their own standpoint are targeted by an "apolitical" postmodernism. In a review of Diana Fuss's *Essentially Speaking*, she writes: "Identity politics emerges out of the struggles of...exploited groups to have a standpoint on which to critique dominant structures, a position that gives purpose...to struggle. Critical pedagogies of liberation...necessarily embrace experience, confession and testimony as relevant ways of knowing" (1991a, p. 180). Resisting the notion that race and experience do not matter, P. Gabrielle Foreman shows that "[r]ace, and the habits of surviving we've developed to resist its American deployment, *is* material in a racist culture which so staunchly refuses to admit it is so. This we know but find almost too obvious to write down. Yet our silent space is rapidly being filled with post-modern, post-Thurgood Marshall concepts of the declining significance of race" (1991, p. 13).

There *is* an identity politics to feminist poststructuralism: an identification with the (white) male text. Elizabeth Meese, for example, writes: "When gender is the focus for examining difference, deconstructive criticism might even be said to be identical with the feminist project" (1986, p. xi). Others spend time cataloguing feminism's convergences with and divergences from this masculine point of reference. Alice Jardine (1985) does this in *Gynesis*,[11] and Hekman (1990) in *Gender and Knowledge*. Some insist that feminism *belongs* to postmodernism. In "The Discourse of Others: Feminists and Postmodernism," Craig Owens[12] mistakenly tries to improve the status of feminism by arguing that it is part of postmodernism:

---

10. *cont. from previous page*
    many feminists of colour and lesbian feminists are complex enough to be easily misread as both essentialist and deconstructionist by those who reject dialectical possibilities.... Today, it is not hard to see diverse, heroic and exciting, practice among ever wider groups of women who are consciously and collectively claiming the right to define themselves/their identity, to speak for themselves, and to name their world; who are articulating their own values and visions; who are committed to building solidarity/sisterhood as they articulate their differences. Nevertheless, postmodern feminists choose not to see the new dialectical possibilities this practice creates and reveals. Their theory remains impervious to the lessons as well as the imperatives of practice."
11. See Toril Moi (1988) for a critique of Jardine's work as a postfeminism which never really had a feminist stage.

The absence of discussions of sexual difference in writings about postmodernism, as well as the fact that few women have engaged in the modernism/postmodernism debate, suggest that postmodernism may be another masculine invention engineered to exclude women. I would like to propose, however, that women's insistence on difference and incommensurability may not only be compatible with, but also an instance of postmodern thought. (1983, p. 61, 62)

Linda Nicholson (1990, p. 6) holds that feminist theory "belongs in the terrain of postmodern philosophy." Jane Flax (1990, p. 42) also absorbs feminism in post-modernism: "Feminist theorists enter into and echo postmodernist discourse..."; "feminists, like other postmodernists" (1990, p. 42). Flax (1990, p. 40) now believes that "the further development of feminist theory (and hence a better understanding of gender) also depends upon locating our theorizing within and drawing more self-consciously upon the wider philosophical contents of which it is both a part and a critique." Flax contradicts her earlier, radical position on female socio-symbolic practice and Marxism: "If we deny our own experience, if we decide *a priori* to fit those experiences into categories which others have decided are politically correct, we lose the very possibility for comprehending and overcoming our oppression" (1977/78, p. 22).

The Adam's rib approach is stated openly in Chris Weedon's *Feminist Practise and Post-Structuralist Theory*, and more implicitly in Nancy Fraser's *Unruly Practices*. In neither of these books do we get a clear sense of real struggle with or significant opposition to male theory, and so their value as critiques is also limited. Rather, the major situatedness of each writer is as expert bringing male theory to the women's movement. This suggests a new Aristotelian formula whereby theory is male and action is female, passive, there to be formed by the male seed or seminar. Female experiences are taken like tribute to be formed and informed by masculine theory. This is not "freedom from unreal loyalties" (Woolf: 1947, p. 205).

Rosi Braidotti's *Patterns of Dissonance* (1991) is a more complex book. Braidotti is stressed by the coincidence that credibility works both ways, and has elaborated the contingency plan AND women AND stir. Given the crisis of philosophical knowledge, she argues that we are all in this together and "the old guiding thread for all of us now, women and men alike, is a tightrope stretched over the void" (1991, p. 15).

What sort of kinship system is postmodernism? Certainly, it is not post-patriarchal. Who does the uptown poststructuralist marketplace buy, sell, exchange, credit, legitimate? Who enters into the exchange of women? In *Yearning, race, gender and cultural politics*, bell hooks asks "what does it mean when primarily white men and women are producing the discourse around Otherness?" (1990, p. 53). The Other is included – in theory! (1990, p. 54). In reality, "few nonwhite scholars are being awarded grants to investigate and study all aspects of white culture from a standpoint of difference" (1990, p. 55). The Other of race is displaced and erased in the postmodern framing of difference, as is the Other/sex. The postmodern condition tolerates no binary opposition of black to white, female to male; it is embarrassed by words like "struggle" and "solidarity": "Words like Other and difference are taking the place of commonly known words deemed uncool or too simplistic, words like *oppression, exploitation,* and *domination*" (1990, pp. 51-52). Kathleen Barry also criticizes the academic marketplace, the de-funding of analyses of racism, sexism and class oppression, and the "defeminism of women's studies" (1991, p. 83). "Immense political energy is devoted to seeing that alternatives are nipped in the bud, rendered ridiculous, and never adequately funded," charges Mary O'Brien with reference to women and health care (1989, p. 213).

In her introduction to *Feminism/Postmodernism*, Nicholson defines postmodernists as critical of objectivity and neutrality and this is, she claims, "even more radical" (1990, p. 3) than the work of scholars involved in "other" political movements, including feminism, Marxism, Black and gay liberation. It is postmodernists, not feminists, who "have extended the field where power has traditionally been viewed as operating, for example, from the state and the economy to such domains as sexuality and mental health" (1990, p. 4). Thus, at least one century of diverse feminist scholarship and practice is unrecognized, ignored, rewritten, trivialized. It appears that a certain authoritative consensus is being promoted and recirculated, a somewhat totalizing postmodern feminist metanarrative about the history and the potential of feminism. Curious how the critical practice is not situated in a study of the culture or the epistemology of postmodernism. Nicholson believes that postmodernism deconstructs the "God's eye view" (1990, p. 2, 3) bias of an Enlightenment methodology. I believe that Nicholson has *read* Derrida, but did not recognize him. Yet Nicholson's book has been well-received by Enlightenment misogynists; as Modleski points out, "postmodern feminists might well wish to ponder how they wound up in this new 'alliance' with anti-feminist humanism" (1991, p. 14).

Gender and Knowledge, Elements of a Postmodern Feminism goes one step beyond the presentation of feminism as an aspect of postmodernism, and portrays postmodernism as the ultimate (post) feminism. But then, "Consent", as Mary O'Brien ironizes, "relies on a perception by the public that, imperfect though a system may be, it is the only game in town" (1989, p. 213). And the game here is the absorption of all critical space by postmodernism. Hekman's project is to postmodernize feminism; hers is not a feminist critique of postmodernism, but a "postmodern approach to feminism" (1990, p. 3). It is no longer a question of extending postmodernism by adding gender; it is feminism which must be purged by postmodernism of Enlightenment, essentialist, absolutist and foundationalist tendencies. Cartesian epistemology, not class or heterosexuality, is the main enemy here, and Foucault, Derrida and Gadamer are brought forward to critique feminism. Indeed, Hekman's major target is not the sexism of social and political thought, but the "women's way of knowing" literature. Daly, Ruddick, Gilligan, Chodorow, Lorde, feminist standpoint theory, the "Marxist feminist camp" (1990, p. 40), the "contradictory" (1990, p. 30) radical feminists, the maternal thinkers, all are distinctly less perfect than Derrida and Foucault: "The strongest case for a postmodern feminism can be made through an examination of the work of Derrida and Foucault" (1990, p. 155). Hekman proposes a "conversation of mankind" *[sic]*

(1990, p. 9) between feminism and postmodernism (1990, p. 123). In this *Taming of the Shrew* it seems that only man may speak of woman and not be a biological determinist. Hekman's assertion that life with men under the darkness of postmodernism would be different than under their "Enlightenment" is not convincing.

Modleski finds that "what distinguishes this moment from other moments of backlash is the extent to which it has been carried out not against feminism but in its very name" (1991, p. x). Modleski's "Postmortem on Postfeminism" (1991, pp. 3-22) outlines the literary/political process in which a feminized backlash undermines feminism and delivers us "back into a prefeminist world" (1991, p. 3). She points to "gynocidal feminisms" (1991, p. 4) fascinated with deconstructions of masculinity; ironically feminism is only valued as a "conduit to the more comprehensive field of gender studies" (1991, p. 5).

I reject both the postmodernist theory/practice dichotomy as well as the male/ theory use of female/experience as matter. (The child is usually matricidal anyway and has delusions of being self or Father-born.) Fraser and Weedon, among others, suggest that if one is truly serious about social change, she must read and use the *male* bodies of work. Surely our activism must be something other than standing as experts bringing masculine formulations to movement matters? Bringing male theory to the women's movement is not feminist critique or intervention; it is a position of compromise within institutions and a form of quietism. It denies and hides the abusiveness of the ideology to which it reconciles itself and others. Joan Scott sees theory as a way of ordering experience and determining political practice. We need, says Scott (1988, p. 33), theory that will enable us to think, analyze and articulate, "And we need theory that will be relevant for political practice. It seems to me that the body of theory referred to as postmodernism best meets all these requirements" (1988, p. 33). Instead, I argue the best methodology for evaluating the practice of theory that is put before us as what feminists must attend to if we are really serious about social change is whether it originates from feminist politics and women's experiences. Not a tributary to or coincidence with male philosophy; women must be the matter and the energy: the future. This is what The Milan Women's Bookstore Collective suggests in their work, *Sexual Difference*:

This book is about the need to make sense of, exalt, and represent in words and images the relationship of one woman to another. If putting a political practice into words is the same thing as theorizing, then this is a book of theory, because the relations between women are the subject matter of our politics and this book. It is a book of theory, then, but interspersed with stories. We believe that to write theory is partly to tell about practice, since theoretical reasoning generally refers to things which already have names. Here we are dealing partly with things that had no names (1990, p. 25).

Certainly, bringing the women's movement and feminist theory to bear on male ideology and practice is a more risky position, and the Milan Collective takes those risks.

In *(Ex)Tensions*, Elizabeth Meese reacts against the charges that feminist deconstructors are fathers', not mothers' daughters, and attacks the pioneers of feminist literary criticism as dominating, severe, austere, restrictive, controlling, orthodox. In particular, she targets the work of Showalter, Baym, Marcus, Robinson, and Auerbach in *Feminist Issues in Literary Scholarship*, edited by Shari Benstock. Meese (1990, p. 9) seems to be furious with Showalter[13] who "urges feminist critics to stick with theory received 'via the women's movement and women's studies'." Meese takes the position that Father Knows Best, or at least what mother does not, and that deconstruction will force Women's Studies' feminism to relinquish its power and "orthodoxy". Thus, Meese reenacts the daughter's rage and rejection of the mother, and the turning towards the Father which ironically recreates her as the same. Luce Irigaray writes the dutiful daughter's process in "And One Doesn't Stir Without the Other" (1981, p. 62):

I'll leave you for someone who seems more alive than you. For someone who doesn't prepare anything for me to eat. For someone who leaves me empty of him, mouth gaping on his truth. I'll follow him with my eyes, I'll listen to what he says, I'll try to walk behind him.

Escape to the House of the Father is not one. It is the path to patriarchal wifehood. Jane Gallop puts the double-cross this way:

Postmodernist thinkers are defending against the downfall of patriarchy by trying to be not male. In drag, they are aping the feminine rather than thinking their place as men in an obsolescent patriarchy. The female postmodernist thinker finds herself in the dilemma of trying to be like Daddy who is trying to be a woman. The double-cross is intriguing and even fun [*sic*], but also troubling if one suspects that it is the father's last ruse to seduce the daughter and retain her respect, the very respect that legitimized the father's rule (1988, p. 100).

The real absurdity of postmodernist feminism is its sexist context. For example, at a recent conference the male commentator[14] criticized Nancy Fraser for her sparse referencing of feminist work. But has he ever spoken against Foucault's or masculine theory's sexism? Those men who do take up feminist texts often only complain that the writer isn't feminist enough. He didn't complain that Foucault is not anti-sexist, which in any case does not involve him in the same political risk as it does Fraser.

The objections to radical feminism's break with tradition are particularly academic, because it is there in the institution, that we must locate ourselves in the discourse in order to write credibly. For it is true that if we read/write/speak of women, very few will attend to what we say, even if the women referred to are not feminists. So that the objection to leaving male theory behind expresses a real fear of being silenced: unless you read/write/speak the boys, no one will listen to you. You will be outside the defined and policed arena of discourse. Now, in the academy, you

---

13. See Modleski (1991, pp. 3-6) for an account of Elaine Showalter's switch to gender studies and "gynocidal feminisms".
14. Tom Wartenberg, speaking at the special session on *Unruly Practices* by Nancy Fraser, at the Society of Phenomenology and Existential Philosophy, 29th Annual Meeting, October 11, 1990, Valhalla, Pennsylvania.

cannot just say anything about male theory. You have to proceed with an immanent critique, that is to say, you have to expertly play the parts against the whole. You show, for example, how certain assumptions in the work actually defeat its stated purpose of human liberation, but once remedied, i.e. salvaged, the theory will work for women. An immanent critique can stay within the masculinist academic circle. In this position women become the technicians of male theory who have to reprogram the machine, turning it from a war machine against women into a gentler, kinder war machine, killing us softly. This is a very involving task and after years of playing this part it is understandable that there may be little desire to admit that the effort was virtually futile. An investment has been made, and the conformity is not wholly outer. What attitudes and feelings does this sexist context produce towards oppositional women who refuse this male material? Does a male-circled woman have the power and security to be generous? Having compromised her freedom, will she be less willing to compromise ours? Perhaps the most pernicious aspect of this arrangement, besides the ways it sets women against one another, is the fact that although the male academy values owning our freedom, it does not have to pay a lot for it. Masculine culture already controls gross amounts of female lives. Still, it seems to want more, but always at the same low price. The exploited are very affordable.

This book points to the missing, hidden parts of postmodernism which have been occluded in the rehabilitation processes others have undertaken. In doing so, I am suggesting that feminist critique cannot ignore the misogyny which is the ideological practice of this theory. It would not be possible to take a piece of the cloth of National Socialist or White supremacist "theory" for liberatory goals, even though status in institutions of higher learning have required this methodology and figures key to post-structuralism, like Heidegger and de Man, have collaborated.[15] These masculine theories are not purely theoretical. What I am showing in the discussion of these texts is that ideological practices are real, and that an essential part of feminist strategy is to be aware of the masculinist ones. Also, not all thought is male and knowing this is also a significant feminist activity.

---

15. Victor Farias's exposé of Heidegger's Nazism caused tremendous debate in France, a debate which is traced in Ferry and Renaut (1988). Derrida's response is worth special attention; a reading of this and his defense of Paul de Man's wartime journalism for the Belgium newspaper under Nazi control is essential in evaluating whether deconstruction is the anti-totalitarian methodology it claims to be. Luc Ferry and Alain Renaut, *Heidegger and Modernity*, translated by Franklin Philip, Chicago: The University of Chicago Press, 1990; Victor Farias (1989), *Heidegger and Nazism*, Temple University Press; and Jacques Derrida (1989b), *Of Spirit, Heidegger and the Question*, translated by Geoffrey Bennington and Rachel Bowlby, Chicago: University of Chicago Press; Jacques Derrida, "Like the Sound of the Sea Deep within a Shell: Paul de Man's War," in *Critical Inquiry, 14*, 3, Spring, 1988 pp. 590-652; David Lehman (1991), *Signs of the Times, Deconstruction and the Fall of Paul de Man*, New York: Poseidon; Thomas G. Pavel (1990), *The Feud of Language, A History of Structuralist Thought*, Oxford: Basil Blackwell, especially "Post-Scriptum: The Heidegger Affair".

Nothing Mat(t)ers

In the men's room(s)

When I was young I believed in intellectual conversation:
I thought the patterns we wove on stale smoke
floated off to the heaven of ideas.
To be certified worthy of high masculine discourse
like a potato on a grater I would rub on contempt,
suck snubs, wade proudly through the brown stuff on the floor.
They were talking of integrity and existential ennui
while the women ran out for six-packs and had abortions
in the kitchen and fed the children and were auctioned off.

Eventually of course I learned how their eyes perceived me:
when I bore to them cupped in my hands a new poem to nibble,
when I brought my aerial maps of Sartre or Marx,
they said, she is trying to attract our attention,
she is offering up her breasts and thighs.
I walked on eggs, their tremulous equal:
they saw a fish peddler hawking in the street.

Now I get coarse when the abstract nouns start flashing.
I go out to the kitchen to talk cabbages and habits.
I try hard to remember to watch what people do.
Yes, keep your eyes on the hands, let the voice go buzzing.
Economy is the bone, politics is the flesh,
watch who they beat and who they eat,
watch who they relieve themselves on, watch who they own.
The rest is decoration.

Marge Piercy (1982, p. 80)
Circles on the Water

1

A SPACE ODYSSEY

> What women need to do, to put it in the simplest way, is to be able to demonstrate that male dominant culture and the male-stream thought which buttresses and justifies it are both, in some sense, prejudiced by the very fact that they are masculine.
>
> One way of doing this, or at least of starting to do it, is to consider male philosophy as an ideology of male supremacy. (O'Brien: 1981, p. 5)

Postmodernists view de Beauvoir's work as hopelessly foundationalist (grounded in a theory of human nature) and transcended by Lacanian psychoanalysis. Nevertheless, she had her own views on the "new" postmodern writing of Robbe-Grillet and others. The violently individualist, amoral, apathetic and misogynist *nouveau roman* was the literary event of the '60s. Hubert Aquin and Alain Robbe-Grillet are two of the better known authors in this genre. In her discussion of Klossowski, de Sade, Bataille and phallic fantasy/ideology, Dardigna cites the following interview with Robbe-Grillet:

There is in all my novels an attack on the body, at the same time the social body, the body of the text and the body of woman, all three stacked together. It is certain that, in the male fantastic, the body of woman is the privileged target. In no way am I ashamed of my sado-erotic fantasies; I give them a major role: the life of the fantastic is what the human being must claim most strongly (Dardigna: 1981, p. 21).

These thriller detective novels of the "God is Dead and I'm okay" period typify a certain masculinity, which professes not heroes, but anti-heroes. Simone de Beauvoir discusses her distress with the *nouveau roman*. "It is a dead world they are building, these disciples of the new school" (1968, p. 637). She charges that in their regressive, schizophrenic, metaphysical work, the justifications and the discoveries coincide: the Revolution has failed, the future is slipping from our grasp, the country is sinking into political apathy, man's [*sic*] progress has come to a halt; if he is written about, it will be as an object; or we may even follow the example of the economists and technocrats who put objects in his place; in any event, he will be stripped of his historical dimension (1968, p. 636).

These are the common characteristics of the new school which "confuses truth and psychology...refuses to admit interiority...reduces exteriority to appearances" (1968, p. 636). De Beauvoir captures the superficiality and contra-mundane aspect of the post-1945, postmodern ideology: "appearances are everything, it is forbidden to go beyond them...the world of enterprises, struggles, need, work, the whole real world, disappears into thin air" (1968, p. 636). She charges that "with the intention of saying nothing, they mask the absence of content with formal convolutions..."(1968, p. 636). De Beauvoir links this "escape into fantasies about the absolute" and "defeatism" (1968, p. 637) to the degraded situation of France and the rise of fascism there.

Those who have stood at the door of the Masters' House of science and subjectivity, of class and state power, have been struck by what O'Brien calls "an ironic sense in which the understanding of how hegemony works might well be clarified in an ethnography of Marxist intellectuals" (1989, p. 233). Maria-Antonietta Macciocchi, a former student of Louis Althusser, looks back at the men of her generation and recalls life among the men of science and subjectivity, class and state power. She chronicles their disappearance as the ending of an era:

Nikos Poulantzas committed suicide on October 3, 1979. Lacan dissolved his school on March 16, 1980. Sartre died on April 15, 1980. Barthes, victim of an automobile accident on February 18, 1980, died in the month of April in the same year. Althusser strangled his wife on November 17, 1980. Lacan died on September 19, 1981 (1983, p. 487).

Certainly, their works influenced, engaged and denounced one another in many ways. Althusser reread Marx and Lacan, Lacan reinterpreted Freud, Barthes' *Mythologies* was indebted to Lévi-Strauss's *Mythologiques*, Sartre influenced Foucault, and Poulantzas tried to write the methodological micro-histories called for by Althusser. Foucault said: "Open Althusser's books" (Bellour: 1971, p. 192) even though he disagreed that Marx represented an epistemological break with Classical thought. Louis Althusser read Lacan[1] as having accomplished for the unconscious what he, Althusser, had done for the theory of the economic structure. Lévi-Strauss sought to interpret the universal unconscious with language, while Freud considered the particular. Their two approaches merge in Lacan's work. Lacan turned to the mathematical sciences to reveal the functions of the unconscious just as Lévi-Strauss described universal codes with the use of mathematics (Ragland-Sullivan: 1987, p. 138). This is not to deny the level of difference and disagreement within that period of

---

1. Louis Althusser, (1984) "Freud and Lacan," *Essays on Ideology*, London: Verso, pp. 141-172.

French political and social theory. Althusser may have written of Freud and Lacan, but in 1980 he violently denounced Lacan as that "magnificent, pathetic Harlequin" (Clément: 1983, p. 21) at one of Lacan's private seminars to which he had gained access. *Anti-Oedipus* (1983) by Félix Guattari and Gilles Deleuze was a rebellion against Father Lacan, which had some success among the Lacanian school. Deleuze was a former pupil and analysand of Lacan; as was Althusser. Some Lacanians followed the forbidden work of Jacques Derrida, who criticized Lacan's phallo-gocentricism in *The Post Card* (1987b). In the section "Le facteur de la verité", Derrida argued that Lacanian psychoanalysis was prescriptive rather than simply descriptive. Derrida and Foucault argued over origin and madness. All of these authors whose roots lay either in scientific Marxism or functionalist structuralism had denounced exis-tentialism, yet at a certain point all were secretly turning to Sartre, and to the Romantic novelist Stendhal, writers who embraced the humanistic, meta-physical, historicist tradition that structuralism rejected (Macciocchi: 1983, p. 491).

Macciocchi deliberately describes Althusser's torments preceding his murder of his wife and his attempt to absolve his subjectivity. In the year before her death, Althusser test drove and pretended to purchase a Rolls Royce in London. In Italy, he spent an evening with an "earthy" woman who confided to a friend, "Yes, nothing but little kisses...he's afraid of the body" (1983, p. 530). At a Terni Workers' Cultural Circle, he spoke for the first time on "The Pleasures of Marxism," performing as at a carnival of denunciation and absurdity in the face of orthodoxy and passivity. After this, he confessed to Macciocchi: "I told the truth, and I saved my soul" (1983, p. 535). She considers: "For the first time, I heard him speak in the first person. However, people turned their backs on him, furious that he was showing the gap between yesterday's utopias and today's realities, that he thereby touched the knot of theoretical reflexion, which was finally the knot of his own despair" (1983, p. 535). Macciocchi traced the "insolent" acts (1983, p. 538) of the twelve-month period prior to Althusser's murder of his wife, Hélène Rythmann, and discovered his growing despair over communism, Marxism, and his work. But Macciocchi focuses on Althusser's epistemological breakdown, and not its patriarchal expression and force: "These three acts were the sundering...[la rupture]...of three inhibitions, of three chastity belts, with which marxism had cast subjects into iron statues. Human passions, the need to imagine, and the liberty of thinking – otherwise known as heresy" (1983, p. 538). The uxoricide is negated, used as a metaphor for Althusser's purported self-destruction, almost in the way Derrida uses the story *Pierrot Murderer of His Wife* to focus on subjectivity.[2] According to Macciocchi:

By killing Hélène, in a final grip of love and hate, he sent to the tomb the Mother, the nurse, the companion, the Jew he had protected from persecution, and also the only voice that could prolong his own. He really wanted to silence himself forever (1983, p. 537).

---

2. See discussion in Chapter 4.

Monique Plaza calls Althusser's murder of Hélène Rythmann "ideology in action" (1984a, p. 75). She argues that "the murder of a woman is within the continuum of the discursive negation of women…ideology against women is not just a matter of words; it is also a matter of death" (1984a, p. 75). When Plaza presented this paper to an international symposium on Ideology at the Polytechnic of Central London in 1981, organizers requested that she remove this discussion of Althusser's murder of his wife (1984a, p. 82). Geraldine Finn argues that we must attend to the political and personal:

We cannot afford to continue to separate the intellectual in a man (I choose my terms carefully) from the emotional: the depression from the ideas; or the political from the personal: the commitment to class struggle from the stormy marriage, the dead wife…Neither Althusser, "France", nor the world's intellectuals and revolutionaries will acknowledge *patriarchy* as the powerful, pervasive and pernicious ideological state apparatus which it is; at the same time, none of them escape its effects (Finn: 1981, p. 28, italics in original).

When Althusser died in 1990, many masculine Marxists and philosophers still found reference to the murder to be in very bad taste. One obituary read:

It is still too early to draw up a balance sheet. The master has left too deep an impression on us. Above all, the man was so close to us, with his exquisite gentleness, his tact…
   Then came the tragedy, which he himself described, partly out of a sense of propriety and partly out of derision, as the "non-event", the killing of his wife, the committal to hospital (Comte-Sponville: 1990, p. 16).[3]

Gregory Elliott is more indignant and feels that Althusser is unjustly attacked and beset: "doubtless *pour décourager les autres*, some have not hesitated to identify the death of Hélène Althusser at her husband's hands as the inevitable denouement of [his theoretical endeavour]" (1991, p. 28). Indeed, Hélène victimizes Louis Althusser by staging a supposed murder, murder rendered now in quotation:

When, in November 1980, defeat came, provoked in part by the political setbacks of the late '70s, the pitiless form it took – the "murder" of his companion of some thirty-five years – condemned him to oblivion thereafter (1991, p. 29).

Melancholic musings on the Master beset by feminism and the woman he murdered…. A Master is Being Beaten.

No manifesto has been endorsed by structuralism, the *nouveau roman*, semiotics, deconstruction, poststructuralism and postmodernism. The Saussurian-dominated intellectual problematic was inaugurated by Lévi-Strauss in reaction to the Marxism and existentialism of Sartre and others. Yet the indefinability and shifting categorization of Lacan, Derrida and Foucault contribute to the confusion surrounding already abstract, slippery texts. It's difficult to know who is what, where, and when.

---

3. I am grateful to Angela Miles who brought this reference to my attention.

This is also complicated by their search for ancestors.[4] John Rajchman (1991, p. 120) remarks that "postmodernism is what the French learned Americans were calling what they were thinking." What follows is a brief presentation of definitions and a history of the categories.

Male-stream literature (*Ésprit*, 1967; Caws, 1968) named the stars of the French structuralist movement: Claude Lévi-Strauss, the founding father from anthropology; Roland Barthes from *belles lettres* and literary criticism; Foucault and Derrida in the philosophical mode; Althusser the structuralist Marxist; and Lacan, the fundamentalist and surrealist Freudian. Pavel (1990, p. 5) argues that the work of Lévi-Strauss, Lacan, Foucault and Derrida has the following common features: the use of linguistic concepts, the critique of humanism, subjectivity and truth and *"the replacement of metaphysics by metacriticism"* (1990, p. 6, italics in original). Of the rise and "fall" of French structuralism and poststructuralism, Pavel writes "in France during the 1960s, the concepts of structural linguistics were transformed into a lasting set of metaphysical notions, which, in turn, played a crucial role in one of this century's most spectacular attempts to achieve intellectual modernization" (1990, p. 1). Lacan makes this proposition clear in "The Meaning of the Phallus":

This passion of the signifier then becomes a new dimension of the human condition, in that it is not only man who speaks, but in man and through man that it [ça] speaks, that his nature is woven by effects in which we can find the structure of language, whose material he becomes, and that consequently there resounds in him, beyond anything ever conceived of by the psychology of ideas, the relation of speech (1985b, p. 78).

Language, sign, and code are the privileged forms of mediation, which is reduced to *exchange*. The post-war emphasis on rational positivism and critique of metaphysics led many philosophers to borrow scientific models from the human sciences, especially linguistics. Meaning and value had no place in the analysis of signifier and signified. Indeed, the new epistemology is primarily linguistic. Central to all this is the notion of structure as the reduction of matter to form. According to Lévi-Strauss, structuralism, unlike formalism, does not distinguish between form and matter. On the contrary, it challenges such distinction: "Form defines itself by opposition to a content which is exterior to it; but structure has no content: it is itself the content, apprehended in a logical organization conceived as a property of the real" (Lévi-Strauss: 1960, p. 122). This is foundational to postmodernism's epistemology: structure is matter, energy is male, and He is the female of form as well.

Edith Kurzweil defines structuralism as "the systematic attempt to uncover deep universal mental structures as these manifest themselves in kinship and larger social structures, in literature, philosophy and mathematics, and in the unconscious psycho-logical patterns that motivate human behaviour" (1980, p. 1). Josué Harari has

---

4. Nietzsche, for example, is understood in conjunction with postmodern anti-narrative critique (Shapiro: 1989) and as a profound influence on the modernist work of D.H. Lawrence, and Gide (Foster: 1981).

determined the following basic outlines of a structuralist position: "(1) the rejection of the concept of the 'full subject' to the benefit of that of structure; (2) the loss of the pertinence of the traditional 'form/content' division in so far as for all structuralist theorists content derives its reality from its structure; and, (3) at the methodological level, a stress on codification and systematization" (1979, p. 27).

Structuralism[5] became fashionable during France's conservative Gaullist period, in a climate of political resignation. Marxists have critiqued its conservatism, anti-humanism, and self-referentiality. Jost Hermand has argued that structuralism's pessimistic emphasis on unalterable structures serves the interests of state interventionist monopoly capitalism:

Serving these functions, structuralism once again reveals its ideological affinity for the establishment. Positivism, with its emphasis on the individual, was an accurate reflection of the principle of free enterprise within the bourgeois system. Structuralism shows that even the bourgeois who are fighting so desperately to maintain their privileged position have become the captives of structures (read "monopolies") (Hermand: 1975, p. 220).

The political engagement typical of Sartre's existentialist stance was abandoned, and according to Hermand, "a period of luxurious *tristesse* set in" (1975, p. 214). In discussing the reception of French structuralism in Germany, Hermand indicates that it was attractive to traditionalists who appreciated the following qualities: "the emphasis on the purely formal, the historical timelessness, the apparent 'scholarliness' of an absolutely objective, even scientific method and, last but not least, ideological independence which seemed to be free of all political affiliations" (1975, p. 213).

Structuralism was ridiculed during the student movement of 1968. French students wrote on the walls of the Sorbonne: "Structures do not take to the streets" (Roudiez: 1975, p. 212). This may be why "everyone" was a structuralist in the early 1960s, but after 1968, few admitted it. Apostles became apostates: Roland Barthes, Jacques Lacan, Michel Foucault, Philippe Sollers and Julia Kristeva of the *Tel Quel* group all repudiated the label. The attempt to modernize the human sciences via structuralism's promise of scientific credentials had met with setbacks. For example, the collaborative projects of followers of Lacan and Lévi-Strauss to establish connections between the "constituent units" of myths and analysands' dreams with computer technologies had failed (Kurzweil: 1980, p. 21). Both Lévi-Strauss and Lacan were concerned with unconscious structures, one at the universal, anthropological level of tribal myth, the other at the individual, psychological level. It was believed[6] that human minds, histories and desires could be input and printed out like pure data, and read like

---

5. See Boyne (1986), Broekman (1977) and Caws (1990) for a standard introduction to and discussion of structuralism and French social/sociological theory.
6. Sherry Turkle (1978, pp. 164-188) discusses Lacan's attempt to render his theories of the unconscious scientifically rational through the use of *mathemes*, mathematical formulas.

algebraic equations, mathematical laws. In spite of the inevitable failure of this project, the work which developed out of structuralism remained part of the century of Saussure and linguistic law:

In France in the 1960s, linguistics, in particular structural linguistics, brought the promise of a true scientific conversion for the humanities. When this project miscarried, linguistics provided the critics of the scientific approach with the conceptual weapons of their discontent. Cultural, epistemological and metaphysical debates were all expressed in a vocabulary bristling with linguistic jargon (Pavel: 1990, p. vii).

Eve Tavor Bannet (1989) champions as *poststructuralist* the work of Barthes, Derrida, Foucault and Lacan, who all dissent from structuralism's notion of universal laws in the human mind and society. She argues that poststructuralism is a reaction to the centralizing features of the technocratic reorganization of France. Robert Young (1981, p. 8) finds that poststructuralism[7] displaces rather than develops structuralism through an immanent critique and interrogation of the latter's fundamental concepts:

Post-structuralism, then, involves a shift from meaning to staging, or from the signified to the signifier.... Broadly, however, it involves a critique of metaphysics (of the concepts of causality, of identity, of the subject, and of truth), of the theory of the sign, and the acknowledgement and incorporation of psychoanalytic modes of thought. In brief, it may be said that post-structuralism fractures the serene unity of the stable sign and the unified subject. In this respect, the 'theoretical' reference points of post-structuralism can be best mapped via the work of Foucault, Lacan and Derrida, who in different ways have pushed structuralism to its limits and shown how its most radical premises open it up to its own deconstruction.

Discussing the theorists who have produced "poststructuralism," Weedon (1987, p. 13) counts Saussure, Althusser, Freud, Marx, Lacan, Derrida, and Foucault. In her terms:

All forms of poststructuralism assume that meaning is constituted within language and is not guaranteed by the subject which speaks it.... Psychoanalytic forms of poststructuralism look to a fixed psycho-sexual order; deconstruction looks to the relationship between different texts; and Foucauldian theory...looks to historically specific discursive relations and social practices (1987, p. 22).

Ellie Ragland-Sullivan (1989, p. 42) argues that poststructuralism is an American, not a

---

7. Anthony Giddens identifies the following as definitive characteristics of structuralism and post-structuralism: "the thesis that linguistics, or more accurately, certain aspects of particular versions of linguistics are of key importance to philosophy and social theory as a whole; an emphasis upon the relational nature of totalities, connected with the thesis of the arbitrary character of the sign, together with a stress upon the primacy of signifiers over what is signified; the decentering of the subject; a peculiar concern with the nature of writing, and therefore with textual materials; and an interest in the character of temporality...(as separate from history)" (1987, p. 196).

French phenomenon, and describes how Jacques-Alain Miller (Lacan's son-in-law and literary executor) shocked an Ottawa conference on "The Reception of Post-Structuralism in Francophone and Anglophone Canada" "by saying that 'post-structuralism' was not a word used in France."

There is no clear conception of the meanings of poststructuralism and postmodernism, their relation, distinction or significance. Profoundly elusive, purposively ambiguous, these are terms which are not used systematically, and about which there is no consensus. Yet they have come to dominate the critical and cultural landscape.[8] For Ihab Hassan (1987, p. xvi), postmodernism and poststructuralism share many affinities, but "postmodernism appears larger, is international, in scope. Art, politics, technology, all of culture, fall within its compass..." Andrew Ross, in *Universal Abandon? The Politics of Postmodernism*, sees poststructuralism as "a late modernist phenomenon" (1989, p. xi) and locates it as a symptom and cause of the larger context of postmodernism (1989, p. xi). Peter Dews (1987, p. xi) considers the "poststructuralist" work of Jacques Lacan, Michel Foucault, Jacques Derrida and Jean-François Lyotard as moving towards a conceptualization of postmodernity, the condition of the "present age".

With respect to deconstruction, Young (1981, p. viii, Preface) writes: "There is not a great deal of consensus about what, if anything, post-structuralism is, apart perhaps from the recognition that it involves the work of Derrida." Rajchman claims that the *nouveau roman* is postmodernist literature about itself, and "postmodernism is sometimes said to be the art of deconstruction" (1991, p. 121). Ragland-Sullivan finds that poststructuralism is associated mainly with the name of Jacques Derrida, whom she criticizes for making "the text – Writing, Language – the condition of itself" (1989, p. 56). She agrees with other writers who support Lacan's claim that "everything in Derrida is already in his [Lacan's] work" (1989, p. 42) with this difference: "Where ambiguities, opacities, slipperiness, and gaps in discourse are a final point for Derrida, this was the place from which Lacan began to ask questions" (1989, p. 62).

Deconstruction is a certain masturbation with the text, playing with the terms at hand. Derrida demonstrates the careful, contingent manipulation of meanings and the endless deferral of sense:

The movements of deconstruction do not destroy structures from the outside. They are not possible and effective, nor can they take accurate aim, except by inhabiting those structures. Inhabiting them *in a certain way*, because one always inhabits, and all the more so when one does not suspect it. Operating necessarily from the inside, borrowing all from the old structure...the enterprise of deconstruction always in a certain way falls prey to its own work (1976, p. 24, italics in original).

---

8. A 1991 Seminar is devoted to "The Genealogy of Postmodernism: Nietzsche, Heidegger, Derrida and Rorty," under the direction of Bernd Magnus, Center for Ideas and Society, University of California, Riverside.

In other words, Derrida *interrupts* (*coitus reservatus*) but does not abstain! Elizabeth Grosz defines deconstruction[9] as the procedure of investigating the binary logic of metaphysical texts through an operation of reading which involves reversal, displacement and indetermination:

Deconstruction is neither a destruction of prevailing intellectual norms and theoretical ideals, nor their replacement or reconstruction by new, more acceptable forms. Deconstruction in its technical sense refers to a series of tactics and devices rather than a method: strategies to reveal the unarticulated presuppositions on which metaphysical and logocentric texts are based (Grosz: 1989, p. xv).

But mostly, deconstruction means never having to say you're wrong. Or a feminist. As Derrida likes it: "I am not against feminism, but I am not simply for feminism" (1989b, p. 228). Deconstruction hopes to endlessly defer feminism.

Western philosophy has been categorized according to classical, medieval, and modern periods. Now a postmodern era has been announced, variously dated as post-Enlightenment; post-September, 1939 (World War II) (Hassan: 1987, p. 88); post-November, 1963 (the assassination of Kennedy) (McCaffery: 1986, p. vii); and post-Heidegger's *Letter on Humanism* (Benjamin: 1988, p. 2). Modernism itself is an elastic period, and "may rightly be assimilated to romanticism, romanticism related to the enlightenment, the latter to the renaissance, and so back, if not to the Olduvai Gorge, then certainly to ancient Greece" (Hassan: 1987, p. 88). Postmodernism then is *2001, A Space Odyssey*, starring both Australopithecus and Astronaut. Hominids and their tools. Their projections?

In *Against Postmodernism, A Marxist Critique*, Alex Callinicos (1990a, p. 5) discusses poststructuralism in the postmodern epoch:

It is necessary to distinguish between the philosophical theories developed between the 1950s and the 1970s and subsequently grouped together under the heading of 'poststructuralism' and their appropriation in the past decade in support of the claim that a postmodern epoch is emerging. The running has been made in this latter development primarily by North American philosophers, critics and social theorists, with the help of a couple of Parisian figures, Lyotard and Jean Baudrillard who appear, when set beside Deleuze, Derrida and Foucault, as the *epigoni* of poststructuralism.

In his chapter, "Toward a Concept of Postmodernism," Ihab Hassan, one of postmodernism's earliest chroniclers and promoters, points to the following who "evoke a number of related cultural tendencies, a constellation of values, a repertoire of procedures and attitudes" (1987, p. 85) that are called postmodernism: Derrida, Lyotard, Foucault, Lacan, Deleuze, Baudrillard [10], Beckett and Robbe-Grillet. Hassan

---

9. See her useful glossary of terms which introduces *Sexual Subversions*.
10. In *Jean Baudrillard, From Marxism to Postmodernism and Beyond*, Douglas Kellner locates
cont. next page

includes in this list Godot and Superman (the movie, I assume, not the book by Nietzsche). John Rajchman (1991) provides a Foucauldian history of the category, postmodernism. Parisian debates have ordered American postmodern discourse, yet "Foucault rejected the category [postmodern]; Guattari despises it, Derrida has no use for it; Lacan and Barthes did not live, and Althusser was in no state, to learn about it; and Lyotard found it in America" (1991, p. 119). "Postmodernist" is what Americans have labelled these diverse writers, "a sign that Paris no longer controls the designation of its own thought" (1991, p. 120).

Given the elusiveness of a chronology for postmodernism and its masked cohort, it seems a definition of the Mystery itself is beyond human capabilities. Charles Bernstein (1987, p. 45) admits there "is no agreement on whether postmodernism is a period, a tendency within a period, an aestheticophilosophical category transcending, indeed deploring, periodization, much less exactly who or what would constitute the definition of the term..." Gaile McGregor calls it "a portmanteau concept yielding something for everyone" (1989, p. 148) and notes that "the literature yields an almost breathtaking range of contradictory assertions about its constitution, its derivation, and its value" (1989, p. 147). John Rajchman (1991, p. 125) remarks that:

Postmodernism is theoretical cannibalism; it is the supermarket approach to ideas. One jumbles together the different theoretical idioms available without commensurating them into a single coherent language.

Some definitions have come forward, nevertheless. J.G. Merquoir (1989, p. 41) finds that the "postmodern label has been attached to at least three things:

(a) a style or a mood born of the exhaustion of, and dissatisfaction with, modernism in art and literature;
(b) a trend in French philosophy, or, more specifically, in poststructuralist theory;
(c) the latest cultural age in the West.

Craig Owens (1983, p. 57) describes postmodernism: "Decentered, allegorical, schizophrenic...however we choose to diagnose its symptoms, postmodernism is usually treated, by its protagonists and antagonists alike, as a crisis of cultural authority, specifically of the authority vested in Western European culture and its institutions." Raulet (1983, p. 205) says it is "a breaking apart of reason, Deleuzian schizophrenia." Hassan's postmodernism at once invokes an abstract "Apollonian

---

10. *cont. from previous page*
   Baudrillard's work as "a variant of poststructuralism" (1989a, p. 90) best read in terms of the poststructuralist debates. Baudrillard becomes a sort of ultra-poststructuralist who takes the fundamental premises to the extreme "to dissolve the concepts and problematic of social theory and radical politics altogether" (1989a, p. 91).

view" and a sensuous "Dionysian feeling": "sameness and difference, unity and rupture, filiation and revolt" (1987, p. 88). Hassan first used the term in order to "explore the impulse of self-unmaking" (1987, p. 86). From a Marxist perspective, Alex Callinicos (1990b, p. 115) characterizes it as the discourse of a satiated but dissatisfied Western generation:

The discourse of postmodernism is therefore best seen as the product of a socially mobile intelligentsia in a climate dominated by the retreat of the Western labour movement and the 'overconsumptionist' dynamic of capitalism in the Reagan-Thatcher era. From this perspective, the term 'postmodern' would seem to be a floating signifier by means of which this intelligentsia has sought to articulate its political disillusionment and its aspiration to a consumption-oriented lifestyle. The difficulties involved in identifying a referent for this term are therefore beside the point, since talk about postmodernism turns out to be less about the world than the expression of a particular generation's sense of ending.

Jurgen Habermas (1985), from a perspective informed by the Frankfurt School and critical theory, defines it as a neoconservative intellectual movement.[11] Elspeth Probyn (1987, p. 349) indicates that postmodernism heralds "the end of history; the implosion of meaning; the negation of totality and coherence; 'the body without organs'; the death of the referent; the end of the social; and the absence of politics" According to Jane Flax:

A wide variety of persons and modes of discourse are often associated with it – for example, Nietzsche, Derrida, Foucault, Lacan…; semiotics, deconstruction, psychoanalysis, archaeology/genealogy and nihilism. All these otherwise disparate persons and discourses share a profound scepticism regarding universal (or universalizing) claims about the existence, nature and powers of reason, progress, science, language and the 'subject/self' (1986, p. 322).

Linda Nicholson (1990) and Susan Hekman (1990) define postmodernism as what women lack and feminists should envy.

Andreas Huyssen's 1984 article, "Mapping the Postmodern," reprinted in *Feminism/Postmodernism*, is recognized as a key document in tracing the category. However, Huyssen himself insists on the ambiguous, relational nature of the term and demurs: "I will not attempt here to define what postmodernism *is*" (1984/1990, p. 236, italics in original). In any case, his focus is the debate regarding postmodernism's relationship to modernism. In this context, Huyssen distinguishes poststructuralism as a critical discourse, from postmodernism, an artistic discourse. He notes the conflation of the two terms in America, the way that poststructuralism "has come to be viewed, in the U.S., as the embodiment of the postmodern in theory" (1984/1990, p. 264). Huyssen wants to retain for postmodernism the role of a theory of the postmodern, and

---

11. For general introduction to the literature surrounding the Habermas/Lyotard debates on modernity, see Jonathon Arac's *Introduction to Postmodernism and Politics* (1986), and David Ingram's Postscript in *Critical Theory and Philosophy* (1990).

contain poststructuralism as a critique of modernism. He allows poststructuralism to be "a postmodernism that works itself out not as a rejection of modernism, but rather as a retrospective reading..." (1984/1990, p. 260). Nevertheless, Lyotard's *The Postmodern Condition* discusses *la modernité*, not *la postmodernité*.

In *The Postmodern Condition: A Report on Knowledge*, Jean-François Lyotard defines postmodernism[12] as an "incredulity toward metanarratives" (1984, p. xxiv) and a resistance to interpretation: "It is necessary to posit the existence of a power that destabilizes the capacity for explanation" (1984, p. 61). For Lyotard, critique, like alienation, is impossible, out of fashion. He takes a position of self-regulation within his own philosophical meditation, such that he both represents and diagnoses postmodernism: this is the simultaneity of the postmodern condition. Lyotard finds that the major characteristic of the postmodern condition, a "historically exceptional" event, is its presentation of the most complex self-regulation of basic human conditions: "life, death, birth, work, the parity of the rich and poor" (1985, p. 12). After curating *Les Immatériaux* at the Centre Georges Pompidou in 1985, Lyotard defined the postmodern condition again:

I shall keep this idea of a slow and heavy change equal in length to that of modernity; and this particularity of technologies to create, in an autonomous fashion, new material materials, new matrices, from their acquired knowledge and not as a function of people's needs. And I would insist precisely on the fact that this development is searching for its legitimation (1985, p. 14).

According to Élie Théofilakis, editor of a collection discussing Lyotard's *Les Immatériaux*, modernity is dead, as is the Western promise to humanity of the control of its destiny through "Knowledge, Emancipation, the Economy, History," (1985, p. ix). Such hard materials on which to base a modern sensibility no longer exist. Simultaneously, technoscience has relegated the last five thousand years to the history of the stone age, and humanity as the measure of all things is only a nostalgia. In fact, "there will never again be any proof of our ends, nor proof of the end" (1985, p. x). As man/nature is replaced by man/technique, "our" previous knowledge and sensibility is displaced, dematerialized; *les immatériaux* create us and we are not longer in control. Even the frontiers of life and death become fluid, mobile. We are already other, indeed, we are the immaculately conceived! Can we say then that postmodernism is the philosophy of the immaculately deceived? The undead?

Fredric Jameson tends to refer to postmodernist and poststructuralist theories interchangeably, but he distinguishes between these conceptualizations and the postmodern condition: postmodernism versus postmodernity.[13] Jameson states that there "is a

---

12. For a trenchant and thoughtful critique of Canadian postmodernism, see Gaile McGregor (1989). Especially useful is her discussion of Linda Hutcheon's work on postmodernism (1988a; 1988b).
13. Contrary to Lyotard and Jameson, Scott Lash (1990, p. 4) sees postmodernism as a strictly cultural paradigm, exclusive of, although compatible with, the post-industrialist capitalist economy. It is a "regime of signification" rather than a "regime of accumulation".

difference between the production of ideologies about this reality and the reality itself. They necessarily demand two different responses" (in Stephanson: 1989, p. 72). It is Jameson's view that postmodernity is the cultural logic of late capitalism (1984) (1990). He sees poststructuralist theory as a symptom of postmodernist culture (1984, p. 61) but expects that a reconstructed postmodernism will address it (1984, p. 92). Similar to Baudrillard's urge to reflect to excess a degraded condition, Jameson hopes to, "undo postmodernism homeopathically by the methods of postmodernism: to work at dissolving the pastiche by using all the instruments of pastiche itself" (in Stephanson, 1989, p. 59). Vincent Descombes describes this as Lyotard's strategy as well:

Lyotard considers it reactionary or reactive to protest against the state of the world, against 'capitalism' if we like. There should be no question of reproaching capitalism for its cynicism and cruelty: on the contrary, that tendency should be stoked. Capitalism *liquidates* everything that mankind had held to be most noble and holy; such a liquidation must be rendered 'still more liquid' (1979/1988, pp. 181, 182, italics in original).

Hassan believes that postmodernism has taken a wrong turn, has become "a kind of eclectic raillery" (1987, p. xvii) and he hopes it will instead reach a posthumanism tempered by a pluralist pragmatism. Hassan turns away from the Disneyland wit of a certain postmodernism, and calls for renewed "human" values and beliefs: "The time for sterility is past, grateful as we must remain to the masters of demystification.... Without some radiancy, wonder, wisdom, we all risk, in this postmodern clime, to become barren" (1987, pp. 229, 230). Thus some postmodernists, sated with Dionysian disruption and decreation, call on their old gods for deliverance. Having danced the tarantella, post-modernism relegitimates and restabilizes masculine traditions of power and prestige, which are always in a state of crisis. The tarantella is a southern Italian ritual dance by women, which lasts several hours, even as long as a day. A wildly passionate, raging and public dance, it exorcises and enacts a ferocious female desire for freedom and pleasure. It is an interlude which concludes with the woman's reinsertion into the rule and prohibitions of masculine culture. I am suggesting that the postmodernist usurpers of "the feminine" are doing a Tootsie tarantella and reinscribing their power in transgressing (women's) boundaries and their boundaries around women.[14]

Let us examine, then, this crisis of indifference. Crisis[15] is key to the thought of

---

14. See Sandra M. Gilbert's introduction to *The Newly Born Woman* by Hélène Cixous and Catherine Clément (1975/1986).

15. From her work on Hispanic modernism in the Americas, Iris Zavala charges poststructuralism with recycling pluralism and apocalyptic "end of ideology" theorizing (1988). "Each *ancien* has had its *moderne*," (1988, p. 83) she notes, and this particular *querelle* is unremarkable. "Forecasts, end-of-time/new-era diagnoses, futurology, apocalyptic theories and practices – millenarianisms – abound at the turn of the centuries" (Zavala: 1988, p. 83). What she does not note is how the anguish of existentialism, the atomic epistemology of structuralisms and the catastrophic surges in Foucauldian time and mind all exhibit signs of masculine crisis. J.G. Merquoir asks: *"What if the idea of a crisis of modern culture, far from mirroring historical reality, were a figment of the humanist imagination?"*

cont. next page

postmodern and poststructuralist man, specifically, the crisis of God's death. Lacan writes: It is clear that God is dead. That is what Freud expresses throughout his myth – since God came out of the fact that the Father is dead, that means to say no doubt that we recognized that God is dead, and that is why Freud thinks so hard about it. But also, since it is the dead Father at the origin that God serves, he too has been dead all along. The question of the Creator in Freud is then to know what must be appended to that which continues to exercise this order today (1986, p. 152).

Both creativity and crisis are being rethought in the space opened up by the death of the Creator. Lévi-Strauss awards creativity to structure, Nietzsche recreates a Superman, while Sartre gives creative potential to the struggle of the for-itself with the in-itself. In this way, the good, the true and the beautiful are redivided and reorganized.

Nietzsche proclaims "the beautiful," as the birth of perfection, and Superman as the progeny/goal of this birth. God is dead, therefore Zarathustra must give birth to himself and his world. This affirmation attempts to ride the waves of uncertainty, and exult in delirium and ambiguity as the sources of creation. Nietzsche proclaimed a postmodern nihilism of action and aesthetic truth. As Megill summarizes, "instead of drawing back from the void, man dances upon it. Instead of lamenting the absence of a world suited to our being, man invents one. He becomes the artist of his own existence, untrammelled by natural constraints and limitations" (1985, p. 34). Nietzsche established art as the new source and possibility of truth. He saw "the world as a work of art which gives birth to itself" (1978, p. 419 aphorism 796). Foucault claims that Nietzsche was the first to understand that "man was dying of the signs born in him" (Bellour, 1981, p. 142). Nietzsche was the first prophet of the death of God and man, he was the harbinger of the new *law of eros*. Yet women have always recognized the similarity between what we are told is divine authority and equally pretentious male authority. This new prophetic activity is a frenzy of possession – of woman, and an acting out of union with the deity: the Original Phallus.

While Nietzsche danced on God's grave, Sartre sought to realize immortality within human time. In spite of the death of God, transcendence is still possible. Physical man becomes metaphysical man through the totalizing process of history. And grace is reincarnated in the existentialist project as praxis and being-for-itself. Sartre, then, is the inheritor of "the good", of value, which comes when one avoids the pitfalls of bad faith. Sartre's search for value is as ideological and patriarchal as Lévi-Strauss' reification of truth.

Lévi-Strauss claimed "truth": God is dead, but his Word is alive and universal. Truth is structure, and it is without value. The ten commandments, the laws of human

---

15. *cont. from previous page*
   (1989, p. 47). In other words, Lyotard, Foucault, et al. use postmodernism to hide the atrocities of their humanism and they are imagining themselves in crisis in order to remain in the theory-academic business. Most critically, Modleski points out: "we need to consider the extent to which male power is actually consolidated through cycles of crisis and revolution, whereby men ultimately deal with the threat of female power by incorporating it" (1991, p. 7).

consciousness, are absolute truths: self-creating, self-validating, and self-perpetuating. Incest is the taboo which is the cornerstone of social relations. Lacan would go even further: the Oedipal taboo is the origin of the superego, of the individual as well as the cultural superego of the collectivity. For Lévi-Strauss, truth is scientific and natural, not historical and dialectical. Like Rousseau, Lévi-Strauss believed that whatever is universally true must be natural. However, since nothing remains to be done, this ultimate truth can only be redemonstrated. The universal absorbs everything, and history is replaced by nature. This is explicit in Lévi-Strauss' attack on existentialism: "Structuralism, unlike the kind of philosophy which restricts the dialectic to human history and bans it from the natural order, readily admits that the ideas it formulates in psychological terms may be no more than fumbling approximations to organic or even physical truths" (1966, p. 689). Or as Descartes wrote in 1641, "the idea of God, which is in us, must have God as its cause" (1958, p. 173). The father of French philosophy was demonstrating his theory of the separation between mind and body, and the existence of God: "By the name God I mean a substance that is infinite, immutable, independent, all-knowing, all-powerful, and by which I myself and everything else, if any such other things there be, have been created" (1958, p. 204). Descartes' *Meditations on First Philosophy*, in which the existence of God and the distinction in man of soul and body are demonstrated, reformulated but centred on Augustine's problem of knowledge and conversation with reason: *I desire to know God and the soul. Nothing more? Absolutely nothing.*[16] Three centuries later, this idea is modernized: structure is God, and the binary code is His Word: light/dark, heaven/earth, male/female. Structure is the new inhuman objectivity, but it is also a historically masculine understanding of matter.

A fear of life and a disembodied approach to nature is an important characteristic of male history and scientific patriarchy. Man's "paranoid somatophobia" (Scheman: 1982) can be traced to Descartes, who demonstrated the isolation of the male self, the existence of a detached ego without connectedness to the natural world. *Cogito ergo sum* expressed the distrust of the body and the senses felt by a self that would only know the natural world through science. Science is the attempt at understanding through separation. Indeed, disengagement and distance are the Nietzschean preconditions for illumination and greatness. These epistemological and ontological formulations have remained at the centre of subsequent French philosophy. And so has god, even when he has been declared dead, for he reincarnates as discarnate structure, language and nothingness. Structure is the body of this apparition; language is the mind and nothingness is the soul.

What is the meaning of the declaration of the death of all absolutes, the assertion of the death of the Father? Freud understood the critical importance of the end of metaphysics for man's desire and law. According to Lacan, the success of Freud's

---

16. *Deum et animam scire cupio. Nihilne plus? Nihil omnino.* From *Soliloquiorum*, lib. I, cap. II, in Descartes (1958, p. ix).

Totem and Taboo is to write the only modern myth possible: "The myth of the murder of the father is clearly the myth of a time for which God is dead" (1986, p. 209). The only *material* in Lacan is murder, in his view, the original Freudian murder which inaugurated civilization and creation. (It has a history, then, this monotonous crisis). It's a matter of being born into and by the Phallus. So God is not dead: masculine philosophy continues to perform sacrifices to him.

Jean Baudrillard blames the failure of the "revolution" on women and change, women's change. He sees puritanical "hysterics" everywhere whom he accuses of exaggeration about sexual abuse (1986, p. 42). The radical nostalgia which pervades his postmodern scribbling is for Rousseau's (1979) Sophie and Lasch's haven in a heartless world. For Baudrillard, a rapist is a violent fetus[17] who longs for ancient prohibitions not sexual liberation (1986, p. 47). Baudrillard's pessimism is actually his hope for a defeat of feminist initiated change and a return to man and god in contract, the eternal sacrifice of woman. His ramblings in his cups of cool whisky (1986, p. 7) are given the status of thought. He considers himself *outré* and daring to criticize feminists but, as anyone who has taken a feminist position knows, misogynous attack is banal and regular. Sorry, Baudrillard: it is *outré* to support and to be a feminist. But is this *in vino veritas*, when Baudrillard proposes a Dionysian sacrifice of woman to the image of beauty, purity, eternity? In *Amérique*, he writes: "One should always bring something to sacrifice in the desert and offer it as a victim. A woman. If something has to disappear there, something equal in beauty to the desert, why not a woman? (1986, p. 66). When queried about this "gratuitously provocative statement" Baudrillard replied, "Sacrificing a woman in the desert is a logical operation because in the desert one loses one's identity. It's a sublime act and part of the drama of the desert. Making a woman the object of the sacrifice is perhaps the greatest compliment I could give her" (Moore: 1989, p. 54). A compliment postmodernism will make over and over, like opera.[18] Commenting on a sacrificial scene in D. H. Lawrence's *The Woman Who Rode Away*, Millett writes:

> This is a formula for sexual cannibalism: substitute the knife for the penis and penetration, the cave for a womb, and for a bed, a place of execution – and you provide a murder whereby one acquires one's victim's power. Lawrence's demented fantasy has arranged for the male to penetrate the female with the instrument of death so as to steal her mana...
>
> The act here at the centre of the Lawrentian sexual religion is coitus as killing, its central vignette a picture of human sacrifice performed upon the woman to the greater glory and potency the male (1971, p. 292).

---

17. Mary Daly (1978, p. 431) has also pointed to Jean-Paul Sartre's identification with fetuses in *Being and Nothingness* (1978).

18. See Catherine Clémen "Dead Women" in her book *Opera, or the Undoing of Women* (1988). Again, it is resistance to male domination which is *outré*: "Carmen, in the moment of her death, represents the one and only freedom to choose, decision, provocation. She is the image, foreseen and doomed, of a woman who refuses masculine yokes and who must pay for it with her life" (1988, p. 48).

This explicates the psychic structure, power and process of "phallic consciousness" (1971, p. 292). In *Parole de Femme*, Annie Leclerc describes masculine philosophy: "Death. Death. Death…For if desire is the only thing on their lips, their hearts harbour only dreams of death…Horror and fascination, death haunts them, these fanatics of desire" (1974/1987, p. 77) The "death fuck" (Millett: 1971, p. 292) is the core of this ideology; it is a murder mystery like a novel by Robbe-Grillet. And the target is not the Father, but woman, as nature and mother: mat(t)er.

It is to the heart of mater/matter that phallic consciousness seeks to penetrate. And in feminine disguise, as we see when Derrida becomes a woman. But this is unoriginal; as Anne-Marie Dardigna (1981, p. 37) notes with respect to Sade's "ejaculating" and "discharging" heroines. In Derrida's work the ontology of language is like one of the questions of first philosophy: a religion of the sacred and the profane where male words are sacred and female flesh is profane. Derrida, of course, profanes the profane to worship the sacred. This epistemology knows only the Word, which is not material, although the Word is *in* man. (Not woman, specifies Lacan.)

Lacan's *mot*erialism[19] is both "the death fuck" (Millett: 1971, p. 292) and Gnostic intercourse as death. By the twentieth century, the theft of any possibility for *women* to speak of feminine sexuality in the novel was underway (Dardigna: 1981, p. 37). For what happened "with the invention of the Sadean heroine was the *assimilation of feminine sexuality*" (Dardigna: 1981, p. 37, italics in original). Lacan strives for a style which would imitate mad, paranoid female ecstasy, as indicated by his fascination with Aimée, a woman who killed a woman.[20] The style of murdering women: "Style is the man himself" incants the *homme fatal* (1966, p. 9). I want to point to the ways in which the ethical and political formulations within these writings reflect a masculine appropriation and definition of the feminine,[21] somewhat like Flaubert's "Madame Bovary, c'est moi."[22]

This masculinization of womb-madness (hysteria, already a male fantasy) is similar to the *melancholia* claimed by the male literary critic and described by Tania Modleski and Julianna Schiesari as male feminization for female negation. They argue that the gendered ideology of melancholia recuperates women's real sense of loss and muteness as a privileged form of male expression, ironically of male *in*expressivity and suffering; beset manhood (Modleski, 1991, p. 9). Further, "[w]hat is of course

---

19. Lacan uses this as a play on mot (word)/materialism. Jacques Lacan (1989), "Geneva Lecture on the Symptom," *Analysis 1*, 14. Thanks to Maira Januus.
20. Lacan's 1932 thesis and early articles deal with women's (a displacement?) murders and attempted murders of other women. His thesis, *De la psychose paranoiaque dans ses rapports avec la personnalité,* studied Aimeé's unmotivated attempt to murder an actress she had never met, and his 1933 article, "Le Crime paranoiaque" took up the crime of the von Papin sisters who had murdered their employer and her daughter. Lacan theorized that these delirious paranoic breaks were motivated by a desire for self-punishment (Dean: 1986).
21. See also Teresa de Lauretis (1985) and Tania Modleski (1986; 1991).
22. Andreas Huyssen discusses this in his study of masculine identification with the feminine (1986, p. 189). But see Barry (1989) for an excellent feminist analysis of Tootsie-Lacan, and Modleski (1991, p.15) on Tootsie-Culler.

besetting manhood today is feminism, which the melancholy male 'hero' responds to by appropriating so that he can make its losses (for which he is thus partly responsible) his losses" (1991, p. 10) and *voilà:* "the problem of misogyny becomes...a problem of self-loathing for the male" (Elaine Hansen in Modleski: 1991, p. 11).

What are some of the practical implications of this theory of form and matter? Semiotics[23] is the applied version, a cousin of abstract poststructuralism. In "Pandora's Box in Aftertimes", the internationally recognized American semiotician, Thomas A. Sebeok, reports on his work (during Ronald Reagan's term) for the Bechtel Group, Inc. This group was engaged to form a Human Interference Task Force and prepare a study for the U.S. Nuclear Regulatory Commission. Sebeok was engaged to devise a semiotic system of communication to prevent human disruption of buried nuclear wastes that would be understandable for up to 10,000 years. Sebeok recommends that the area be cursed and a legend and ritual developed and re-enacted annually so that "superstition" may grow and "the uninitiated will be steered away from the hazardous site for reasons other than the scientific knowledge of the possibility of radiation and its implications;" (1986, p. 168). The secret of the radioactively cursed area would be held by an elite few: "The actual "truth' would be entrusted exclusively to an – as it were – "atomic priesthood', that is, a commission of knowledgeable physicists, experts in radiation sickness, anthropologists, linguists, psychologists, semioticians, and whatever additional administrative expertise may be called for now and in the future" (1986, p. 168). The scientist of semiotic systems and communication recommends, as his fail-safe code, a curse and a priesthood. Semi-idiotics? This is the future envisioned by priests of expert masculinity, logos and rationality: word without end, deadly secrets, disguises, clandestine initiations. "Membership in this elite 'priesthood' would be self-selective over time" (Sebeok: 1986, p. 168).

What sort of political action emerges from these ideas about the world? Michel Foucault wrote a series of articles in the Milan newspaper *Corriere della Sera* chronicling his trips to Iran and his ardent praise[24] for the Ayatollah Khomeini's original, mythical and supposedly anti-political discourse (1978, p. 1). The Ayatollah, said Foucault, is a man who says nothing but no, who is non-political, and there will never be a "Khomeini" government (1978, p. 1). An Iranian woman responded: "It seems that for a Western Left sick of humanism, Islam is preferable...but elsewhere! Many Iranians, like myself, are at a loss, desperate at the thought of an 'Islamic government'" (Eribon: 1989, p. 305). Foucault responded that Mme. H. was unintelligent, hateful, and did not understand Islam (Eribon: 1989, p. 305). White western men understand Islam better than Iranian women?

---

23. Robert Young (1981, p. 3) describes semiology as "a science of signs, whereas structuralism is a method of analysis." Semiotics is how semiology has come to be known in America, following the influence of C.S. Pierce.
24. See also the interview with Michel Foucault, "Iran: The Spirit of a World Without Spirit" in the collection edited by Lawrence Kritzman (Foucault: 1988, pp. 211-224).
25. See especially pp. 41-43 of Descombes (1989).

Vincent Descombes (1989) analyzes Foucault's defense of his support for Khomeini which appeared in *Le Monde* as "Inutile de soulever?"[25] Descombes summarizes Foucault's political strategy: "What importance can there be in this death, that shout, or that uprising and in return, what do I care about any general principle in any particular situation?" (1989, p. 41). Descombes considers that this article reveals Foucault's fundamental views about the individual and the collective. Committed revolutionary activity is not the source of Foucault's acts, rather, he indulges in a desire to participate enthusiastically in disruption. Singularity takes all privileges; Foucault is enraged by all constraints, limits, obstacles to the wilful and spontaneous expression of the singular (man). According to Foucault's formulations, the question of whether the individual is abusive can never be raised. Any action against the universal, or collective others, is good. In Foucault's system, argues Descombes, there is no place for political judgement (1989, p. 43). "Foucault has managed to join in one sentence a surrealistic ethic demanding a state of permanent exception for the individual and a supercilious cleric. It's an unexpected alliance of the marquis de Sade and Julien Benda" (1989, p. 43).

Dario Fo, active in Italian political theatre, also speaks to the empty gestures of the contemporary postmodern era: "In Italy postmodernism is a fashion that is already dead. Fashion is by nature ephemeral: it is what results when there is not a fundamental, real reason, ideology, or morality behind a discourse. In other words, when discourse doesn't make an argument" (Stephanson and Salvioni: 1986/7, p. 167). Fo's Gramscian critique of postmodernism's cultural vision and point of reference reintroduces notions of connection and creative formation, indeed, of self-other relations: "Culture is also a moral term. We are not just talking about literature but about a concept of life and the quality of life. Culture means the search for a positive relation between people, for an active moral attitude of solidarity" (Stephanson and Salvioni: 1986/7, p. 164).[26]

The implosion of consciousness and responsibility, the death of meaning, is being proclaimed by postmodernism. All this is occurring as feminist critiques of the economy of patriarchal ideological and material control of women emerge from women's liberation movements. In her article, "The race for theory," Barbara Christian charges that this new white male theory and language "surfaced, interestingly enough, just when the literature of peoples of colour, black women, Latin Americans, and Africans began to move to 'the centre'" (1988, p. 71). I argue that postmodernism's declaration of the death of God the Father is a denial of the practice of male supremacy, past and present. It is my contention that postmodernism is a masculine ideology based on a notion of consciousness as hostile, and an epistemology of negation which is one of separation, discontinuity and dismemberment. Narcissistic

---

26. The work of the Milan Women's Bookstore and Italian feminism is not necessarily within his consideration, since his reference is to a masculine class analysis. For a preliminary feminist critique of Gramsci, see Brodribb (1989b).

and romantic, these *idéologues* (late Enlightenment nominalists) imitate divine process. They are engaged in a process of disengagement. As such, it is not possible to reclaim or rehabilitate postmodernism for feminist uses. To simply add woman to the recipe for the "death of man" and the "end of meaning" would be Sophie's[27] choice. Wisdom is not manic, and the fateful, fatal law of eros is simply male ideology and not proto-feminist theory. In the post-world of male theories and conference circuits, the death of woman is the ticket to masculine redemption and resurrections; and such performances never acknowledge the death of women from male violences.

At the centre of contemporary French and derivative social and political thought is a violent, oppositional and static model of consciousness. These theories of subjectivity and power are inadequate because they have neither grasped nor admitted the nature of patriarchal ideology, or attended to the critiques from feminist theory. These theories of structure, subject and power are ideological. Reading them *is* torture: recalling that *to torture* originally meant to separate the mind from the body.

This phenomenon, developed in France but labelled in North America, has been seen as creative, innovative, liberating and varied, as ambiguity opening up space. I suggest it is a new Napoleonic Code and can be understood as a movement with specific parameters, common themes and ideologies relating to the historical context of masculinist orientations to form and matter. It is unexceptional, unoriginal and but for its hegemony, uninteresting. Therefore, I am criticizing these philosophies in an historical as well as a substantive way. I am attempting to evaluate whether postmodernism is the philosophy of the "prophets of prick and prattle" as Mary O'Brien maintains.[28] In fact, Jacques Lacan says:

In other words – for the moment, I am not fucking, I am talking to you. Well! I can have exactly the same satisfaction as if I were fucking. That's what it means. Indeed, it raises the question of whether in fact I am not fucking at this moment (1977, pp. 165-166).

Their prophecy is the death of God; nevertheless, the law of postmodernism is Father Knows Best and the phallus is its symbol. Feminism is the Devil, staked out and variously pilloried as bourgeois deviation, biological determinism, foundationalism and essentialism. Accordingly, opposition to the ontological teleology of masculinist body and culture is sin and women's autonomy lacks grace.

I define poststructuralism/postmodernism as a neurotic symptom and scene of repression of women's claims for truth and justice. Postmodernism is the attempted masculine ir/rationalization of feminism. I prescribe a listening cure for this masculinity *in extremis*, this masculine liberal philosophy in totalitarian form. How

---

27. *Sophie's Choice*, a 1982 CBS Fox movie directed by Alan J. Paluka, where Sophie, played by Meryl Streep, chooses suicide and a manic depressive man over life with a boring, protective one. In other words, she chooses Dionysus over Apollo, postmodernism over the Enlightenment.
28. Mary O'Brien, personal discussion, 1982.

can one recognize a PMS (postmodern/poststructuralist) man? An individual suffering

from the PMS Political, Personality and Discursive Disorder exhibits at least three of the following delusions:[29]

1. Does not know how to listen. Cannot deal with narrative structure.
2. Is bored, fascinated and melancholic.
3. Thinks his word is God. Or at least, confuses his penis with a deity.
4. Is narcissistic, constantly gazing into mirrors, surfaces, looking glasses. Even when not looking directly in a mirror, sees his reflection everywhere.
5. Cannot make a commitment. Fears the political engagement of others.
6. Despises matter but appropriates its form in a contrary and fetishistic way.
7. Thinks any critique of sexism is easy, superficial, unfair, and cheap.
8. Worst feeling: connection to and responsibility for another.
9. Favourite feeling: exterior control and interior flux.
10. Favourite acts: repetition, sacrifice.
11. Favourite authors: de Sade, Nietzsche.

Postmodernism is the cultural capital of late patriarchy. It is the art of self-display, the conceit of masculine self and the science of reproductive and genetic engineering in an ecstatic Nietzschean cycle of stasis.

---

29. Of course, those manifesting PMS disorder will also score very highly on the scale of the Delusional Dominating Personality Disorder (DDPD) elaborated by Paula Caplan and Margrit Eichler (1990). For a political theory diagnosis, see Christine Di Stefano (1983).

2

NOTHINGNESS AND DE/GENERATION

Seyton: The Queen, my Lord, is dead.
Macbeth: She should have died hereafter:
There would have been a time for such a word.-
To-morrow, and to-morrow, and to-morrow,
Creeps in this petty pace from day to day,
To the last syllable of recorded time;
And all our yesterdays have lighted fools
The way to dusty death. Out, out brief candle!
Life's but a walking shadow; a poor player,
That struts and frets his hour upon the stage,
And then is heard no more: it is a tale
Told by an idiot, full of sound and fury,
Signifying nothing.
(*Macbeth*, Act V, Scene V)
(Shakespeare: 1964, p. 159).

Gayle Rubin's article, "The Traffic in Women: Notes on the 'Political Economy' of Sex" (1975), was one of the first works of feminist structuralism in English. Rubin used structural anthropology and psychoanalysis to develop a theory of the sex/gender system. Her structuralist analysis focused on relationships: the social relations which constitute and define female identity. Social relationships and identity are interdependent and part of a complex process, but Rubin negates subjectivity and epistemological questions of an etiological nature. As a structuralist, Rubin is anti-essentialist and the essence she is against is female.[1]

The theories of Claude Lévi-Strauss and Sigmund Freud were important to Gayle Rubin because "In reading through these works, one begins to have a sense of a systematic social apparatus which takes up females as raw material and fashions

---

1. See Rubin's contribution to the sadomasochistic sexuality reader, *What Colour is Your Handkerchief?* (1979)

domesticated women as products" (1975, p. 158). While she intends to bring a "feminist eye" (1975, p. 159) to their work, she believes that Lévi-Strauss and Freud provide conceptual tools for describing the sex/gender system. Against this argument it is my contention that these tools and Rubin's theory are profoundly phallic. Structuralism and psychoanalysis also seem attractive to Rubin because they allow an escape from biology: "The 'exchange of women' is a seductive and powerful concept. It is attractive in that it places the oppression of women within social systems, rather than in biology" (1975, p. 175). However, it is not necessary to repudiate the body and materialism in order to oppose sexist ideologies of reproduction. Indeed, such antimatter is the common ground of patriarchal ideology. Before accepting Lévi-Strauss's or Freud's conceptual tools, Rubin should at least consider the significance of these gifts, a significance which is explicit in her own quotation from Mauss's essay on gift giving and the Big Man: "An aspiring Big Man wants to give away more goods than can be reciprocated. He gets his return in political prestige" (1975, p. 172).

Freud and Lévi-Strauss are more attractive than Marx, Rubin argues, because their work makes sexuality visible. The different experiences of men and women could then emerge in a critical study of the social organization of sexuality, and particularly Lévi-Strauss's *The Elementary Structures of Kinship*:

It is a book in which kinship is explicitly conceived of as an imposition of cultural organization upon the facts of biological procreation. It is permeated with an awareness of the importance of sexuality in human society. It is a description of society which does not assume an abstract, genderless human subject. On the contrary, the human subject in Lévi-Strauss' work is always either male or female, and the divergent social destinies of the two sexes can therefore be traced. Since Lévi-Strauss sees the essence of kinship systems to lie in an exchange of women between men, he constructs an implicit theory of sex oppression (Rubin: 1975, p. 170-171).

Structure tyrannizes over experience: culture is imposed on sensuality and the body, ideology descends upon substance in a metaphysical and idealistic way. Sexuality, as one moment of female reproductive experience, is given primacy because it is the universal masculine position in reproductive consciousness (O'Brien: 1981). In contrast to Rubin's assertion, Lévi-Strauss's theoretical society is an abstract, universal, male-gendered one, *without* individual male *or* female subjects. It is abstract because it is not material: the relations of kinship are established without births. A hereditary roster of kingships would allow the social destinies of the two sexes to be traced, but that does not make it an implicit theory of sex oppression.

Rubin believes that the dual articulation of the theory of the gift and the incest taboo provides a theory of women's oppression. The incest taboo is a mechanism to establish alliances between groups; it "imposes the social aim of exogamy and alliance upon the biological events of sex and procreation" (1975, p. 173). This motiveless structure is again unrelated to immediate experience: procreation is an event which does not relate to serious political action or agency, on the part of men or women. The agent in this sentence is a cultural structure: the incest taboo, which imposes a set of relations on matter. The motive is to establish kinship. Rubin tries to use Lévi-Strauss's study of kinship as an economics of sexual systems: "the subordination of women can be seen as a product of the relationships by which sex and gender are organized and produced. The economic oppression of women is derivative and secondary" (1975, p. 177). Lévi-Strauss and Freud permit a break with orthodox Marxism, and a discussion of sexuality. Rubin can then isolate the sex/gender system from the mode of production, and propose a women's movement that is "analogous to, rather than isomorphic with" the movement of the working class (1975, p. 203).

Rubin argues that the division of labour by sex exaggerates sexual difference, creates gender, and enforces heterosexuality (1975, p. 178). This structural analysis leaves Rubin at a loss to explain *why* "marital debts are reckoned in female flesh" (1975, p. 182), or *why* constraints on homosexuality mean male dominance. Rubin claims that Lévi-Strauss's theory of kinship and the incest taboo is a theory of the control of female sexuality. But this is not the case. In "Women on the Market," a section of *This Sex Which Is Not One*, Luce Irigaray critiques Lévi-Strauss[2] and remarks: "Are men all equally desirable? Do women have no tendency toward polygamy? The good anthropologist does not raise such questions" (1977/1985d, p. 171). Why do women not exchange men to create social relationships among us? Clearly, this is because kinship is not an abstract concept for women: it is experienced materially as well as socially in the process of birth (O'Brien: 1981).

Rubin sees structuralism and psychoanalysis as feminist theories *manqué*. Her critique remains superficial and wholly immanent because she does not challenge the profound masculinity of the epistemological and ontological presuppositions in these works. Rubin's anti-intellectualism replaced the need for a thorough investigation of the partiality of the conceptual tools she was thrilled to highjack. Geraldine Finn (1989), however, provides a thoroughly anti-sexist reading of Lévi-Strauss in "Natural Woman, Cultural Man: the Anthropology of Male Hysteria and Father Right,". Finn begins with the nature/culture split as masculine ideology and then shows how "culture' is a mechanism for "men's insertion in systems of kinship" (1989, p. 24). Lévi-Strauss's search for a material infrastructure to the exchange of women is part of the operation of this "magical thinking" (1989, p. 24). Drawing from *The Politics of Reproduction*,[3] Finn shows the designs of Lévi-Strauss's laws: to replace the "natural links of kinship which privilege women in general and mothers in particular, with the artificial links of alliance governed by rules which privilege men in general and fathers in particular" (1989, p. 27).

---

2. For a critique of Lévi-Strauss, see also Nancy Hartsock (1983) and Trinh T. Minh-ha's (1989) section, "The Language of Nativism: Anthropology as a Scientific Conversation of Man with Man." It is curious that a work which targets the Great Masters and "has a grandmother in its belly", like Trinh Minh-ha's does, should be taken over/up as poststructuralist, and marketed as "Post-Feminism".
3. "The custodianship of magic is not, as Lévi-Strauss thinks, an innate masculine attribute. It is the first historical attempt to mediate the contradictions within the male process of reproduction" (O'Brien: 1981, p. 157).

Miriam Johnson is critical of Gayle Rubin's and Juliet Mitchell's "phallo-centric analyses" (1987, p. 122). Both "ignore women's mothering and attempt to link Freud's description of Oedipus complex to Lévi-Strauss's theories about the consequences of incest taboos for the exchange of women" (1987, p. 122). According to Johnson, unexamined Freudian assumptions lead Rubin to the conclusion that "kinship arrangements which put women at a disadvantage depend on heterosexuality in both men and women" (1987, p. 125).

Like Rubin, Simone de Beauvoir accepts the "profound work" (1949/1974, p. xx) of Lévi-Strauss on kinship and binarity, and supplements this with a Hegelian master/slave dialectic. De Beauvoir reviewed *The Elementary Structure of Kinship* in *Les Temps Modernes* with humility and great enthusiasm. She accepted the notion of a strict passage from Nature to Culture that was inaugurated when men formed reciprocal relations with other men; women are secondary beings not because we are exchanged but because we have not followed this existentialist path to authenticity and greatness. The universal taboo reflects the original attitude of the existent:

To be a man, is to choose oneself as a man by defining one's possibilities on the basis of a reciprocal relation to the other; the presence of the other is not accidental; exogamy, far from being limited to registering it, on the contrary constitutes it; by it the transcendence of man is realized and expressed. Exogamy is the refusal of immanence, the demand for a *dépassement*; what matrimonial regimes assure man through communication and exchange is a horizoning towards which he can project himself; through their bizarre appearance, they assure him a human beyond (1949, p. 949).

Glad to be of service! The exchange of women expresses transcendence for men. In de Beauvoir's interpretation, the incest taboo reveals a universal attitude of the existent: man chooses himself as a man and defines his possibilities by establishing a reciprocal relationship with the other man. Exogamy constitutes the presence of the other man, it is the refusal of immanence, and the recognition of the necessity of transcendence, a human horizon towards which man may project himself (de Beauvoir: 1949). Culture and the Other inaugurate human existence for hostile brothers-in-law. But such a masculine civilization demands a sacrifice (Blaise: 1988). All this masculine generation of systems of kinship – immortality and the transcendence of female contamination – demand a blood sacrifice. O'Brien illuminates how "...the male understanding of blood – death and discontinuity – triumphs over the female understanding of blood – life and integration" (1981, p. 156).

In "Sacrifice as Remedy for Having Been Born of Woman," Nancy Jay (1985) skillfully outlines the affinity between blood sacrifice and patrilineal descent. Her study of sacrificial practices cross-culturally illuminates the Judeo-Christian sacrificial tradition in particular. The "logic of sacrifice" (1985, p. 293) opposes sacrificial purity to the contamination of childbirth, and is used to organize patrilineage and transcend maternal biological descent and mortality:

Where participation in "eternal" social continuity is a paternal inheritance, mortality itself may be understood as a maternal inheritance. (As Job said, "Man that is born of woman is of few days, and full of trouble.... Who can bring a clean thing out of an unclean?" 14:1 and 4). Sacrificially constituted descent, incorporating women's mortal children into an "eternal" (enduring through generations) kin group, in which membership is recognized by sacrificial ritual, not merely by birth, enables a patrilineal descent group to transcend mortality in the same process in which it transcends birth. In this sense, sacrifice is doubly a remedy for having been born of woman (1985, p. 297).

The centrality of sacrifice, and decapitation in particular, to contemporary French theory is traced by Carolyn Dean in "Law and Sacrifice: Bataille, Lacan and the Critique of the Subject" (1986). She traces literary theory's metaphors of physical violence to the particular discursive configuration which inaugurated French psychoanalysis, and observes that "Textual production depends on a mutilated author, on a process of cutting rather than on a more conventionally conceived process of healing..." (1986, p. 43). But this law of sacrifice goes beyond French literary theory; it is fantasy, philosophy, ideology.

Traditionally, Lévi-Strauss and Sartre are seen as major opponents in the history/structure, nature/culture debate. Both search for matrices: foundational myths or total systems to explain Man and his history. Their debate is over the very foundation of the dialectic. Sartre argues that it arises from the opposition between man and his surroundings, while Lévi-Strauss insists it is between man and Man as the messenger of universal structures from the beyond. Their approaches to matter and nothingness are commonly masculine in orientation and development.

Structuralism became philosophically fashionable with the publication in 1962 of Claude Lévi-Strauss' *The Savage Mind*: it was no longer the purely linguistic method of analysis developed by Saussure. This work broke with contemporary existentialism's formulations of being and knowledge. A major element of this text was a refutation of Sartre's conception of history, particularly as formulated in *Critique de la Raison Dialectique* which appeared in 1960. This reappraisal of *Being and Nothingness* was influenced by the events of the Algerian war and was an attempt to renovate Marx's theory of history for the post-war world. Sartre focuses on the oppositions between existence and knowledge. Sartre believed that "Knowledge is a mode of being; but for a materialist it is out of the question to reduce being to knowledge" (1976, p. 823). Sartre expresses his conception of history and consciousness and cites Marx:

"Men make their own History...but under circumstances...given and transmitted from the past." If this statement is true, then both determinism and analytical reason must be categorically rejected as the method and law of human history. Dialectical rationality, the whole of which is contained in this sentence, must be seen as the permanent and dialectical unity of freedom and necessity (1976, p. 35).

Sartre promised that the second volume of *The Critique of Dialectical Reason*, released in 1986, would "approach the problem of totalisation itself, that is to say, of history in its development and of Truth in its Becoming" (Sartre: 1976, p. 824). For Sartre, the crisis in Marxist culture is the lack of a concept of Truth.[4]

The totalising thought of historical materialism has established everything except its own existence. Or, to put it another way, contaminated by the historical relativism which it has always opposed, it has not exhibited the truth of History as it defines itself, or shown how this determines its nature and validity in the historical process, in the dialectical development of *praxis* and of human experience (1976, p. 19).

In order to grasp the problem of how to "speak the truth" without absolutizing it or falling into an historical relativism, Sartre distinguishes between scientific and dialectical reason:

The modern scientist sees Reason as independent of any particular rational system. For him, Reason is the mind as an empty unifier. The dialectician, on the other hand, locates himself within a system: he defines *a* Reason, and he rejects *a priori* the purely analytical Reason of the seventeenth century, or rather, he treats it as the first moment of synthetic, progressive Reason. It is impossible to see this as a kind of practical assertion of our detachment; and equally impossible to make of it a postulate, or a working hypothesis (1976, p. 20).

Lévi-Strauss rejects Sartre's distinction:

The discovery of the dialectic subjects analytical reason to an imperative requirement: to account also for dialectical reason. This standing requirement relentlessly forces analytical reason to extend its programme and transform its axiomatic. But dialectical reason can account neither for itself nor for analytical reason (1966, p. 253).

For Sartre, only dialectical reason can understand human history and its totalizing movement through praxis: matter is mechanical and inert, but mind is dialectical and active. It is possible to criticize Sartre's model, however, without turning to animism, animatism, or Lévi-Strauss. The structuralist "dialectic" is static: men/Man are the unconscious bearers of a universal totem. Women are neither particular nor universal in this account, but our subjugation is necessary to the establishment of civilization. Lévi-Strauss's argument about the relationship of consciousness to nature is therefore not original: "male-stream thought" has always concluded that male superiority is natural. Lévi-Strauss's particular contribution to patriarchal ideology is his binary coded model of nature and culture (sky/earth, man/woman, and the social relations of marriage) as structure. He rejects the Sartrean for-itself but simply reformulates the in-itself as passively structured: if Sartre says matter is nothing except the site of struggle, necessity and nausea, Lévi-Strauss argues that matter is entirely negative-form. Lévi-Straussian Man is competitive, hostile and uncooperative, and requires the formation of alliances through the exchange of men's sisters. However, he also transfers this

---

4. Such a notion is rejected absolutely by Derrida and deconstruction.

drive to power from men as a group to a primordial structure. His theory of culture refers to the body, but the embodiment is male, and the sexuality is already constructed as patriarchal. Lévi-Strauss has mistaken "exchange of women" for the Word of God. The meaning of the enslavement of women as supposedly necessary to culture is not his concern.

Structuralism emphasizes synchronicity, as opposed to the diachronic conception of time.[5] J.M. Domenach criticizes the non-temporal aspect of the anthropologist's philosophy: "Contrary to certain of Samuel Beckett's plays where time passes without anything happening, we could say here that much happened without time passing: meetings, alliances, conflicts..." (1973, pp. 693-694). Certainly, Sartre's question regarding "the problem of totalisation itself, that is to say, of history in its development and of Truth in its becoming" (1976, p. 824) is outlawed by the epistemological priority of the synchronic over the diachronic in the structuralist model. Sartre's theory of temporality and the dialectic is not synchronic. It is, however, no less patriarchal. Like other marxisms, it has appropriated the dialectic for masculine experience. *Act* as opposed to *action* is the distinction between Lévi-Strauss's synchronicity and Sartre's diachronicity. And both acts and actions can be patriarchal. What I wish to emphasize here is the implication of this conceptualization of time and action for the development of structuralism generally.[6]

Lévi-Strauss's focus on the intelligibility of structure in *The Elementary Structures of Kinship* was based on a rejection of Sartre's position on the primacy of existence over consciousness. In *The Savage Mind*, Lévi-Strauss denounced Sartre's theory of history, and accused him of transcendental humanism:

---

5. Althusser's work reflects this structuralist conception of the totality and the self-validation of systems. Gaston Bachelard deeply influenced Althusser's work. His synchronic conception of time is a sort of proto-structuralist tendency. In *L'intuition de l'instant*, a study of G. Roupnel's *La Silöe*, Bachelard contrasts Roupnel's focus on *l'instant* with Bergson's discussion of *la durée*. Bachelard appreciated Roupnel's belief that time has only one reality: that of the instant: "time is a reality compressed into an instant and suspended between two voids" (1966, p. 13). Bachelard's theory of temporality is based on a duration which is composed of instants without duration. His argument for the primordial character of the instant and the mediating and indirect nature of duration retains Roupnel's original sense of duration as a void. Sense and meaning are contained in the immediate experience which is the instant. Clearly, this synchronic epistemology is not dialectical. This extraordinarily narrow and sychronic tendency suggest the masculine temporal consciousness which O'Brien (1981) describes as relating to masculine reproductive consciousness.

6. Foucault's genealogical history of *asujetissement* (meaning the making of subjectivity and becoming subject to, governed) takes up the question of subjectivity, power, sexuality and institutional forms to catalogue anonymous discursive formations. *The Order of Things* stands as a negative epistemology asserting the death of man, an etiology of *ex nihilo* creativity, and an ontology of *rerum concordia discors*. Foucault's approach to temporality and sense is also a *discontinuity* in sign and structure. Most relevant to any discussion of temporality is *The Order of Things*, first published in 1966. Foucault describes knowledge formations as tables or squares: tables that are destroyed, enigmatic dislocations, unforeseeable destructions, rather than mediation or dialetical processes of history. Change occurs when "knowledge takes up residence in a new space" (1973a, p. 217).

We need only recognize that history is a method with no distinct object corresponding to it to reject the equivalence between the notion of history and the notion of humanity which some have tried to foist on us with the unavowed aim of making historicity the last refuge of a transcendental humanism: as if men could regain the illusion of liberty on the plane of the 'we' merely by giving up the 'I's' that are too obviously wanting in consistency (1966, p. 262).

Kant maintained that the form of knowledge is determined by categories of the mind and that the meaning or content of knowledge comes from sensory perception. Lévi-Strauss stands Kant on his head: the categories of the mind are determined by the form of knowledge: structure and the genetic code. Lévi-Strauss emphasizes structure of mind and the laws of communication which have been ordered by the laws of nature, not by historical praxis.

But in order for *praxis* to be living thought, it is necessary first (in a logical and not a historical sense) for thought to exist: that is to say, its initial conditions must be given in the form of an objective structure of the psyche and the brain without which there would be neither *praxis* nor thought (1966, p. 263).

The aim of structuralist philosophical anthropology is to find a commonality of conceptualization behind the apparent diversity of human societies and to dissolve rather than constitute man. Man is dissolved into nature, because Lévi-Strauss has made possible "the reintegration of culture in nature and finally of life within the whole of its physico-chemical conditions" (1966, p. 247). The opposition between nature and culture is only of methodological importance:

We have had to wait until the middle of this century for the crossing of long separated paths: that which arrives at the physical world by the detour of communication, and that which as we have recently come to know, arrives at the world of communication by the detour of the physical (1966, p. 269).

To the traditional Marxist conception of culture as bounded, in the final analysis, by economic structures, Lévi-Strauss tries to provide a supplementary understanding of culture as emerging from universal, unconscious structures. He wishes to show "not how men think in myths, but how myths operate in men's minds without their being aware of the fact" (1975, p. 12). Sociobiology, the technocratic reformulation of Social Darwinism, also proceeds by reductionism and abstraction. E.O. Wilson's *Sociobiology: The New Synthesis* seems relevant here:

The transition from purely phenomenological to fundamental theory in sociology must await a full, neuronal explanation of the human brain. Only when the machinery can be torn down on paper at the level of the cell and put together again, will the properties of emotion and ethical judgment come clear...cognition will be translated into circuitry.... Having cannibalized psychology, the new neurobiology will yield an enduring first set of principles for sociology (1975, p. 575).

Responding to Piaget's critique that his theory of structure lacks a concept of genesis, Lévi-Strauss demonstrates that structures do have a genesis, but on the condition that we understand "each anterior state of a structure is itself a structure" (1981, p. 627). Social reality is a process of construction, "but the process consists of structures which are undergoing transformation to produce other structures, so that *structure itself is a primordial fact*" (1981, p. 627, italics in original). In the Beginning, then, there are "matrices giving rise to structures all belonging to the same set..." (1981, p. 627). This is contrary to Sartre's marxism and his theory of praxis and engagement with the practico-inert. If Lévi-Strauss admits that the structure requires an Other to grasp it, perceive it, this other is not a subject, but only a structured brain that is part of the natural order. The Straussian opus is the self-discovery of structure. Lévi-Strauss's four volumes[7] of the *Introduction to a Science of Mythology* bring history to a close in the true Hegelian Spirit. Since structural interpretation alone can account for itself and other kinds of interpretation, the work of Lévi-Strauss absorbs and transcends all previous thought:

In so far as it...[structural interpretation]...consists in making explicit a system of relationships that the other variants merely embodied, it integrates them with itself and integrates itself with them on a new level, where the definitive fusion of content and form can take place and will therefore no longer lend itself to new embodiments (1981, p. 628).

Criticizing the social sciences as powerless and self-deluding, Lévi-Strauss points to the redeeming scientific nature of his own enterprise:

What structuralism tries to accomplish in the wake of Rousseau, Marx, Durkheim, Saussure and Freud, is to reveal to consciousness *an object other than itself*; and therefore to put it in the same position with regard to human phenomena as that of the natural and physical sciences, and which, as they have demonstrated, alone allows knowledge to develop (1981, p. 629a, italics in original).

The task of consciousness then is to alienate itself scientifically, but with the knowledge that while it is nothing, it is also everything.

Perhaps the major distinction between Sartre and Lévi-Strauss is their mood before the void: Sartre's is one of heroic anguish and resistance, while Lévi-Strauss is moved to scientific sang-froid and surrender. Teleology replaces theology in creation, but ends in nothing. Both post-war philosophies end in nothingness or nothing. For Sartre, nothingness is the beginning of authentic existence, and man uses the absurdity of death to struggle and create over and against the hostility of inert matter. In Lévi-Strauss's view, structuralism rediscovers organic truths. One difference is that structuralism does not

---

7. *The Naked Man* was the last in this series, which included *The Raw and the Cooked, From Honey to Ashes*, and *The Origin of Table Manners*. The French editions and dates of publications are as follows: *Le cru et le cuit*, 1965; *Du miel aux cendres*, 1967; *L'origine des manières de table*, 1968; and *L'homme nu*, 1981.

raise the question of ethics, because there is no freedom. Structure is the centre of Lévi-Strauss's epistemology. It is not unknowable, but it is unstoppable. Structuralism is existentialism without the existent, without the freedom and anguish of subjectivity. Indeed, Lévi-Strauss the noble scientist despises the self-indulgence of existentialist "debauchery" (Lévi-Strauss: 1981, p. 630). Structuralist consciousness "is able to gauge the immensity of its task and to summon up the courage to embark upon it" (1981, p. 630). It has the courage to embrace and not lament alienation, and to experience itself as a product. And postmodernism, according to Stanley Rosen (1985, p. 101), will be "the attempt to assert Nietzsche's doctrine in noble nihilism while surpressing nobility."

Lévi-Strauss argues that Hamlet's dilemma is not within his power to resolve. Sartre's body and mind are at war with nature, for he is within the anti-physis tradition of heroic man. Lévi-Strauss asserts that the contradiction that preoccupied existentialism, to be or not to be, is the binary code of the natural world itself.

The four-volume *Introduction to a Science of Mythology* is meant to end like a Wagnerian opera, with a twilight of the Gods, or more specifically, the twilight of Man. The final image which remains with our noble scientist is a celestial event, a sunset, in which the heavenly body glows with a thousand colours before disappearing as though it had never been. And this will be so for all life, since evolution creates forms, yet always with a view to their destruction once the fireworks of their zenith have passed. Lévi-Strauss, by showing the objective character of myth, has demonstrated the mythic character of Man, the universe and nature. These mythic objective realities will simply collapse upon themselves and disappear once they exhaust the resources of their combinatory systems. Thought is law, not the existential choice of Sartre's subject. The fundamental opposition of Hamlet's dilemma is not in his power to resolve:

Man is not free to choose whether to be or not to be. A mental effort, consubstantial with his history and which will cease only with his disappearance from the stage of the universe, compels him to accept the two self-evident and contradictory truths which, through their clash, set his thought in motion, and, to neutralize their opposition, generate an unlimited series of other binary distinctions which, while never resolving the primary contradiction, echo and perpetuate it on an ever smaller scale: one is the reality of being, which man senses at the deepest level as being alone capable of giving a reason and a meaning to his daily activities, his moral and emotional life, his political options, his involvement in the social and the natural worlds, his practical endeavours and his scientific achievements, the other is the reality of non-being, awareness of which inseparably accompanies the sense of being, since man has to live and struggle, think, believe and above all, preserve his courage, although he can never at any moment lose sight of the opposite certainty that he was not present on earth in former times, that he will not always be here in the future and that, with his inevitable disappearance from the surface of a planet which is itself doomed to die, his labours, his sorrows, his joys, his hopes and his works will be as if they had never existed, since no consciousness will survive to preserve even the memory of these ephemeral phenomena, only a few features of which, soon to be erased from the impassive face of the earth, will remain as already cancelled evidence that they once were, and were as nothing (Lévi-Strauss: 1981, pp. 694-695).

Being and not-Being are beyond the control of subjectivity. Since man has not been in the past, and will not be in the future, the present is as nothing. Lévi-Strauss roots dualism in the opposition of life and death, and then reduces its subjectivity to an empty space between them. He awaits an end when the final word of human history will be spoken: *nothing*.

Lévi-Strauss's neo-Kantian structuralist anthropology of binary, combining mental structures is Social Darwinism supplemented by a return to the catastrophism of Cuvier, a nineteenth-century paleontologist. Sudden discontinuity and a dynamic in which opposition is essential is also favoured by Foucault, who tried to chart an "almost uninterrupted emergence of truth as pure reason" (1973b, p. ix) in the history of the rigorous sciences. The sudden genesis and extinction of structures is *The Order of Things*. Darwin's *The Origin of Species* also interprets life processes as the survival of fittest forms. In his section, "Extinction caused by Natural Selection," Darwin muses how in the "Struggle for Existence" each new species will exterminate those most similar to it (1900, p. 82). Thus, "The extinction of old forms is the almost inevitable consequence of the production of new forms" (1900, p. 276). This accords with the simultaneous "succession of the same forms of life throughout the world" (1900, p. 264) and his theory of natural selection, or the origin and binary combination of forms:

The old forms which are beaten and which yield their places to the new and victorious forms, will generally be allied in groups, from inheriting some inferiority in common; and therefore, as new and improved groups spread throughout the world, old groups disappear from the world; and the succession of forms everywhere tends to correspond both in their first appearance and final disappearance (1900, p. 264).

Clearly, laws of origin, variation and destiny preoccupy the structuralist alchemists, who have found the philosopher's stone in language, the new totemism. The theme from the religious era that resonates most with the thought of structuralism is absolute finality: the end or purpose to which all is shaped, is to be nothing. A prefigured, inescapable, predetermined ending, signifying nothing. For Sartre, nothingness, the great hole left by the death of God, opens the possibility for heroic self-creation, an almost Nietzschean celebration of the possibilities for existential Superman. Sartre's alienated man toiled on a "thankless threatening earth" (1976, p. 126). The negative reciprocity of isolated individuals competing for scarce resources is Sartre's marxist foundation of history and dialectics. Matter is responsible for antagonisms between men and the alienation of the self in the encounter with the practico-inert. Sartre writes: "all men are slaves in so far as their life unfolds in the practico-inert field and in so far as this field is always conditioned by scarcity" (1976, p. 331). Foucault and Derrida both imagine life as death/decay, a devouring, deadly matter, the Darwinian view of "nature red in tooth and claw". To Lévi-Strauss, the void is something to be merged with, in a final dispersal of content by binary form. Lévi-Strauss, Sartre and Foucault are preoccupied with the precarious form of being, and the contradiction of life and death. They choose the latter as the foundation of their ontology and epistemology.

But there is another "nothingness" born of language and war, and that is *neutrality;* in my view, the essence of Derrida's deconstruction strategy. From negation to neutrality: *i uomo e mobile.* For there is the mask of the collaborator, the indeterminateness of appearances, the arbitrary regime of signs…? Paul de Man was foremost amongst the Yale deconstructionist school and a key figure for Jacques Derrida, Shoshana Felman, Barbara Johnson and others. In 1987, Ortwin de Graef, a graduate student in Belgium, discovered over one hundred articles written by de Man in 1941 and 1942 for a pro-Nazi, anti-Semitic newspaper. This news came just as Derrida's book on Heidegger and the "question" of his Nazism appeared, and while Derrida (1987a) was deliberating on the evil genius of God at a seminar in Toronto.

The responses to the revelations of Paul de Man's wartime journalism should be key texts for students of deconstruction who must evaluate its claims to be a methodology against totalization and totalitarianism. In *Response: On Paul de Man's Wartime Journalism*, Werner Hamacher argues that de Man's collaboration was "*not* founded on pro-Nazi sympathies but rather on a realism to which force appears as an authority that produces facts and justice" (1989, p. 454, italics in original). Thus, the triumph of the will is that it forces reality into existence. Nothing but force creates. Reality is the force of circumstance; nothing outside it matters. Is deconstruction nothing but a stage where everything but consequences are produced? Being, events and ethics are forced, all evidence is circumstantial, all charges unsubstantiated: no material witnesses.

Some defenders of de Man claim his fascist allegiance reflected momentary ambition rather than deep commitment – excusing him as a collaborating opportunist, rather than a "real" fascist. Shoshana Felman uses the same excuse as Rousseau, whose maid (Marion) was fired when he blamed her for a theft he had committed: de Man was not really denouncing the Jews, he was trying to save himself (1989, p. 723). National Socialism evoked his nostalgia for his mother; promising a "renewed relation to the *mother tongue*, beyond the loss marked by the mother's suicide" (1989, p. 710; italics in original). It's his mother's fault. Other justifications argue that his practice and interest was literary rather than political – an argument which completely occludes the social relations which mediate textual production.[8] In "Like the Sound of the Sea Deep Within A Shell: Paul de Man's War," Derrida muses that he will now perhaps have to say "what *responding* and taking a responsibility can mean" (1988, p. 592, italics in original). Yet "Like the Sound of the Sea" is an exercise in justification through the indeterminacy of guilt and the conceit of evasiveness. He emphasizes that de Man was a "very young journalist" – and journalists write in haste, and what he wrote "almost half a century ago" "during less than two years will be read more

---

8. Dorothy Smith's (1990) Marxist and feminist analysis of discursive *production and practices* indicates these relations, in contrast to Foucault's autonomous and autogenerative discursive practices and Derrida's repetition of traces and erasures.

intensely than the theoretician, the thinker, the writer, the professor, the author of great books that he was during forty years" (1988, p. 591).

In these writings, de Man approved the removal of Jews to camps, and longed for the manifestation of a Hitlerian *Volk*. Derrida's long and circular article questions the authenticity of the most anti-Semitic article, speculates on the agony de Man must have felt, itemizes "reading mistakes" (1988, p. 647) that can occur from a non-deconstructionist analysis of the wartime journalism, and finally detours into a diatribe against deconstruction's detractors and those who "if they want still to accuse or take revenge, will finally have to read de Man, from A to Z" (1988, p. 639). Even Malcolm Bradbury notes the ironies of Derrida's response:

The discourse so often used to decanonize and de-fame other writers was put to work to canonize and re-frame the master of deconstruction. More significantly, the vacancies of his theory – it is avowedly not esthetic, moral or ethical, and submits creation to the eternal condition of pure discourse – became a way to pronounce de Man's early writings undecidable, slipping away from their apparent meaning and their crucial historical location (1991, p. 9).

In *Paul de Man: Deconstruction and the critique of aesthetic ideology*, Christopher Norris argues that de Man's subsequent work was a deconstruction of his wartime journalism and a reaction against the totalizing truths of totalitarianism's final solution. Deconstruction then is self-renewal, and the vindicating lesson of collaboration? Terry Eagleton criticizes the argument about a reparative, renunciatory, mature opus by pointing to a certain continuity in de Man's work: "a resolute opposition to emancipatory politics. The early extreme right-wingism mutates into the jaded liberal scepticism about the efficacy of any form of radical political action, the effects of which will always proliferate beyond our control" (1989, p. 574).

De Man never confessed, addressed or took responsibility for this "journalism", and Derrida excuses this: "would that not have been a pretentious, ridiculous, and infinitely complicated gesture?" (1988, p. 638) Apparently, de Man in America spoke of this perhaps only once, in a letter to Harvard authorities in 1955, after he had been anonymously denounced. As central as its roots is this contemporary response to the "question". Having deconstructed history, pronouncements, and responsibility, there can be no verdict, no truth saying, and certainly no guilt. Only indeterminateness: what is collaboration, anyway? Temporization is the response to the questions of identity, its temporality, meaning and consequences.

De Man's anti-individualism and political authoritarianism indicate clearly that he was not an apolitical "man of letters": he commits himself to Hitlerism and the full implications of the fascist revolution which he chided French writers for not apprehending as a totality. In "French literature faced with the events," published January 20, 1942 in *Le Soir*, he criticizes noted French fascist writers for not going far enough, and remaining within the question of the individual rather than the formation of a new totality, new collectivity. These authors are "preoccupied with saving man before saving the world" (1988, p. 187):

We can see in this attitude the persistence of the French individualist spirit, more analytic than organizing, and which will never be able to abandon itself without second thoughts to the intoxication of common efforts. The only change which has been accomplished, a primordial change, it is true, has not been expressed in a conscious fashion by any of the writers cited, but it can be felt in the fundamental thought which inspired each of the essays in question. Individualism survives, but it no longer plays a determining role. It no longer imposes itself like a sovereign power before which all the other necessities must bow. They have finally realized that by acting in such a way, the bases and coherence of society are undermined. They have finally realized, in France, the necessity of an organizing power and have implicitly recognized that the future State must surpass narrowly individualist preoccupations. The problems which they pose are no longer to know which political forms the sacred laws of the individual will dictate to the reigning power, but to elucidate the much more modest question: how to insert the human being in a strongly centralized and disciplined order (1988, p. 187).

The French, according to de Man, are evolving in their conception of an organizing power, but are still at the stage of being "incapable of conceiving of its structure" (1988, p. 188). This resonates with Mussolini's concept of the state: "Anti-individualistic, the Fascist concept is for the State: it is for the individual only in so far as he coincides with the state" (1952, p. 10). Fascism "exacts discipline and an authority which descend into and dominate the interior of the spirit without opposition" (1952, p. 12). This "interior colonization" (Millett: 1970, p. 25), this demand for discipline and obedience from undifferentiated selves is the expression of a rugged and militaristic masculinity. National Socialism, for example, conceives of the *Volk* as a political unity expressed through the Führer. As the essence, manifestation, and bearer of people's will, the Führer demands unquestioning obedience.

Rita Thalmann challenges traditional analyses of the roots of National Socialism to convincingly demonstrate its origins in masculine culture:

Apart from the determinists for whom the history of the Third Reich is merely the modern expression of "Teutonic rage," most specialists interpret it, depending on their ideology, either as the highest stage of capitalism in crisis, or as an accident, a tragic deviation from Western civilization. Never as the extreme logic of a cultural schema founded on the fundamental inequality of the human species.... Yet a simple reading of National Socialist ideologies allows one to realize the extent to which the cultural schema of sexual bipolarity is at the root of the Nazi world view (1983, pp. 45-46).

Thalmann also discusses the importance of an autonomous women's movement and politics: "while the Third Reich marked an incontestable regression of the movement for female emancipation, this regression had already begun when they chose political integration, to the detriment of the struggle for their specific rights" (1983, p. 55). Her material indicates that only a feminist-defined political practice – and one which recognizes women's specificity – can challenge and resist fascist domination. Katharine Burdekin's anti-fascist dystopia, *Swastika Night*, (1940) treats the "Reduction of

Women" to breeding animals who will not resist rape as central to this political ideology (Patai: 1984a). Women are allowed to participate in the "Holy Mystery of Maleness" (1940, p. 9) by bearing children, yet birth is something which defiles men and is transcended by a second birth into the fascist polity.

Nothing matters to both Lévi-Strauss and Sartre. *Nothing* is generative in these *ex nihilo* epistemologies. What really matters is why these patriarchal thinkers are searching for matrices of history, transcendence and matrimony, yet they spurn matter.[9] Matrix, from *mater*, womb, is something within which something else originates or develops. Why does it matter? If matter is "a subject under consideration," "a source especially of feeling or emotion," and especially, a "condition affecting a person or thing, usually unfavourably?"[10]

In contrast to this *ad nihilo* teleology, recent feminist perspectives on temporality shift from the masculinist death-determined future to a birth-determined one. This is the case for Forman (1989), O'Brien (1989a), and Irigaray (1984), although Irigaray uses the metaphors of procreativity only to introduce an amorous heterosexual ethical birth. Her ethics of sexual difference remain within the patriarchal chain which signifies womb as crypt. Frieda Forman's work on women's time consciousness exposes the specific masculinity of Heidegger's Being-Toward-Death. She brings to light the ways in which "for us the future as generative is as much a condition of our lives as is our mortality.... As a collective, women do not only live *in* time (from birth to death), they also *give* time and that act makes a radical difference to Being-in-the-World" (1989, p. 7, italics in original). In "Periods," Mary O'Brien argues that "The birth of a child is the cord which links and breaks and reconstitutes the integrity of history and nature, of linear time and cyclical time. These are not two different time modes but the dialectic vitality of human existence" (1989a, pp. 15-16). I am arguing that what is needed is not "feminist" postmodernism, but feminist thoughts on energy, matter and relativity that do not lead to annihilation.

In "Resolute Anticipation: Heidegger and Beckett," (1989b) Mary O'Brien uses Samuel Beckett's *Waiting for Godot* as a dramatization of Heidegger's *Being and Time*. Heidegger raised the question of Being as the forgotten issue in philosophy. O'Brien does not follow the philosopher into his cave of transcendental Being and everyday being. Rather, she is concerned with the ontological and existential presuppositions of a male *Dasein*. She argues "there can be no authenticity for a he-Dasein who does not recognize that temporality is a continuous *species* experience grounded actively and materially in birth processes, and not the passivity of simply

---

9. *A Feminist Dictionary* defines mater: "Mother. The root *ma* plus the suffix *-ter* yield *mater*, a very old linguistic form which is among the earliest words we can reconstruct historically. Its cognates are found across the Indo-European languages and include in English 'mother', 'mama', 'matriarch', 'maternal', 'material', 'matrix', and 'matter'. The centrality of these worlds is one kind of evidence for the view that a matrilineal Indo-European culture and 'mother-tongue' antedate the patriarchal culture of more recent history" (Kramarae: 1985, p. 260).

10. *Webster's New Collegiate Dictionary*, Springfield, Mass.: G. & C. Merriam Co., 1979, p. 703.

"waiting' for Being to visit one's subjectivity" (1989b, p. 85, italics in original). As O'Brien notes, the very foundation of being in the world, being born, is absent from the play. Beckett dramatizes Heidegger's "throwness" (1989b, p. 86). Vladimir and Estragon "find themselves" in a world in which they were not born. In this waiting room of Beckett's stage, I argue that structuralist he-Dasein attends to his timeless desire: to receive the Word. Vladimir and Estragon threaten to kill themselves if they do not receive word from Godot tomorrow.

It is O'Brien's analysis and not Beckett's dramatization that illuminates for us the masculinity of this static leap for authenticity. There are no women: "There is no dialectic of birth and death, of subject and species, no tension of natural and historical time, no being and no Being" (1989b, p. 88). Godot is a structure, immovable, enigmatic and thanatically eternal. Actually, the message has been sent, and Vladimir and Estragon have heard it. The message is: *NOTHING*, the last word of Lévi-Strauss' *Mythologiques* and the preoccupation of Sartre's being. Estragon and Vladimir, Sartre and Lévi-Strauss do not recognize the sterile masculinity of nothingness. These theories of masculine subjectivity and substance speak only to the unborn and the undead, those without past or future. Time can only be destructive of matter, never generative; time's potency is death, never potential birth. In masculine epistemology, time, space and matter are realities external to Pure Desire and have been theorized in relationship to an original nothingness and a future destruction. Descartes' *Masculine Birth of Time* (Farrington: 1951) portends the annihilation of matter. Existentialism and structuralism turn the tree of life into a hanging post: no new embodiments. This preoccupation with empty, timeless space and the nothing which is everything is the *post*structuralist, *post*modernist, *post*coital, *post*mortem scene.[11]

He-Dasein attends to his timeless desire: to receive the Word and master time, by mating with nothingness/death: Matador.[12] What is at issue, then, is an intimate and ideological process: the purification of masculine desire and the degeneration of time.

---

11. And the excremental cultists recite: "The postmodern scene begins and ends with transgression as the 'lightning-flash' which illuminates the sky for an instant only to reveal the immensity of the darkness within: absence as the disappearing sign of the limitless of the void within and without; Nietzsche's 'throw of the dice' across the spider's web of existence" (Kroker and Cook: 1986, pp. 8-9). *The Postmodern Scene, Excremental Culture and Hyper-Aesthetics* is a prayer to the postmodern cult of despair, authored by representatives of a Canadian journal which is among the strongest endorsers of postmodernism internationally. See also the critique of *The Canadian Journal of Political and Social Theory* by Gaile McGregor (1989). Indeed, Callinicos points out that "postmodernism found some of its most extravagant enthusiasts in Canada" (1990, p. 1). A certain postcolonial mentality?

12. "Lover of death" in Spanish, or "killer of bulls". Of a certain masculinity, Leclerc writes: "Man is aggrieved, not at the cessation of his pleasure, but at the cessation of desire. Deprived of the only tangible proof of his virility, he falls back into the anguish of his indeterminacy, an anguish which never leaves him. His pleasure deprives him of his sense of maleness.

    Robbed of his virility, cut off, therefore, from the only kind of humanity he desires, he feels himself to be totally abandoned, totally alone. Man is the creature for whom pleasure is *desolating*" (1974/1987, p. 77, italics in original).

3

EXISTENCE AND DEATH

The madman jumped into their midst and pierced them with his eyes. "Whither is God?" he cried; "I will tell you. *We have killed him* – you and I. All of us are his murderers. But how did we do this? How could we drink up the sea? Who gave us the sponge to wipe away the entire horizon? What were we doing when we unchained this earth from its sun? Whither is it moving now? Whither are we moving? Away from all suns? Are we not plunging continually? Backward, sideward, forward, in all directions? Is there still any up or down? Are we not straying as through an infinite nothing? Do we not feel the breath of empty space? Has it not become colder? Is not night continually closing in on us? Do we not need to light lanterns in the morning? Do we hear nothing as yet of the noise of the grave diggers who are burying God? Do we smell nothing as yet of the divine decomposition? Gods, too, decompose. God is dead. God remains dead. And we have killed him.... Is not the greatness of this deed too great for us? Must we ourselves not become gods simply to appear worthy of it? There has never been a greater deed; and whoever is born after us – for the sake of this deed he will belong to a higher history than all history thereto" (Nietzsche: 1974, p. 181, aphorism 125).

[Nietzsche]...took the end of time and transformed it into the death of God and the odyssey of the last man; he took up anthropological finitude once again, but in order to use it as a basis for the prodigious leap of the superman; he took up once again the great continuous chain of History, but in order to bend it round into the infinity of the eternal return.... It was Nietzsche, in any case, who burned for us, even before we were born, the intermingled promises of the dialectic and anthropology (Foucault: 1973b, p. 263).

Foucault called Sartre the last Hegelian and the last Marxist: *Critique of Dialectical Reason* was "the magnificent and pathetic effort of a man of the nineteenth century to think the twentieth century" (in Bonnefoy: 1966, p. 8). The new non-dialectical culture which succeeds humanism is heralded by Nietzsche's prophecy of the death of God and man, and can be traced through Heidegger, Russell, Wittgenstein and Lévi-Strauss. According to Foucault, "The non-dialectical thinking which is forming itself will not question the nature of existence, but the nature of knowledge…and its relationship to non-knowledge" (in Bonnefoy: 1966, p. 9).

Several months after Bonnefoy interviewed Foucault, Sartre responded to the vogue of structuralism and Michel Foucault's assault in particular. Sartre found that the denial of history was the fundamental characteristic of the new generation of French intellectuals. The success of *The Order of Things* suggested to Sartre that it was in no way original, that it was a book that was expected. "Foucault gives the people what they needed: an eclectic synthesis in which Robbe-Grillet, structuralism, linguistics, Lacan, and *Tel Quel* are systematically utilized to demonstrate the impossibility of historical reflection" (1971, p. 110). Sartre understood these works as a new form of bourgeois ideology, "the latest barrier that the bourgeoisie once again can erect against Marx" (1971, p. 110). The Marxist theory of history, a dialectical and materialist account of the relations of production and praxis, is suppressed but not surpassed in Foucault's work. There, Sartre saw that history itself becomes unknowable and uncertain, historical reflection is "doxology", but structure is an object of scientific verifiability.

However, Sartre did not reject a structuralism which understood its methodological limitations. He endorsed the Saussurians who took a synchronic approach to the study of language as a system of oppositions. This synchronic permission seems to contradict his Marxist conception of the totalizing movement of history, but in fact it is related to his belief in the relative autonomy of superstructures (1971, p. 110). Sartre believed that linguistic synchronicity would lead to a conceptualization of thought and language which is not one of identity. A synchronic, structural study of the already constituted totality of linguistic relations would lead to an analysis of the "practico-inert" but must then pass over to a dialectical understanding of how structure is produced through praxis.

Sartre claimed that in *The Order of Things* Foucault did not ask the really interesting questions: "how each thought is constructed out of these conditions, or how men pass from one thought to another. To do that, he would have to interpose praxis, therefore history, and that is precisely what he denies" (1971, p. 110). Sartre insisted on the existence of the subject, and dismissed the common denominator of new French intellectuals: "They wish us to believe that thought is only language, as if language itself were not *spoken*" (1971, p. 111, italics in original). Lacan was targeted for using the notion of the disappearing or decentred subject in order to reject history; structure is primary, and passive man is constituted within and by it. The ego is simply a terrain for contradictory forces and points of recognition. Sartre does not deny that the subject is decentred, and he quotes Marx as prior to Foucault and Lacan in announcing that the concept of "man" is obsolete: "I do not see man, I see only workers, bourgeoisie, intellectuals" (1971, p. 113). But for Sartre, "What is essential is not that man is made, but *that he makes that which made him*" (1971, p. 115). It is this *dépassement* and the process of totalization which are the proper subjects of philosophy: "The real problem is this *dépassement*. It is knowing how the subject, or subjectivity, constitutes itself by a perpetual process on [*sic:* of] integration and reintegration on a base prior to it" (1971, p. 113). It is the "philosophical technicians" of absolute and ahistorical truth who are dépassé. According to Sartre, the new generation simply states the existence of ruptures, unable to account for change.

In Sartre's view, Althusser did not comprehend the notion of contradiction between man and the practico-inert structure. "Althusser, like Foucault, sticks to the analysis of structure" (1971, p. 114). Sartre points out structuralism's logical fallacy: "Man is perpetually dephased in relation to structures which condition him because he is something other than what makes him what he is. Therefore I do not understand how one can stop at structure! For me, that is a logical scandal" (1971, p. 115). Epistemologically, the structuralists accept an atemporal formulation of *concept* which is autonomous to the development of things; Sartre defines *notion* as a synthetic process which is homogeneous. He discovers a Cartesian rejection of time among the new generation:

They don't want a *dépassement*, or at any rate a *dépassement* made by man. We return to positivism. But it is no longer a positivism of facts but a positivism of signs. There are totalities, structural wholes which constitute themselves through man; and man's unique function is to decipher them (1971, p. 114).

Foucault was not dissuaded, and would continue to justify his archaeological methodology and the study of the discourse of discourses:

on the same plane and according to their isomorphisms, practices, institutions and theories.... I seek the common knowledge which made them possible, the historical and constituent layer of knowledge. Rather than seeking to explain this knowledge from the point of view of the practico-inert, I seek to formulate an analysis of what one could call the "theorico-active" (in Bellour: 1971, p. 138).

Sartre compared Foucault to Althusser as rendering invisible the relationship of things to lived experience. Anthropology has replaced philosophy, system has negated subject, and language replaces praxis. Foucault, unlike Althusser, does not try to suggest a means of transforming the structure in dominance. As Jeanne Parain-Vial notes, "For Foucault, this notion [the structure in dominance] is not even explicative, it is a positive category of unification. Foucault even avoids posing the problem of causality, and keeps to pure description" (1969, p. 192). She finds that Foucault does not specify, in *The Order of Things*, whether structures of language are identical to or different from mathematical structures: "Is Foucault promising us a philosophy of being and language for the future, or is he demanding from linguistic structure the key category which would dispense with metaphysical reflection and which henceforth would risk engendering a new scientism?" (1969, p. 189). Parain-Vial argues that Foucault does not use structure in the scientific sense as model, only as essence in Kantian rather than linguistic terms. Kant's transcendental *cogito* is empty and static, much like Foucault's *epistemes*.

Like Althusser, Foucault was convinced that humanism was the unnecessary baggage left over from problems the seventeenth century was unable to solve, replete with obsessions which do not merit philosophical reflection, such as "the problem of the relationship of man to the world, the problem of artistic creation, of happiness" (in Chapsal: 1966, p. 15). Foucault's politics is to endorse Althusser's attempt to purge the French Communist Party of the humanist-Marxist tendency, as he asserts in the Chapsal interview (1966, p. 15). He reacts against the charge that his new system of thought is cold and abstract:

It is humanism which is abstract! All these cries from the heart, all these claims for the human person, for existence, are abstract: that is to say, cut off from the scientific and technical world which alone is our real world.... Now, the effort currently made by the people of our generation is not to lay claim to man *against* knowledge and *against* technology, but it is precisely to show that our thought, our life, our way of being, right up to our most daily way of being, are part of the same systematic organisation and thus raise the *same* categories as the scientific and technical world (in Chapsal: 1966, p. 15, italics in original).

Foucault's work was similar to contemporary structuralist tendencies in its elimination of the subject and rejection of phenomenology and existentialism. He makes this clear in an interview with Paolo Caruso published in 1969:

We re-examined the Husserlian idea that there is meaning everywhere, a meaning that surrounds us and permeates us even before we open our eyes and are able to speak. For those of my generation, meaning does not appear alone, it's not "already there", or rather, "it is already there" but under a certain number of conditions that are formal conditions. And from 1955 we dedicated ourselves mainly to the analyses of the formal conditions of the appearance of meaning (in Caruso: 1969, pp. 94-95).

Foucault acknowledged Sartre's passion for politics, but insisted that his own generation had instead discovered a passion for concepts and systems. In this interview for *La Quinzaine littéraire*, Foucault takes his distance from Merleau-Ponty, Sartre, and the generation surrounding *Les Temps Modernes*.[1] The generation of those who were under twenty years of age during the war applauded the courage of the existentialists who reacted to the absurdity of life and the bourgeois tradition by finding meaning everywhere. "But we, we found something else, another passion: the passion of the concept and what I will call the 'system', (in Chapsal: 1966, p. 14). System is defined as an "ensemble of relations which maintain and transform

---

1. Foucault became associated with the journal *Critique* and the newspaper, *Libération*, which as it happens, was founded by Sartre.

themselves independently of the things which they link" (in Chapsal: 1966, p. 14). Foucault himself stopped believing in "meaning" when he discovered the work of Lévi-Strauss and Lacan. Meaning is self-sufficient in structure, which is an absolute object of intelligibility.

The point of rupture came the day when Lévi-Strauss for societies and Lacan for the unconscious showed us that *meaning* was probably no more than a sort of surface effect, a reflection of light, a surface, a foam, and that which crosses us profoundly, that which is before us, that which has supported us in time and space, was the *system* (in Chapsal: 1966, p. 14, italics in original).

History has no voice, no intelligible meaning, but structure *is*. Foucault makes explicit his annihilation of the subject:

What is this anonymous system without a subject, what is it that is thinking? The "I" has exploded (see modern literature) – now is the discovery of the "there is". There is an *on*.[2] In a certain way, we have returned to the point of view of the seventeenth century, with this difference: not putting man in the place of God, but an anonymous thought, a knowledge without a subject, a theoretical without an identity (in Chapsal: 1966, p. 15).

Or, as he says in *Language, Counter-Memory, Practice*: "What matter who's speaking?" (1969/1977a, p. 138). The anonymity and nihilism of Foucault's position is also evident in the way in which it is a theory, or rather a description, of pure relations. The form of forms of relations is still the privileged structuralist concept, an entirely synchronic, non-dialectical formulation without potential. Even the *cogito*, Descartes' atomized, closed domain of interiority, is missing in Foucault.

In the English preface to *The Order of Things*, Foucault rejected the designation of *structuralist*: "In France, certain half-witted 'commentators' persist in labelling me a 'structuralist.' I have been unable to get it into their tiny minds that I have used none of the methods, concepts, or key terms that characterize structural analysis" (1973b, p. xiv). Nevertheless, Foucault has long been discussed in those terms in the French literature.[3] J.M. Domenach referred to "the three musketeers of structuralism, and there are four of them, fittingly enough – Claude Lévi-Strauss, Jacques Lacan, Louis Althusser and Michel Foucault" (1967, p. 771). Sartre and Derrida are other "tiny minds" who have characterized Foucault as a structuralist. Parain-Vial argues that Foucault's distrust for lived experience is what brings Foucault close to structuralism, while his affirmation that man is not the truth of truth distances him from it (1969, p. 184).

---

2. *On* is the indefinite pronoun in French, often translated as rendered in the passive voice. *On dit que* becomes either "It is said that" or "They say that".

3. One example: Editorial, *Ésprit*, Numéro spécial: "Structuralisms, idéologie et méthode," vol 35, no. 360, Mai, 1967, p. 769: "Depuis, le structuralisme s'est developpé, et il s'y est ajouté le 'système' de Michel Foucault."

Foucault's archaeological, rather than historical, enterprise is to elucidate the epistemological field, or *episteme*, to describe the representations, conceptualizations or configurations which inform the empirical sciences. *Madness and Civilization* and *The Birth of the Clinic* are attempts to analyze the conditions under which a scientific object constructs itself (in Caruso: 1969, p. 95). *The Order of Things: An Archaeology of the Human Sciences*, was first published in 1966 as *Les Mots et les Choses*. Foucault wrote *Madness and Civilization* as the history of difference; *The Order of Things* is, he says, "the history of resemblance, of the same, of identity" (in Bellour: 1971, p. 137). It is perhaps his major epistemological work, a speculative philosophy of history which asserts the death of Man. According to Foucault, the epistemological ground is stirring under our feet, and Man as an object of knowledge will disappear "as soon as that knowledge has discovered a new form" (1973b, p. xxiii).

Foucault's search in *The Order of Things* for the forms which ground scientific concepts can be seen as a systematic work of tremendous lucidity, originality and erudition. Jeanne Parain-Vial suggests that Foucault borrowed a great deal without acknowledgement from Jacques Roger's *Les Sciences de la Vie dans la pensée française du XVIII siècle* (1969, p. 176). In contrast, Canguilhem defends Foucault's work as original because it is the first to constitute the *episteme* as an object of study. Language is a traditional topic in philosophy, but Foucault has shown that it is not only a grille which experience must pass through, but a grille which must be defined and decoded (Canguilhem: 1967, p. 610). Pamela Major-Poetzl suggests that Foucault has done for philosophy, history, and cultural theory what Einstein has achieved for science. She heralds Foucault's work as a "first step in the formation of a new science of history independent of the nineteenth-century model of evolutionary biology" (1983, p. ix). Major-Poetzl compares Foucault's archaeology to Einstein's field theory in that it shifts:

...attention from things (objects) and abstract forces (ideas) to the structure of "discourses" (organized bodies of knowledge and practice, such as clinical medicine) in their specific spatiotemporal articulations. Although Foucault, like Einstein, has not been able to eliminate the concept of things entirely and build a theory of pure relations, he has been able to relativize "words" and "things" and to formulate rules describing epistemological fields ("epistemes") (1983, p. 5).

This is a clear, if naïve statement of Foucault's essential positivism and his notion that the social world is regulated by laws and is as interpretable as the natural world. Jeanne Parain-Vial questions even the originality of Foucault's enterprise:

If the role of discourse is to put in order, the question can be formulated thus: where does the order come from that orders the means of putting in order? All that is not very new.... Nothing structuralist or new in the second affirmation of Foucault: the principles of classification are multiple and scientific concepts, even the objects of science, are determined by these principles and by the orientation of the perspective that they impose (1969, pp. 189, 191).

Parain-Vial looks at Foucault's concept of *episteme*:

These *epistemes* are not mentalities; nor are they structure-schemas, nor structure-models. They appear rather as simple concepts, matrix-concepts, which "equip the look" of the reflecting subject, specifications of a resemblance which determines for an ensemble of given sciences or for particular thinkers the secondary concepts which they will use (1969, p. 191).

She sees his epistemological enterprise as original only when it is the most untenable: "when it considers these *epistemes* as exclusive, successive, relatively unconscious, and particularly explicative of the totality of scientific and philosophical concepts of an era" (1969, p. 191).

In his work, Foucault is ambivalent and purposefully obscure about who thinks, who conceptualizes. It is his belief that this radical mystification and quality of absence will open up the space for a critique of knowledge and power. He refuses to formulate or directly address philosophical questions about the being of language and knowledge, or the knowledge of being. The anonymous "discoursing subject" also resented any attempt to question his motives or link his public and private life. "Foucault is extremely resistant, indeed actually hostile, to any attempt to discuss his personal motives. He not only regards his private life as irrelevant to his public role, but he is opposed on principle to efforts to impose psychological norms on his discourse" (Major-Poetzl: 1983, p. 42).

Is Foucault's work fertile for feminist use? While the emphasis on discursive practices does shimmer with a promise of politics, Foucault's work is epistemologically and ontologically static. What is the practice of his politics? Monique Plaza finds that Foucault's work on rape for the French Commission for the Reform of the Penal Code placed rape in the field of sexuality and penalty, setting the rapist at the centre of concerns with processes of institutional power. Foucault, Plaza argues, obliterated the struggles and signs of the women against violence against women movement (Plaza: 1981). In "Ideology Against Women," she summarizes her objections:

Although Foucault has partially called heterosexual power into question and has questioned the "naturalness" of sexuality, he cannot see from his position as a man how this power essentially injures women. And in a debate which opposes the interests of rapists – that is, of men – to the interests of rape victims – that is, of women – he defends the interests of his class and acts in solidarity with it; he defends the right which men want to keep – raping women, that is, subjugating them, dominating them.
 Here we can see how the intelligentsia of the Left, by defending the interests of the class of men, produces a counterideology, which is in fact a "new look" ideology against women (1984a, p. 77).

Nancy Hartsock argues that postmodernism, and her particular focus is Foucault, "represents a dangerous approach for any marginalized group to adopt" (1990, p. 160). She wonders, "Why is it that just at the moment when so many of us who have been silenced begin to demand the right to name ourselves, to act as subjects rather than objects of history, that just then the concept of subjecthood becomes problematic?" (1990, p. 160). Foucault is like the colonizer who resists within the paradigm of colonialism; his position and perspective is irrelevant to the dominated. Hartsock finds that in Foucault's view, power "is everywhere, and so ultimately nowhere" (1990, p. 170). The subjugated are secondary, disruptive forces whose worlds and potentials are not primary. This is not helpful to the marginalized who must "engage in the historical, political and theoretical process of constituting ourselves as subjects as well as objects of history" (Hartsock, 1990, p. 170).

The editors of *Feminism and Foucault, Reflections on Resistance* consider whether theirs is "yet another attempt to authorize feminism by marrying it into respectability?" (Diamond and Quinby: 1988, p. ix). They decide that Foucault helps challenge feminist "orthodoxy" and this is helpful in our historical conjuncture "when feminism is on the defensive politically" (1988, p. ix). Foucauldian analysis will help feminism be humble in anti-feminist times! (Have there been times when feminism has not been under attack?)

Some insist they find Foucault attractive because his work is interdisciplinary (but so is Women's Studies). It resists classification as philosophy, history, or sociology, and rejects the traditional methodologies of those disciplines. For example, Foucault speaks of "a 'political economy' of a will to knowledge" (1980a, p. 73). His archaeology of knowledge has been appealing to feminists who have recognized the limits of trying to work within the economically deterministic paradigms of orthodox marxism and Althusserian structuralism. Althusser's essay on ideology is rejected by Foucault, who writes that ideology is not a king who creates subjects for economic relations of production. Instead, he speaks of a process of subjectification. He argues against the thesis that sexuality has been repressed for purely economic reasons, and describes the proliferation of sexualities and their codification in power, a discursive practice accomplished with the intercourse of knowledge and pleasure. Sex has not been repressed, according to Foucault, it has been provoked, stimulated, formed. In *The History of Sexuality*,[4] presented as "the re-elaboration of the theory of power" (1980b, p. 187), Foucault approaches the question of ideology and power by denigrating both the juridical-liberal and Marxist views. He urges us to cut off the head of the king; that is, to refuse a substantive, singular locus of power which descends from a centre. While the project of asking not what is power, but how it is exercised, is an important and necessary one, Foucault's only answer to "what is power" is "it moves." He reverses the Copernican revolution and replaces Man with the Sun/Son, still an androcentric energy.

---

4. The original French title of this volume is *La Volonté de savoir*. The English translation, *The History of Sexuality*, wrongly emphasizes the sexual at the expense of the will to know, which was Foucault's reference to Nietzsche's *The Will to Power* and the Greek axiom, Knowledge is Power.

Foucault's project is to overthrow conventional conceptions of power as a purely repressive mechanism: we "must conceive of sex without the law, and power without the king" (1980a, p. 91). He forces a re-examination of the repressive hypothesis. "Do the workings of power, and in particular those mechanisms that are brought into play in societies such as ours, really belong primarily to the category of repression? Are prohibition, censorship, and denial truly the forms through which power is exercised...?" (1980a, p. 10). He couples and uncouples knowledge/power/knowledge to argue for a new understanding of the mechanics of power: the power of discourse and the discourse of power, taking into account specifically the deployment of sexuality. Foucault plans to cut off the head of the King, to destroy the idea that there is one central, substantive locus of power:

[M]y main concern will be to locate the forms of power, the channels it takes, and the discourses it permeates in order to reach the most tenuous and individual modes of behaviour, the paths that give it access to the rare or scarcely perceivable forms of desire, how it penetrates and controls everyday pleasure – all this entailing effects that may be those of refusal, blockage, and invalidation, but also incitement and intensification: in short, the "polymorphous techniques of power." And finally, the essential aim will not be to determine whether these discursive productions and these effects of power lead one to formulate the truth about sex, or on the contrary falsehoods designed to conceal that truth, but rather to bring out the "will to knowledge" that serves as both their support and their instrument (1980a, pp. 11, 12).

Foucault does not ask: "What is the will to know?" He inquires how it practices. His history of the Catholic pastoral and of the sacrament of penance illustrates confession as incitement to discourse, a process which he traces to the beginning of the seventeenth century. This transformation of desire into discourse was expanded from the ascetic to the general community, from the monks to all Christians. According to Foucault, this is also the similarity between the seventeenth century pastoral and the writing of de Sade. Truth is simply a medium for the expression of sexuality, where confession constitutes subjects. But Foucault does not only catalogue and ridicule the foolishness and naiveté of Victorian sexual discourse: he aims "to locate the procedures by which that will to knowledge regarding sex, which characterizes the modern Occident, caused the rituals of confession to function within the norms of scientific regularity" (1980a, p. 65). The sexual confession was inscribed in scientific discourse through the inscription of speech as an object of scientific interpretation, the understanding of sex as omni-causal, the idea of the truth of sex as hidden from the subject, a clandestine, dark secret to be extracted by interrogation. Truth lay not in the confession, but in analysis, codification, interpretation. Confession was medicalized, sex was diagnosed, not damned. This has been the one-hundred-and-fifty-year process of production of a *scientia sexualis* and discursive practice. In the West, the *ars erotica* is only latent, it continues to exist only in the pleasure of analysis, in all senses. The injunction to confess is the command to be free. The critical importance of this position as a critique of previous scholarship is the argument that there can be no freedom, truth, or pleasure without their political history. Foucault mocks these absolutes of traditional philosophy:

Confession frees, but power reduces one to silence; truth does not belong to the order of power, but shares an original affinity with freedom: traditional themes in philosophy, which "a political history of truth" would have to overturn by showing that truth is not by nature free – nor error servile – but that its production is thoroughly imbued with relations of power (1980a, p. 60).

Foucault does not measure levels of repression or permission, rather, he shows how power creates lines of penetration. For example, a medical regime advanced, multiplied, and chased desire to the limits, thereby extending and expanding power's space. At the same time, this process specified individuals and incorporated perversions in a psychological, medical categorization of differences within a classification with the strategy of imprinting these categories on the individual modes of conduct and bodies. This is why Foucault argues:

We need to take these mechanisms seriously, therefore, and reverse the direction of our analysis: rather than assuming a generally acknowledged repression, and an ignorance measured against what we are supposed to know, we must begin with these positive mechanisms, insofar as they produce knowledge, multiply discourse, induce pleasure, and generate power; we must investigate the conditions of their emergence and operation, and try to discover how the related facts of interdiction or concealment are distributed with respect to them. In short, we must define the strategies of power that are immanent in this will to knowledge (1980, p. 73).

Foucault is applauded for saying this about power: "Would power be accepted if it were entirely cynical?" (1980a, p. 86) Earlier, Kate Millett wrote on sex and politics: "No tyranny exerts its possibilities without mitigation" (1971, p. 100). Yet she focused on male power over women, still not a popular or cited critical position.

The reason Foucault chooses sexuality as the centre of this discussion is because he believes it best illustrates the flaws of the theory of power as repressive. Or, as he announces, "Power in the substantive sense, *'le' pouvoir*, doesn't exist" (1980b, p. 198). Thus, sexuality is not repressed, as Reich argued, it is endlessly discussed, formulated, and informed. The loud critique of sexual repression has really been a simple tactical shift in the deployment of sexuality, and for these reasons the repressive hypothesis offers neither a history of sexuality nor its liberation. The new form of power as repression was, for Foucault, a new form of pleasure, both for the gazing subject and for the sexual body it wrapped in its embrace. Power was fed by the pleasure it questioned and controlled, pleasure was animated by the probing intensity of the power exercised. Perhaps this is Foucault's politics? There is a double impetus then in the mechanism of control: pleasure and power.

The pleasure that comes of exercising a power that questions, monitors, watches, spies, searches out, palpitates, brings to light; and on the other hand, the pleasure that kindles at having to evade this power, flee from it, fool it, or travesty it. The power that lets itself be invaded by the pleasure it is pursuing; and opposite it, power asserting itself in the pleasure of showing off, scandalizing, or resisting. Capture and seduction, confrontation and mutual reinforcement: parents and children, adults and adolescents, educator and students, doctors and patients, the psychiatrist with his hysteric and his perverts, all have played this game continually since the nineteenth century. These attractions, these evasions, these circular incitements have traced around bodies and sexes, not boundaries not to be crossed, but *perpetual spirals of power and pleasure* (1980a, p. 45; italics in original).

He thinks our pleasure's our pain; incest and its taboo is a game of pleasure and power.

Do the workings of power, its mechanisms, really belong primarily to the category of repression, Foucault asks, or have subjects been talked into it, seduced into subordination, finding pleasure in the penetration by power? Can it be said that our desire and disobedience are rooted in a passion for the phallus, Lacan's only signifier? Foucault's concept of power is ideological. The intimacy of violence is not its enjoyment. Of course, if we say we don't like that, we are told there can be no escape. Even our resistance is already inscribed, constituted, contained, absorbed, impossible. Is that so? Does this mean that we can only perform with the pleasure and power of Judith, who slept with King Holofernes to cut off *his* head? Because that is what he desires, if there is no other history.

Foucauldian feminism is ill-advised: how can we speak with The Master's voice, tell our lives in his categories? Denise Riley's[5] (1988) *"Am I That Name?" Feminism and the Category of "Women" in History* is written against the claim of Black abolitionist Soujourner Truth: "Ain't I a woman?" At the 1851 Akron Convention on Women's Rights, Truth stood fiercely for women's strengths, diversity and collectivity. Riley positions herself in opposition to those who "proclaim that the reality of women is yet to come, but that this time, it's we, women, who will define her" (1988, pp. 4-5). Indeed, Riley's future – and past – is not female but Foucault. Her history is an unconvincing portrayal of deconstructed and decontextualized feminist straw-women. Riley's text is indeed inspired by the pale, pure Desdemona, wife of Othello who asked "Am I that name?" We should remember that it was her fate to be strangled, without a personal or political voice. Desdemona did not speak out, take action, or suspect Iago's plot against her. She fretted in her boudoir rather than joining with her maidservant, Emilia, clearly a more interesting character who said: "Why, we have galls; and though we have some grace,/Yet we have some revenge." (Act IV, Scene III, Part II, *Othello*)

Foucault sees feminism as a sexual liberation movement caught up in the apparatus of sexuality which he describes in *The History of Sexuality*. In an interview, "Power and Sex," he is asked whether it is true that he said that the pro-life and pro-choice

---

5. See Liz Stanley's critique of Denise Riley's approach in "Recovering *Women* in History from Feminist Deconstruction." Briefly, Stanley points to the assumptions in deconstruction which silence women's experiences: "One is the failure to see heterosexuality as a metanarrative binding the category *women* to the category *men*. Another is the tacit denial of aged, black, lesbian, disabled, and working-class women's struggles to name themselves as such. Also women, not just feminists, theorise their own lives and experiences in actually complex deconstructionist terms which recognize multiple fractures within the category *women*." (1990, p. 151, italics in original) See also Tania Modleski (1991) pp. 20-22 for a critique of Riley.

movements "employ basically the same discourse" (Foucault: 1977/1988, p. 114). He responds:

They claimed that I was putting them all in one bag to drown them like a litter of kittens. Diametrically false: that is not what I meant to say. But the important thing is, I didn't say it at all. But a statement is one thing, discourse another. They share common tactics even though they have conflicting strategies (1977/1988, p. 114).

In his view, feminism has responded wrongly to the sexualization and medicalization of the female body. Rather than learning the history of the "immense 'gynecology'" (1977/1988, p. 115) which Foucault planned to write, "the feminist movements responded defiantly" (1977/1988, p. 115). Foucault characterized feminists as saying:

Are we sex by nature? Well then, let us be so but in its singularity, in its irreducible specificity. Let us draw the consequences and reinvent our own type of existence, political, economic, cultural (1977/1988, p. 115).

Condescending and derisive, Foucault considered feminist histories of and writing on "feelings, behaviour and the body" to be unsophisticated. For, "Soon, they will understand that the history of the West cannot be dissociated from the way its "truth' is produced and produces its effects. The spirit likes to descend on young girls" (1977b, p. 153). By "spirit" he means a "primitive" focus on lived, named experience rather than anonymous structure. Actually, Foucault is objecting to a feminist concern with women's specificity and female embodiment and what he fears is a refusal of the androcentric universal. Certainly, he is not citing or deferring to Simone de Beauvoir's "One is not born, but rather becomes, a woman" (1974, p. 301) which both named women's experience and theorized its context. Foucault does not grant originality or complexity to women's scholarship, nor did he favour women scholars. But guess what's missing from the glossy, 1988 presentation of this interview, originally published in 1977? "The spirit likes to descend on young girls" (1977b, p. 153) which appears in the *Telos* version has been edited out. Is this part of the production of the true discourse on Foucault? When he hired his male lover instead of the more qualified woman to the department he chaired in Clermont, he said "We don't like old maids" ("*Nous n'aimons pas les veilles filles*)" (Eribon: 1989, p. 168). It seems Foucault does not accept that patriarchy structures the way "truth" is produced, professors are hired, or "knowledge" marketed.

Foucault's theories of discourse and his theories of power both originate in a notion of self-constructing structures and a conception of the social which has no notion of the individual. Certainly, he has no patience for a feminist individual or a feminist notion of the social. Foucault is preoccupied with the precarious nature of being, with the seed of death in life, and he chooses annihilation as the foundation of his particularly masculinist metaphysics. He poses a system of meaning and non-meaning, and asks what is the nature of discourse and how does it practice in this system where the only certitude is death? *The Order of Things*, as the principal work of Foucault's epistemology, provides access to the particular nihilism that pervades all his work: the ontology of annihilation. When he emphasizes power and discursive *practices*, this is still a malevolent power which is capable only of contagion and destruction. It is especially destructive of resistance, which becomes a co-dependent of oppression. This is the masculinist mask of Foucault's fatal discourse, which is also a mask of power.

In *Michel Foucault, Beyond Structuralism and Hermeneutics*, Hubert Dreyfus and Paul Rabinow insist that there is an epistemological break between the periods of the archaeology of knowledge and the genealogy of power. They insist that Foucault repudiated his position, and that he was not a structuralist. Now, the Rabinow and Dreyfus book has been approved by Foucault; he added an "annex". But even if Foucault finds that Dreyfus and Rabinow have the correct interpretation of Foucault, we cannot simply take the word of the author/s. The reification of discourse that we find in *The Order of Things* remains a constant theme in his work although it manifests itself under a different mask: discourse becomes reified power, which is also anonymous, absent, total, omnipresent, and supreme, and something which is irresistible.

The Order of Things claimed to "reveal a *positive unconscious* of knowledge" (1973b, p. xi, italics in original), a project not dissimilar to Lévi-Strauss's ethnological work on mythical structures. As Major-Poetzl points out, "whereas Lévi-Strauss analyzed the myth-science of primitives and their largely unconscious systems of social classifications, Foucault analyzed the science-myths of Europeans and their systems of classifying words and things" (1983, p. 32). Like Lévi-Strauss, Foucault uses a work of art, *The Maids of Honour* by Velasquez, to uncover the *a priori* of a culture. Foucault hopes to illuminate the law of representation in its pure form from the painting. *The Order of Things* is not a history of ideas, but a description of the limits and conditions of the epistemological fields and their ordering of empirical knowledge. Foucault's archaeological method is to lay bare the fundamental organizing codes which fix the positivities or empirical ordering of a culture's values, conversations, and sciences. It is possible, according to Foucault, to observe the "almost uninterrupted emergence of truth as pure reason" (1973b, p. ix) in the history of the rigorous sciences. *The Order of Things* presents not a search for the spirit of a century but a regional and specific study of the relationship between the knowledges of life, language, and economic production to their philosophical discourses, across the period from the seventeenth to the nineteenth century. Naturalists, grammarians and economists of each *episteme* used the same rules of formation in their theories, and were more closely related to each other than to their own science of a previous *episteme*. Foucault describes discontinuity, leaving aside the question of causality. He felt this step was critical to the development of "a theory of scientific change and epistemological causality" (1973b, p. xiii).

The book begins with laughter, Foucault's laughter, as his preconceptions about the Same and the Other are disturbed by another's reading of a Chinese encyclopedia. The strangeness and unimaginability of that other way of thinking, defining, classifying, arranging, shocks Foucault, and he is provoked into questioning the *episteme* or *tabula* "that enables thought to operate upon the entities of our world, to put them in order, to divide them into classes, to group them according to names that designate their similarities and differences – the table upon which, since the beginning of time, language has intersected space" (1973b, p. xvii). Foucault's goal in writing *The Order of Things* is to announce the end of the modern *episteme*, and to be present at the dawn of its successor. His secondary thesis is that changes in the conceptualization of order and resemblance demonstrate how, in Western culture, the relationships between words and things have been formulated. Foucault does not speak of shifts or transformations but rather of abrupt changes in the *epistemes* of Western culture and the relationship between language and being. The order of the Renaissance, for example, was enforced by the law of resemblance: Renaissance thought was a symbolic and magical thinking of sympathy and affinity. Language was God's signature and was, like nature, fixed and primordial, if mysterious. Language, the gift of God, was a truth which awaited demonstration. Meaning on the other hand, was divined. In the Renaissance space of knowledge, "To search for a meaning is to bring to light a resemblance. To search for a law governing signs is to discover the things that are alike" (1973b, p. 29). At the start of the seventeenth century and the Classical era, similarity ceased to be reliable. The notion of resemblance is replaced by the notion of representation. Foucault emphasizes Cervantes's *Don Quixote* as significant of the rupture. Don Quixote marks the boundary separating the system of signs and symbolic similitudes from the Classical era of quantifiable identities and differences. Foucault describes Don Quixote as the hero of the Same, a negative Renaissance image whose quest for resemblance and likeness verges on madness. With this rupture, the question of how the sign is related to what it signifies is posed for the first time.

The Renaissance system of analogical hierarchy was replaced by Classical analysis. Qualitative resemblance is displaced by measured, quantitative difference. Double representation is now the "mode of being" (1973b, p. 221) of the positivities of Life, Labour and the Word. This is a system of "representations whose role is to designate representations, to analyze them, to compose and decompose them in order to bring into being with them, together with the system of their identities and differences, the general principle of an order" (1973b, p. 221). Language leaves being to enter the age of neutrality and calculation. Analysis is truth. Language does not speak: it calculates. This *episteme* encloses the sciences of the Classical age: general grammar, natural history, studies of the accumulation of wealth. Foucault's meticulous study of the experience of language in the Classical period is juxtaposed with a description of the knowledge of living beings and economic facts. These are the lengthy sections on speaking, representing, and classifying. However, Foucault's aim is to understand the conditions under which these sciences could be constituted as objects of study, and to identify the limits within which the *episteme* developed.

In the nineteenth century and the modern age, the study of the action of producing appearance and law is primary. Literature and linguistics are born, logic becomes independent of grammar. Language is not a means of knowledge, but an object of science, and it, too, obeys its own laws. The Renaissance asked how to recognize that a sign demonstrates what it signifies. The Classical period seeks to know how a sign is linked to what it signifies, and finds the answer in the law of representation; the modern period responds with theories of meaning and the sign. This modern attitude is not a return to Renaissance resemblance and harmony, however, because the First Book (The Bible) has been lost. The being of language was a trinity in the Classical *episteme*, and it was comprised of the significant, the signified, and the conjuncture. But the modern period solidified language in a binary system of signifier and signified, where questions of representation were replaced with questions of signification. The absolute, raw quality of language as one of the world's ineffaceable forms is now gone. "The profound kinship of language with the world was thus dissolved. The primacy of the written word went into abeyance…. Discourse was still to have the task of speaking that which is, but it was no longer to be anything more than what it said" (1973b, p. 43). Most importantly, man is constituted as an object of science in the nineteenth century. Foucault describes the characteristics of the modern *episteme* which permitted the emergence of man:

It is within this vast but narrow space, opened up by the repetition of the positive within the fundamental, that the whole of this analytic of finitude – so closely linked to the future of modern thought – will be deployed; it is there that we shall see in succession the transcendental repeat the empirical, the cogito repeat the unthought, the return of the origin repeat its retreat; it is there, from itself as starting-point, that a thought of the Same irreducible to Classical philosophy is about to affirm itself (1973b, pp. 315, 316).

Classical man had tried to surpass his finiteness metaphysically, but the modern biological sciences denounced metaphysics as a veil of illusion, the philosophy of work called it ideological, alienated thought, and the philosophy of language saw it as a cultural episode. Now, the truth of truth is man. Knowledge itself becomes an object of science. But man is shadowed by himself, his unknowability. Man and the unknowable are contemporary. To think the unthinkable is the modern injunction. And the discovery of the unconscious is the consequence of the constitution of man as an object of study.

The most important procedure in Foucault's "step by step" archaeological methodology is to demonstrate the new organizing principles which arrange these empirical facts on the surface of the table of language. For example, Identity and Difference no longer order the space of "our" knowledge: the modern era sees the emergence of Analogy and Succession. According to Foucault, the rupture took place between 1795 and 1800. The new forms of knowledge (philology, biology and economics) had more in common with one another than with what have been seen as their forerunners (general grammar, natural history, analysis of wealth). In the section, "The Limits of Representation," Foucault begins to sketch out the mutation of Classical Order into modern History. This occurs when labour becomes an absolute unit of measure, and when Adam Smith "formulates a principle of order that is irreducible to the analysis of representation: he unearths labour, that is, toil and time, the working-day that at once patterns and uses up a man's life" (1973b, p. 225). Toward the end of the eighteenth century, the principle of representation lost its power to establish the way of being of knowledge. The unity of Classical thought was fractured, transcendental subjectivity and the empirical world were separated, philosophy and knowledge were no longer transparent to one another.

In the nineteenth century, the field of knowledge could not sustain uniform reflection: each positivity, economics, biology, linguistics, had to have the philosophy that it required (1973b, p. 279). Economic sciences, for example, are based on the end of history, while biology claims the infinity of life. Language as it becomes an object of knowledge, turns back upon itself not in a sixteenth-century movement to interpret the divine Word, but in a movement that turns "words around in order to see what is being said through them and despite them" (1973b, p. 298). If the past believed in meaning, the present, Foucault argues, has discovered the *significant* (1973b, p. 299). The pure sciences emerged, and the way of being of objects became linked with subjectivity through the reduction of philosophy to a reflection on its own development and "what it means for thought to have a history" (1973b, pp. 219, 220). Kant's questioning of the limits of representation marks the beginning of modernity. Knowledge and thought withdraw from the space of representation, which now appears metaphysical in its limitlessness and origin. Foucault accuses Hegel, in particular, of metaphysical thinking: "…Hegelian phenomenology, when the totality of the empirical domain was taken back into the interior of a consciousness revealing itself to itself as spirit, in other words, as an empirical and a transcendental field simultaneously" (1973b, p. 248).

The displacement of language from its representative function has gone unnoticed, in Foucault's view. Modern thought compensated language's loss of immanence in the world by lodging it in the unconscious and in the transcendental act of pure knowing. Formalism and the discovery of the unconscious moved together. Structuralism and phenomenology met and proceeded across the common ground of divine grammar, resulting in "the attempt, for example, to discover the pure forms that are imposed upon our unconscious before all content; or again, the endeavour to raise the ground of experience, the sense of being, the lived horizon of all our knowledge to the level of our discourse" (1973b, p. 299). Foucault characterizes the common *episteme* of structuralism and phenomenology in the elevation of language to the divine and rejects them both.[6] Foucault sees Marxism as based on the same conditions of existence and arrangements of knowledge as bourgeois thought: "the historicity of economics…the finitude of human existence…and the fulfilment of an end to History" (1973b, p. 262). The promise of the dialectic and anthropology were sent up in flames by Nietzsche,

---

6. See his vehement rejection of the phenomenological approach which leads to "transcendental consciousness" (1973b, p. xiv).

and this light illuminates what may be the space of thought in the next *episteme*. Foucault's question is not the Classical: What is thought? or the modern one: What is man? but the postmodern question: What is language? "The whole curiosity of our thought now resides in the question: What is language, how can we find a way round it in order to make it appear in itself, in all its plenitude?" (1973b, p. 306). Foucault's imagery is fiery, all-consuming, and apocalyptic when he emphasizes Nietzsche's question: "Who is speaking?" (1973b, p. 305) and Mallarmé's answer: the being of the word itself. He is not quite sure whether this question marks the culmination of modern thought reaping the fragmentation of Classical order, or whether it signals the dawning of a new *episteme* birthed by volcanic eruption.

Is it a sign of the approaching birth, or, even less than that, of the very first glow, low in the sky, of a day scarcely even heralded as yet, but in which we can already divine that thought – the thought that has been speaking for thousands of years without knowing what speaking is or even that it is speaking – is about to re-apprehend itself in its entirety, and to illumine itself once more in the lightning flash of being? Is that not what Nietzsche was paving the way for when, in the interior space of his language, he killed man and God both at the same time, and thereby promised with the Return the multiple and re-illumined light of the gods? (1973b, p. 306).

The specular and spectacular mirror stage?[7] In Lacan's theory, (1936/1977) the child recognizes absence, lack and realizing it is not merged with the mother/world, emerges into a break from the Real and seeks images of the original (the imagery) and language (the symbolic). Here the child in the mirror phase is Foucauldian structure, grasping the lightning chain of signifiers in his Apocalyptic birth.

Nietzsche's return is used as a Frankensteinian moment of self-illumination by the demiurge of knowledge: a static Being of Discourse recognizes itself when modern thought's question "Who is speaking?" flashes across both Renaissance resemblance and Classical representation, symbol and sign, and the Science of Being is known. From a position of stasis, man re-apprehends being in a flash of lightning. Yet, since there is no memory, no *aletheia* in Foucault's epistemology, there can be no new futures.

There is no intentional, subjective time in Foucault's Darwinian science of history. His discursive practices are governed by a spatializing logic as universal as Hegel's. There is no work in Foucault's time, no labour. Space is not perceived, and time is not experienced. Temporality is absent in Foucault's writing because he rejects lived experience as a foundation for knowledge, and time is experienced. Foucault's archaeology of knowledge and genealogy of power are natural "sciences", marked by a Nietzschean theory of evolution: the struggle for life *and* the will to power. The key works of Charles Darwin, *The Origin of Species by Means of Natural Selection or the Preservation of Favoured Races in the Struggle for Life* and *The Descent of Man and*

---

7. Jacques Lacan (1936), Le stade du miroir comme formateur de la fonction du Je, *Écrits*, Paris: Seuil: 1966, pp. 93-100; *Écrits: a Selection* (1977) translated by Alan Sheridan, London: Tavistock, pp. 1-7.

Selection in Relation to Sex were also preoccupied with the forms, variations and origins of life. Foucault's structural Darwinism studies the descent of competitive, Malthusian formations.

"Man" is a creature of some not entirely omniscient deity: "Before the end of the eighteenth century, *man* did not exist - any more than the potency of life, the fecundity of labour, or the historical density of language. He is a quite recent creature, which the demiurge of knowledge fabricated with its own hands less than two hundred years ago" (Foucault: 1973b, p. 308).[8] Who are these demiurges, these splendid, flawless unities of knowledge which gave birth to "man" but topple into the yawning chasms which border each *episteme*? *Epistemes* are the spaces for the deployment of new modes of being of the empiricities Life, Labour and Language. Yet these two dimensional tables have no depth. The modern *episteme*, for example, has a length of about 1795-1950, and is wide enough to sustain the inscription of those positivities which support all our forms of empirical knowledge. Successive but discontinuous, these *epistemes* are telegrammatic instants flashing across empty space. They are instants in time suspended between voids. Between them falls the shadow, the abyss. *Epistemes* are like the scenes of Robbe-Grillet's disorder of words and things, asserting the desolating beauty of discontinuity and displacement. "The chasm" (1973b, p. 250), the "abyss" (1973b, p. 251ff.) into which the shattered structures "topple" (1973b, p. 251) surrounds these places. What really swallows the incarnated word, the positivities of man's knowledge? In Foucault's thought, the abyss is the place of broken meanings, perhaps it is also the bottomless pit of the old cosmogonies, a matrix of meanings not man's own that threaten his knowledge with chaos? Who is this non-being whose nothingness has "the power to annihilate" (1973b, p. 285)?

Foucault follows the tracks of demiurges, searching for the rules of law and order and autonomous, creative forces that are his motor of history, the motor of man's history. His concern with the structure of *epistemes*, or fields of knowledge, suggests a strong belief in Order – an order which Lacan sought for the unconscious, Saussure for linguistics, Lévi-Strauss for myth, and Einstein for physics.

Death and finality order Marxist epistemology, as Foucault illustrates in his discussion of the shift of the ordering principles of the Classical *episteme*:

The equivalence of the objects of desire is no longer established by the intermediary of other objects and other desires, but by a transition to that which is radically heterogeneous to them; if there is an order regulating the forms of wealth, if this can buy that, if gold is worth twice as much as silver, it is not because men have comparable desires; it is not because they experience the same hunger in their bodies, or because their hearts are all swayed by the same passions; it is because they are all subject to time, to toil, to weariness, and, in the last resort, to death itself. Men exchange because they experience needs and desires; but they are *able* to exchange and to *order* these exchanges because they are subjected to time and to the great exterior necessity (1973b, p. 225, italics in original).

---

8. If one points out that need, memory and desire were subjects of Classical thought, Foucault counters that nevertheless, "there was no epistemological consciousness of man as such" (1973b, p. 309).

Necessity does structure the Marxist dialectic, yet this particularly masculine appreciation of time and life is historically masculine and cannot be restricted to the nineteenth and twentieth centuries. In Foucault's own epistemology, men, objects and desires are neutral and universal points of reference. What is of interest in the above passage is Foucault's sense of struggle and finitude. Gilles Deleuze, who has celebrated the Foucauldian oeuvre and collaborated with him extensively, finds that the passage in *The Order of Things* dealing with nineteenth century biology actually expresses "a fundamental aspect of Foucault's thought" (1988, p. 152), that is, a Nietzschean view of life and history.[9] This is the passage in question: "there is being only because there is life…the experience of life is thus posited as the most general law of beings…but this ontology discloses not so much what gives beings their foundation as what bears them for an instant towards a precarious form" (1973b, p. 278). Life is like Nietzsche's truth, a woman and one who is fluid, capricious and threatening to man's boundaries:

Life is the root of all existence, and the non-living, nature in its inert form, is merely spent life; mere being is the non-being of life. For life…is at the same time the nucleus of being and of non-being: there is being only because there is life, and in that fundamental movement that dooms them to death, the scattered beings, stable for an instant, are formed, halt, hold life immobile – and in a sense kill it – but are then in turn destroyed by that inexhaustible force. The experience of life is thus posited as the most general law of beings, the revelation of that primitive force on the basis of which they are; it functions as an untamed ontology, one trying to express the indissociable being and non-being of all beings. But this ontology discloses not so much what gives beings their foundation as what bears them for an instant towards a precarious form and yet is already secretly sapping them from within in order to destroy them. In relation to life, beings are no more than transitory figures, and the being that they maintain, during the brief period of their existence, is no more than their presumption, their will to survive. And so, for knowledge, the being of things is an illusion, a veil that must be torn aside in order to reveal the mute and invisible violence that is devouring them in the darkness. The ontology of the annihilation of beings assumes therefore validity as a critique of knowledge: but it is not so much a question of giving the phenomenon a foundation, of expressing both its limit and its law, of relating it to the finitude that renders it possible, as of dissipating it and destroying it in the same way as life destroys beings: for its whole being is mere appearance (1973b, pp. 278, 279).

For Nietzsche, truth is a woman; for Derrida, life is a woman, for Foucault, death is a woman, or at least, a mother. Words and things are tissued from a matrix of life which spoils and infects them at the origin.[10] The ontology of the annihilation of beings is *The Order of Things*. Destruction is the destination of all existence which is vanity,

---

9. This is from the section, "Appendix On the Death of Man and Superma," in Gilles Deleuze (1988) *Foucault*, Minneapolis: University of Minnesota Press pp. 124-132.

10. For more information on Foucault and the origin, see Michel Foucault, "The Retreat and the Return of the Origin" in *The Order of Things*, pp. 328-335, New York: Vintage Books, 1973; and "Nietzsche, Genealogy, History" in Paul Rabinow, (Ed.) *The Foucault Reader*, pp. 76-100, New York: Pantheon Books, 1984. An interesting counterpart and feminist discussion of O, Origin and Women is Hélène Cixous's *Vivre l'Orange/To Live the Orange*, Paris: des femmes, 1979.

discontinuity and decay. The corruption of the flesh is the original cause in Foucault's system, and the seed of death in life is central to his epistemology. Foucault confuses immortality with discourse, and mortality with life. Death is surely an aspect of life, but Foucault's Christian conceptualization fixes corruption as our ontology, and attributes the cause of death to birth.

Actually, Foucault's epistemology – life destroys beings – may be more medieval than modern. The Cathars were medieval Christian heretics who practiced an exceptional asceticism, and held that matter is evil and Being precedes matter. The Christ of the Cathars was not subject to birth or death. Although the exact details of their faith were suppressed by the Inquisition, the Cathars are believed to have rejected intercourse and any act that would perpetuate *matter*, the essence of evil in the world. Giving birth would be the greatest sin and impurity. Without birth, there would be no decay of precarious forms. Cathars sought to attain perfection and re-enter the light of the good Creator, leaving behind a world soiled by the Demiurge's introduction of generation and therefore putrefaction. Sheila Ruth formulates the masculinist ego in "Bodies and Souls/Sex, Sin and the Senses in Patriarchy: A Study in Applied Dualism:"

[E]ternal life, godhood, goodness and salvation stand in strict opposition to physical existence, sense, sensuality, death and ultimately woman, who for men incorporates them all. The question of woman and death is the key to understanding this mindset, since dualism is a strategy in patriarchy for avoiding death. It begins in a primary terror: Death is bad, the worst thing conceivable; nothing is more awful. At all costs, it must be conquered, negated. It proceeds: bodies are the things that die, visibly, right before our eyes, displaying to us in painfully vivid terms our own mortality. Our bodies, which betray us to death, are therefore bad. In that case, if we wish not to die, we must separate from our bodies (1987, p. 157).

Woman represents carnality, sin and death, and she defies God and eternal life. De Beauvoir is more sombre and pessimistic on this point, but she also notes man's equation of woman and death. The degradation and vilification of woman and nature is related by de Beauvoir to the fact that woman, as the source of biological continuity, embodies the natural process of birth and death. In a 1979 interview she argued that men resent women, since they are of women born. Consequently men associate women with nature, and mortality. De Beauvoir believed that feminist politics could not deal with man's hatred of woman as the representative of death since, "It is above all an individual matter. I do not believe that feminism will prevent men from hating women because women are their mothers, consequently their death, in a manner of speaking" (Simons and Benjamin: 1979, p. 340).

Gad Horowitz (1987) takes up the Foucauldian question of prediscursive bodily matter and its conjugation with and necessary but negative relationship to discursive power. Horowitz (1987, p. 62) notes that for Foucault, "Human material, although it requires discursive formation in order to be, always contains resistance to any specific discursive formation." Horowitz recognizes that in Foucault's ethical system, primal matter contains resistance, but Horowitz does not link this to the extraterrestrial discursive system of power and domination which is the other half of the co-dependency relationship. For Foucault, matter contains resistance; it is passivity and inertia. In his mechanics of sado-masochism, only the power of domination is given energy, movement, formative force. Horowitz misses this Aristotelian heritage which is the bedrock of Foucault's "excessive antiessentialism" (1987, p. 65). Horowitz is probably correct when he says that the "bodies and pleasure" section is simply Foucault's way of specifying for the sexual sphere, the nature of the resistance to power that is always and everywhere the concomitant of power: "If there were no 'deployment of sexuality' (power) there would be no 'bodies and pleasure' (resistance)" (1987, p. 68). But more significantly, Foucault's law of pleasures/power is similar to Lacan's signifying chain originating *ex nihilo* and universally inscribed in nature, in the unconscious: a Sadeian ethics of decreation and fission/*frisson*.

Foucault claims to be against a metaphysical interpretation of the body and history, his forms are precarious, sapped by life. In "Nietzsche, Genealogy and History," he puts forward a genealogy of the descent of discursive practices: "genealogy, as an analysis of descent, is thus situated within the articulation of the body and history. Its task is to expose a body totally imprinted by history and the process of history's destruction of the body" (1984, p. 83).[11] What is Foucault's body? "The body is the inscribed surface of events (traced by language and dissolved by ideas), the locus of dissociated self (adopting the illusion of a substantial unity), and a volume in perpetual disintegration" (1984, p. 83). The morphology which interests Foucault is that of the will to power/knowledge.[12] And so, Foucault turns to Nietzsche.

Certainly, Nietzsche has been called a Nazi. Walter Kaufmann was the first to attempt to discredit this view. But even if he was not a fascist, it is at least necessary for us to consider the views of Hedwig Dohm, a feminist of Nietzsche's time, who found that he had "nothing more to offer...than the common prejudices of his age and sex" (Kennedy: 1987, pp. 193-194). Derrida might say that this was not what Nietzsche meant, and the erasures and absences must be teased out. But Ellen Kennedy, in "Nietzsche: Woman as Untermensch," has a much plainer reading of the nihilist. She takes him at his word, concluding: "Both the ground for women's subordination in women's biology and Nietzsche's coherently masculine state of adventurers and warriors are founded on a Darwinistically derived master-sex" (Kennedy: 1987, pp. 197-198). Her reading[13] spurns Derrida's vulgarization.

---

11. For a discussion of the concept of the body in Foucault and Nietzsche, see Scott Lash, "Genealogy and the Body: Foucault/Deleuze/Nietzsche," *Theory, Culture & Society*, 2(2), pp. 1-17.
12. As he says in "History of Systems of Thought": "Our objective this past year was to initiate a series of individual analyses that will gradually form a 'morphology of the will to knowledge'", (1970/1977a, p. 199).
13. Other feminist critiques of Nietzsche include: Kelly Oliver, "Nietzsche's Woman, the Poststructuralist Attempt To Do Away with Women," *Radical Philosophy*, Spring, 1988, 48, pp. 25-29; and Amy Newman, "Aesthetics, Feminism and the Dynamics of Reversal," *Hypatia,* Summer, 1990, 5 (2), pp. 20-32.

Nietzsche in no way expected women to become Supermen, or to participate in nihilistic affirmation. There is no essence, the world is irrational, there is only existence, which resides in man's will, his will to power. Nietzsche asserts that there are no gods, but sings hymns to Dionysus in *Ecce Homo*: "Have I been understood? – *Dionysos against the Crucified*" (1986b, p. 134). Is this new idol to be worshipped by women? Are his rituals and practices fortunate for feminists? Nietzsche argues that the *Übermensch* is to be a godless man; but woman must not be godless. The god of woman must be Superman, and this worship must be maintained by fear. Nietzsche rejects the efforts of democratic male liberals who support feminist causes, wanting "to turn women into free-spirits and *literati*: as if a woman without piety would not be something utterly repellent or ludicrous to a profound and godless man" (1987, p. 149). The woman who struggles for equal rights "unlearns *fear* of man: but the woman who 'unlearns fear' sacrifices her most womanly instincts" (1987, p. 148). According to Zarathustra, woman's happiness is to fear and to delight in man's will: "The man's happiness is: I will. The woman's happiness is: He will" (1986a, p. 92).

Nietzsche is considered to be a sexual sadist by the naive readers of his work who plainly take him at his word. "Are you visiting a woman? Do not forget your whip!" (1986a, p. 91) is the most famous phrase. But the text must be quoted at length:

Today as I was going my way alone, at the hour when the sun sets, a little old woman encountered me and spoke thus to my soul: 'Zarathustra has spoken much to us women, too, but he has never spoken to us about woman.' And I answered her: 'One should speak about women only to men!' 'Speak to me too of woman,' she said; 'I am old enough soon to forget it.' And I obliged the little old woman and spoke to her thus: Everything about woman is a riddle, and everything about woman has one solution: it is called pregnancy. For the woman, the man is a means: the end is always the child. But what is the woman for the man? The true man wants two things: danger and play. For that reason he wants woman, as the most dangerous plaything. Man should be trained for war and woman for the recreation of the warrior: all else is folly (1986a, p. 91).

Zarathustra speaks to a woman who has no memory to guard the silence about women, which must remain essentially a male subject and subject to man. In his arrogance, women only know themselves through the male word.

Anthony Stephens (1986) argues that the current hagiographers, particularly Deleuze, Derrida, Foucault and Habermas, do not address the questions of authority and responsibility in Nietzsche's work. Derrida and Foucault, in particular, have used Nietzsche to break with the dialectical and historical vision of Marxism, and Deleuze's ahistorical resurrection of Nietzsche has meant that, "No longer to be stuffed inside a closet, its thumpings and roarings ignored, the 'Übermensch' is once more allowed to parade around as if it threatened no one" (Stephens: 1986, p. 105). Many commentators have preferred to discuss the integrity of the literary object, the structural tensions in the organization of the text. The usual excuse for avoiding the questions of authority and responsibility, particularly in the above passage, is that Zarathustra's words were said by a female character in fiction, and cannot be psychologized or held to reflect on the author in any way. As Stephens points out: "the progress towards a relatively greater integrity of the literary object somehow leaves the words without an author; the plea for devulgarisation deletes the dimension of authorial responsibility entirely, leaving Nietzsche as an authority for...? Who knows? Perhaps going to women with bunches of flowers instead" (1986, p. 99).

Nietzsche fancied himself as an immoralist fighting the theologians, but both the immorality and the theology are primordially patriarchal, as they are in the work of de Sade. I argue that the reason for the post-war Nietzsche renaissance which Stephens so ably describes, but does not adequately account for, is precisely this appeal to and continuity with patriarchy. Nietzsche is held up as a philosopher of affirmation and transcendence, a hero of annihilation. Yet his affirmation is a denial, and it is a denial particularly of women. It is also a denial of history, in favour of an Eternal Return or endlessly repeated synchronicity. Interesting how the philosophers of desire feel that history and woman must be denied together.

What is Nietzsche's account of the feminine, of woman and women? The question of Nietzsche's misogyny, and whether it might have any influence on his philosophy, is not debatable but is still debated. The tradition of outlawing feminist complaints about Nietzsche's misogyny is best represented by Walter Kaufmann:

Nietzsche's writings contain many all-too-human judgments – especially about women – but these are philosophically irrelevant; and *ad hominem* arguments against any philosopher on the basis of such statements seem trivial and hardly pertinent (1974, p. 84).

And what of Nietzsche's metaphysical misogyny, when he attributes the essence of evil to woman? Parable 48 of *The Anti-Christ*:

...God created woman. And then indeed there was an end to boredom – but also to something else! Woman was God's *second* blunder. – 'Woman is in her essence serpent, Heva' – every priest knows that; '*every* evil comes into the world through woman' – every priest knows that likewise (1969, p. 164).

Sarah Kofman in *Nietzsche et la scène philosophique* finds that the accusation of misogyny is unfounded.[14] Nietzsche is simply caustic about *certain* women, the feminists in particular (1979, p. 288). Kofman refers to the following passage, parable 5 of "Why I Write Such Excellent Books" in *Ecce Homo*:

Has my answer been heard to the question how one cures – 'redeems' – a woman? One makes a child for her. The woman has need of children, the man is always only the means: thus spoke

---

14. One uncritical endorsement of Nietzsche's "feminine" is Jean Graybeal (1990), *Language and "the Feminine" in Nietzsche and Heidegger*, Bloomington: Indiana University Press. Nietzsche is "in touch" with "the feminine", according to Graybeal, who does not pause to consider the masculinity and oppressiveness of his categorization of "the feminine" in the world and in language; nor does his misogyny occur to her as full of consequences for "the feminine".

Zarathustra. – 'Emancipation of woman' – is the instinctive hatred of the woman who has *turned out ill*, that is to say is incapable of bearing, for her who has turned out well – the struggle against 'man' is always only means, subterfuge, tactic…. At bottom the emancipated are the *anarchists* in the world of the 'eternal-womanly', the underprivileged whose deepest instinct is revenge (1986b, p. 76).

For Kofman, this is merely a passage condemning *ressentiment* in both men and women. But in spite of the protests of Kaufmann and Kofman, Nietzsche is indeed a misogynist. We must take him at his word, especially when the words are threats. Misogyny is also worth taking seriously in someone who sees himself as "the first psychologist of the eternal-womanly" (Nietzsche: 1986b, p. 75), as he says in parable 5 of "Why I Write Such Excellent Books," in *Ecce Homo*. Indeed, women must not lose a fear of male revenge against female weakness and womanly virtues which are antithetical to the warrior state of the Superman. Woman must overcome her spirit for revenge and her *ressentiment* by affirming and becoming generous and hearing the Superman: "Let the flash of a star glitter in your love! Let your hope be: 'May I bear the Superman!'" (1986a, p. 92).

In Nietzsche's work, women are craven beings with a natural slave mentality. Yet it seems odd that while woman lacks a will to power, her "natural" submission must continually be reinforced by making her *afraid* of man. Otherwise, she triumphs, but perhaps only over the man of the herd? Superman eludes woman's dominion and guile, and keeps her in fear. Man must overcome himself to overcome woman. But is it only as Superman that man can overcome woman? Woman is man's basest passion; his marriage to his creative potential is holy:

Your love for woman and woman's love for man: ah, if only it were pity for suffering and veiled gods! But generally two animals sense one another. But even your best love too is only a passionate impersonation and a painful ardour. It is a torch which should light your way to higher paths. One day you shall love beyond yourselves! So first *learn* to love! For that you have had to drink the bitter cup of your love. There is bitterness in the cup of even the best love: thus it arouses longing for the Superman, thus it arouses thirst in you, the creator! A creator's thirst, arrow, and longing for the Superman: speak, my brother, is this your will to marriage? I call holy such a will and such a marriage (1986a, p. 96).

It is shameful that the man who aspires to love and to be Superman must couple with she who is "a little dressed-up lie" (1986a, p. 96). A tremendous will is therefore necessary for man to create something that is not part of the stupid herd from this coupling. Thus, Superman must grit his teeth, swallow the bitter cup, and aim upward. And yet it must be so, for there are no Superwomen, and no woman worthy of being Superman's wife or mother. The only bride for Superman is eternity, as this passage from *Thus Spoke Zarathustra* attests:

Oh how should I not lust for eternity and for the wedding ring of rings – the Ring of Recurrence! Never yet did I find the woman by whom I wanted children, unless it be this woman, whom I love: for I love you, O Eternity! (1986a, p. 246).

But man has not yet eternity for his wife, he has woman: "Yes, I wish the earth shook with convulsions when a saint and a goose mate together" (1986a, p. 96). Is Superman so easily seduced then, and by a goose? Could Dionysus be compromised by so weak and insipid a creature? The shroud which Nietzsche uses to make less bitter the cup of man's essential powerlessness to give birth in spite of the most Dionysian or Herculean self-love, is the shroud of a joyous fatalism/fetalism before an eternal return which robs particular women of the power of generation and puts it in the hands of universal Superman. With his will to power, he alone can know such an affirmation of the whole. Only Superman can delight in the eternal return, which says that woman is nothing, finite bodies and births are nothing. But Superman's own nothing is something else: he is a creator because he has embraced the fetishes of procreativity over the abyss of nihilism. The finite, the small, the particular: woman is loathesome to Nietzsche.

Such a spirit who has *become free* stands amidst the cosmos with a joyous and trusting fatalism, in the *faith* that only the particular is loathsome, and that all is redeemed and affirmed in the whole – *he does not* negate any more (1954, p. 554).

"He does not negate anymore" should be "he is not negated anymore", for what Nietzsche affirms is his triumph over death. Nietzsche's joyous fatalism before the "whole" is that he can overcome it by a massive will to power. The eternal recurrence is his hope for the transcendence of both finitude and the annihilation of his particularity through its eternal return as masculine time without end.

Lévi-Strauss's theory of time is similar to that of Nietzsche's, except that Nietzsche proclaims an endless synchronicity, and Lévi-Strauss was more nihilistic in his finitude. The particles of matter may be broken down to the infinitesimally small, and recombine, but the number of these recombinations is as finite as the matter it disperses and forms. In contrast, Nietzsche conceives time as infinite, and recombinations of specific moments and bodies will occur again and again, endlessly. The eternal return is Nietzsche's dynamic synchronicity. Unlike Lévi-Strauss's final moment of ultimate binary combination, there is no finality in Nietzsche, no "nothing" at the end, but a continual return to the same. Nevertheless, the Superman is similar to Lévi-Strauss's and Sartre's idea that while man is nothing, he is also everything. Superman:

who has organized the chaos of his passions and integrated every feature of his character, redeeming the ugly by giving it a meaning in a beautiful totality...would also realize how inextricably his own being was involved in the totality of the cosmos: and in affirming his own being, he would also affirm all that is, has been, or will be (Kaufmann in Nietzsche: 1974, p. 320).

Superman's "Yes" is an attempt to absorb eternity in his own being: imitating the formless chaos of the abyss with his uterus-fetish. But this is a static and not a dialectical creativity. There is no creation of new beings since matter/mater is rendered ultimately finite and sterile.

But the abyss is not easily mastered. It is a dangerous labyrinth from which man may not emerge, a tormented sea on a dark night. Its aspects are creation and woman. Nietzsche must leap from peak to peak over the abyss, along the teeth of the *vagina dentata*, insatiable cavity of death and rebirth. In parable 27 of *Twilight of the Idols*, he is humming to himself to mask his fear: "Women are considered deep – why? because one can never discover any bottom to them. Women are not even shallow" (1969, p. 25). In Nietzsche's "Women and their action at a distance" in *The Gay Science*, Man is tormented beside a thundering sea, when "suddenly, as if born out of nothing" a ghostly sailboat "appears before the gate of this hellish labyrinth" (1974, p. 123). And hell has always yawned – a cognate of yoni, the female genitals. In this dream of death, Nietzsche is on a ship, which is always "she", cradle and coffin, taking the Norseman's soul back to the sea Mother.[15] David Farrell Krell in *Postponements, Woman, Sensuality and Death in Nietzsche*, argues that "*Distanz*, the aura of the feminine, here invades the very essence of heroic masculinity" (1986, p. 9). This insight appends rather than informs Krell's discussion of the passage. In fact, the ghostly feminine ships terrify and inspire Nietzsche in their movement: "A spiritlike intermediate being: quietly observing, gliding, floating? As the boat that with its white sails moves like an immense butterfly over the dark sea. Yes! To move *over* existence! That's it! That would be something!" (1974, p. 123). These intermediate beings in feminine ships are *fetuses*. To exist, they must leave the womb – take their distance. "The most powerful effect of women is, in philosophical language, action at a distance, *actio in distans*; but this requires first of all and above all – *distance*" (1974, p. 124). Keeping woman at a distance allows Nietzsche to approach the abyss, the labyrinth, just as Theseus took her thread/cord and moved away from Ariadne to enter the labyrinth and slay the minotaur. And who is the minotaur Nietzsche hears?

Do I still have ears? Am I all ears and nothing else? Here I stand in the flaming surf whose white tongues are licking at my feet; from all sides I hear howling, threats, screaming, roaring coming at me, while the old earth-shaker sings his aria in the lowest depths, deep as a bellowing bull, while pounding such an earth-shaking beat the hearts of even these weather-beaten rocky monsters are trembling in their bodies (1974, p. 123).

But birth is into a life where spare time will end with man being "dashed against the rocks." How to return to return again is the central preoccupation: to move *over* existence and not be swept under by it, the secret is held by the quietly observing, floating intermediate beings in feminine ships. Only Superman/Zarathustra can think the "'most abysmal thought'" (1986b, p. 108, aphorism 6).

Theseus took an even greater distance when he abandoned Ariadne on Naxos and sailed off (in a boat with white sails moving like a butterfly over the dark seas?).[16]

---

15. Barbara Walker describes the ship as an early womb symbol (1983, p. 934).
16. What is never noticed is that Theseus was later destroyed by Aphrodite and the cursed love of Ariadne's sister, Phaedre.

The *distanz* that Nietzsche/Theseus want to take is a space/time relationship; specifically, a female movement over existence. Existence, a certain manifestation in and through space and time, elapses. And man is dashed against the rocks.

Nietzsche feels that he knows how to deal with truth and woman, unlike the theologians who were maladroit in their approach.[17] Superman can enter the abyss with bravado because he is wearing several masks and he is both the most negative and the most affirmative of men: a male mother. *His* contemplative spirit gives birth to itself. The following passage from Book II, aphorism 72 of *The Gay Science* makes this clear: "Pregnancy has made women kinder, more patient, more timid, more pleased to submit; and just so does spiritual pregnancy produce the character of the contemplative type, which is closely related to the feminine character: it consists of male mothers" (1974, p. 129). Nietzsche yearns to give birth to Superman, to himself, a work of art. He wants to have eternity's children: "Never yet did I find the woman by whom I wanted children, unless it be this woman, whom I love: for I love you, O Eternity!" (1986a, p. 246). But there is danger other than the gaping abyss. Nietzsche/ Dionysus fears the maenads[18] may tear him to pieces when they find him mimicking the Mother, being and becoming eternally feminine in Her fetishes. This fear is revealed in *Ecce Homo*, in aphorism 5 of "Why I write such excellent books":

Dare I venture in addition to suggest that I *know* these little women? It is part of my Dionysian endowment. Who knows? perhaps I am the first psychologist of the eternal-womanly. They all love me – an old story:[19] excepting the *abortive* women, the 'emancipated' who lack the stuff for children. – Happily I am not prepared to be torn to pieces: the complete woman tears to pieces when she loves…. I know these amiable maenads…. Ah, what a dangerous, creeping, subterranean little beast of prey it is! And so pleasant with it! (1986b, pp. 75, 76).

These abortive women Nietzsche fears are those who will make him abort his child, which is himself, the child of eternity.[20] For what are the Dionysian myths he clings to in particular? They are described in *Twilight of the Idols* in "What I Owe to the Ancients," aphorism 4:

---

17. See the preface to *Beyond Good and Evil* by Friedrich Nietzsche. It is the impudent theologians who search for Truth, and do not understand "her" ferocious, protean, unknowable character.

18. Traditionally understood to be the devotees of the God Dionysus. They were believed to tear human and animal flesh and devour blood and wine in bacchic rituals. See figures in Chapter 6. In "The Maenad in Early Greek Art," Sheila McNally traces the changing relationship between the satyr and the maenad from 580 to 470 B.C. The rapport of harmony, excitement and affection changed to one of hostility and abduction, she claims. McNally sees this as representing a shift in the organization of men's experiences of *eros* and *logos* and a transvaluation of reason, nature and culture. Interestingly, she maintains that the maenads were outside social contracts, and unlike other women, had no male "protectors". The maenad had to rescue herself from difficulty and indeed "no other female in Greek art defends her chastity so fiercely as the maenad" (McNally: 1984, p. 107). While there are no satyrs in Euripides' *Bacchae*, they may appear in Nietzsche as either the *Untermensch*, or *Übermensch*.

19. Here we find Lacan is not original in his use of this taunt. An old story, indeed.

20. Nietzsche's execrable book of poetry, *Dithyrambs of Dionysus* (1984) means *doubly-born Dionysus*.

What did the Hellene guarantee to himself with these mysteries? *Eternal* life, the eternal recurrence of life; the future promised and consecrated in the past; the triumphant Yes to life beyond death and change; *true* life as collective continuation of life through procreation, through the mysteries of sexuality. It was for this reason that the *sexual* symbol was to the Greeks the symbol venerable as such, the intrinsic profound meaning of all antique piety. Every individual detail in the act of procreation, pregnancy, birth, awoke the most exalted and solemn feelings. In the teachings of the mysteries, *pain* is sanctified: the 'pains of childbirth' sanctify pain in general-all becoming and growing, all that guarantees the future, *postulates* pain.... For the eternal joy in creating to exist, for the will to life eternally to affirm itself, the 'torment of childbirth' *must* also exist eternally.... All this is contained in the word Dionysus: I know of no more exalted symbolism than this *Greek* symbolism, the symbolism of the Dionysian. The profoundest instinct of life, the instinct for the future of life, for the eternity of life, is in this word experienced religiously – the actual road to life, procreation, as the *sacred road* (1969, pp. 109, 110).

Dionysus is the word for pregnancy. The pain that Nietzsche would love to feel is the pain of eternal birth and rebirth of himself, thus affirming negation joyfully.

Traditional Nietzsche scholarship finds that it is "man" who speaks as Ariadne to the god Dionysus. In "Dionysus Versus the Crucified," Paul Valadier articulates this moment as the divinization of the human spirit in the affirmation of sense and mind. According to Valadier, Dionysus's malleability is fundamentally opposed to the rigidity of the ascetic ideal which "keeps a certain distance from life due to its fear of life" (1977, p. 248). There is a difference in attitude towards destruction that distinguishes Dionysian creativity and becoming from Christian asceticism and Nietzsche describes this in Book Five of *The Gay Science*:

The desire for *destruction*, change, and becoming can be an expression of an overflowing energy that is pregnant with future (my term for this is, as is known, "Dionysian"); but it can also be the hatred of the ill-constituted, disinherited, and underprivileged, who destroy, *must* destroy, because what exists, indeed all existence, all being, outrages and provokes them (1974, p. 329, aphorism 370).

Nietzsche then reaches out across the abyss to a new superabundance, he is pregnant with the future. This is where classical scholarship fails in its interpretation of the Dionysian ideal. Valadier finds that Ariadne's lament is a lyrical invocation of a venerated god. The mask of Ariadne means that "man must assume an authentically 'feminine' attitude in welcoming Dionysus. Far from affirming Dionysus on the basis of a powerful pride, he is called forth in an amorous, feminine lament" (1977, p. 249). Book Four of *The Will to Power* shows the distinction between the Crucified and Dionysus. Dionysus stands for "the religious affirmation of life, life whole and not denied or in part; (typical – that the sexual act arouses profundity, mystery, reverence)" (Nietzsche: 1978, p. 542, aphorism 1052). Based on this passage, Valadier concludes that Nietzsche is using the feminine as a guise for the affirmation of the spiritual through the sexual. Valadier puts man and eternity in the places of Ariadne and

Dionysus. Man is Ariadne, and Dionysus is eternity: "Ariadne's relation to Dionysus is a remarkable complement to the relation between man and He who is" (Valadier: 1977, p. 249). In spite of Kaufmann's ribald commentary which accompanies his translation of this passage, it is not the sexuality of Greek vases that Nietzsche means. As the earlier parable in Book Two indicates, he is swept away by the mystery and power of procreation:

The Christian priest is from the first a mortal enemy of sensuality: no greater antithesis can be imagined than the innocently awed and solemn attitude adopted by, e.g., the most honourable women's cults of Athens in the presence of the symbols of sex. The act of procreation is the mystery as such in all nonascetic religions: a sort of symbol of perfection and of the mysterious design of the future: rebirth, immortality (1978, p. 94).

Valadier uses simply a receptive feminine aspect of Nietzsche's imagery, and occults the power of procreation and the centrality of it in Nietzsche's theory of the eternal return.

The song to eternity in Part III, aphorism 4 of "The Seven Seals" of *Thus Spoke Zarathustra* reverses the relation of feminine man to virile god. Valadier is referring to this particular section:

Oh how should I not lust for eternity and for the wedding ring of rings – the Ring of Recurrence! Never yet did I find the woman by whom I wanted children, unless it be this woman, whom I love: for I love you, O Eternity! (1986a, p. 246).

According to Valadier, this passage "describes a virile relation between man and eternity – the latter symbolized as woman and mother, the former as male and father" (1977, p. 249). In Valadier's view, this reversal, this play of feminine, masculine, then feminine is simply pointing out "the contrasting nature of man's relation with eternity (or with the gods)" (1977, p. 249). It is simply a series of masks which Nietzsche uses to describe the correct approach to the gods and becoming (the gods?). But the true inversion here is of the uterus. It is Nietzsche's fetish to wear the mask and clothing of woman, in order to win the heart of the effeminate god he loves. Ariadne was originally a Cretan goddess and not a mortal, such that Dionysus's marriage to her may have marked a link with a pre-Hellenic nature religion of the Minoans. This would account for Dionysus's association with fruitfulness and generation. Both Nietzsche as Ariadne and Dionysus as the consort to the maenads have usurped feminine qualities.[21] For what Nietzsche craves as Ariadne is not a gay relationship with Dionysus, but a

---

21. "The madness which is the Dionysian Final Solution for women is confusion – inability to distinguish the female Self and her process from the male-made masquerade. Dionysus sometimes assumed a girl-like form. The phenomenon of the drag queen dramatically demonstrates such boundary violation. Like whites playing 'black face', *he incorporates the oppressed role without being incorporated in it*" (Daly: 1978, p. 67, my italics)

lesbian one. A lesbian relationship in which he can parthenogenetically become pregnant with himself. What traditional scholarship sees as a dynamic romanticism of the will is really a desire for self-pregnancy. This makes Nietzsche both his mother and his father: he has no father, and no mother that bore him.[22] He seeks to be twice born in the eternal return, as Dionysus was. The god's mother, Semele, gave birth to him prematurely and died when her lover, Zeus, appeared before her in his lightning magnificence and incinerated her. Zeus's revelation of his divinity destroyed Semele,[23] and he sewed Dionysus in his thigh until his second birth. Nietzsche's so-called affirmation of the passions and of life and the body is of a masculine nature, which is using female fetishes to affirm male motherhood. The original title of "The Plaint of Ariadne" was "The Travail of the Woman in Childbirth" (Krell: 1988, p. 19). The travail of childbirth becomes the travail of the creator.

Whose body is at (the) stake here? Why does Nietzsche despise women, both the virtuous and the maenads? Nietzsche fears and wants to destroy the maenads, those who could tear Dionysus to pieces. They threaten this birth in and of the masculine feminine. Dionysus and Nietzsche have both gone beyond their powers, and this sacrilegious sacrifice of woman and the taking and wearing of her skin and body tempt Kali, the original destroyer they so shamelessly imitate. His affirmation of his femininity is a denial of women, of real pregnancy, and woman's role in conception. Mother becomes a silly goose that lowers the tone of the male seed. Nietzsche and Dionysus, these two *hommes roses*[24] delight Foucault and Derrida because they claim to show how man can become where God was, now that God is dead.

But this absorption of the feminine is not without precedent. Tantrism predates Nietzsche's transvestism by several thousand years. Based on the principle that women's spiritual energy is greater than man's, Tantrism holds that emotional and sexual mating with a woman is man's only path to divinity. *Maithuna* is the essential ritual, it is *coitus reservatus* or sex without male orgasm. This preserves man's vital fluids. But more importantly, Tantric-trained men seek to absorb the fluids of the woman's orgasm through their penises. "The vital fluids thus conserved would be stored in a man's spinal column, mount through the *chakras* up to his head, and there flower forth with the inspiration of divine wisdom" (Walker: 1983, p. 973). The transvestism of Derrida, Dionysus and others is as contemporary as the Pope and as

---

22. A different discussion of Nietzsche's automaternity can be found in David Farrell Krell, "Consultations with the Paternal Shadow: Gasché, Derrida and Klossowski on *Ecce Homo*," in David Farrell Krell and David Wood, eds., *Exceedingly Nietzsche, Aspects of Contemporary Nietzsche Interpretation*, (pp. 80-96) London: Routledge, 1988.

23. Formerly an earth goddess, she was only a mortal in the Greek panoply.

24. Diane Lamoureux's term refers to men who appropriate feminist language to patronize women. What a new and bitter form of displacement! It seems that now men are not only better mothers than women (the movie *Kramer vs Kramer*), better women that women (*Tootsie*), but now *les hommes roses* are better feminists than women, and they are Prince Charming as well!

ancient as the Roman Magna Mater cults.[25] Dressing in women's clothing, men seek access to the sacred symbols and knowledge of birth: generation and generations, the creation of space and time. Regarding the wearing of female clothing by priests and prophets, Walker argues that "their original objective was to make themselves resemble women so the spirits would find them acceptable" (1983, p. 1014). Shamans, priests, and magicians of many cultures still seek power through female fetishes,[26] some even observe menstrual rituals (1983, p. 1015). Most Gods require a female source of power in order to *act*. This is behind Nietzsche's understanding of the action of women at a distance. Even God required Mary in order to produce Jesus, required mater/matter for the eventual appearance of the holy spirit. Dionysus is not eternity, *He* is not eternity, as Nietzsche understands very well. The truth is the future is female.[27] And he is haunted with the shape-shifting, malleable inconstancy of this truth. The Nietzchean becomes mad, fearing and embracing eternity.

But isn't Nietzsche for life, and against the ascetic ideal of the priests who fear life? In parable 18 of *The Anti-Christ*, he rails against the perversity of those who choose death:

The Christian conception of God – God as God of the sick, God as spider, God as spirit – is one of the most corrupt conceptions of God arrived at on earth: perhaps it even represents the low-water mark in the descending development of the God type. God degenerated to the *contradiction of life*, instead of being its transfiguration and eternal *Yes*! In God a declaration of hostility towards life, nature, the will to life! God the formula for every calumny of "this world", for every lie about "the next world"! In God nothingness deified, the will to nothingness sanctified! (1969, p. 128, italics in original).

And yet he wills nothing for woman. Nietzsche rejects an end to creation, and the Christian repression of his virile sensuality, he does believe in something: a feminine sacrifice of the female. For the difference between Dionysus and Christ is not in their martyrdom, it's more a question of style. This is indicated in Book Four, aphorism 1052 of *The Will to Power* (1978, p. 543):

Life itself, its eternal fruitfulness and recurrence, creates torment, destruction, the will to annihilation.... The tragic man affirms even the harshest suffering: he is sufficiently strong, rich, and capable of deifying to do so (1978, p. 543).

---

25. Born in 1842, Daniel Paul Schreber was the President of the Judges Court of Appeal in Saxony. *Memoirs of my nervous illness* (1955) is an account of his severe hallucinations and periods at psychiatric asylums. Schreber's delusions of becoming female and his procreative fantasies of self-impregnation were described as homosexual anxieties by Freud. A chilling, sexist interpretation of Schreber is: *Psychosis and Sexual Identity: Towards a Post-Analytic View of the Schreber Case*, edited by David B. Allison, et.al., (1988).

26. This is also documented by Allen and Hubbs: "The identification with the feminine in order to assume her power is most strikingly ilustrated in the widespread custom among male shamans of wearing feminine attire." Sally G. Allen and Joanna Hubbs (1987), "Outrunning Atalanta: Feminine Destiny in Alchemical Transmutation," in Sandra Harding and Jean F. O'Barr (Eds.) *Sex and Scientific Inquiry* (pp. 79-98). Chicago: The University of Chicago Press, p. 83.

27. See O'Brien (1989a) and Forman (1989) on temporality.

Sex and danger are associated in the mythology of the male psyche as death and rebirth. Barbara Walker describes the association of spiders and witches in medieval Europe: "the folk tale of the Spider and the Fly suggested the once widespread belief that flies are souls in search of a female entity to eat them and give them rebirth" (1983, p. 958). The god on the cross is a curse on life, a signpost to seek redemption from life; Dionysus cut to pieces is a *promise* of life: he will be eternally reborn and return again from destruction (1978, p. 543). But even as Christ and Dionysus merge in Nietzsche's final metaphors, so is the covenant re-established. Nietzsche denounces Spinoza's spinning of a metaphysical God, because he wants Superman to spin himself, his own work of art. Nietzsche must celebrate both sex and death, since he is antithetical to the ascetic religions which denied sex in order to deny death. But he celebrates the rebirth of masculine sex and death. He dresses as a woman to fool the devouring abyss, to pass. Yet to truly embrace his fate, surely he must face the abyss as a man and not as a God? And in order to become anti-sexist, which of course was never Nietzsche's goal, his postmodern disciples must stop thinking of him and themselves as gods.

4

Neutrality and De/meaning

Accordingly I shall now suppose, not that a true God, who as such must be supremely good and the fountain of truth, but that some malignant genius exceedingly powerful and cunning has devoted all his powers in the deceiving of me; I shall suppose that the sky, the earth, colors, shapes, sounds and all external things are illusions and impostures of which this evil genius has availed himself for the abuse of my credulity; I shall consider myself as having no hands, no eyes, no flesh, no blood, nor any senses, but as falsely opining myself to possess all these things. Further, I shall obstinately persist in this way of thinking; and even if, while so doing, it may not be within my power to arrive at the knowledge of any truth, there is one thing I have it in me to do, viz., to suspend judgment, refusing assent to what is false. Thereby, thanks to this resolved firmness of mind, I shall be effectively guarding myself against being imposed upon by this deceiver, no matter how powerful or how craftily deceptive he may be (Descartes: 1958, p. 181).

Columbine, my charming wife, the Columbine in the portrait, was sleeping. She slept over there, in the big bed: I killed her. Why?.... Ah, here is why! My gold, she filched; my best wine, she drank; my back, she beat, and hard, too: as for my forehead, she decorated it. A cuckold, yes, that's what she made me, and exorbitantly, but what does that matter? I killed her – because I felt like it, I am the master, what can anyone say? To kill her, yes...that pleases me. But how shall I go about it?... Of course, there's the rope – pull it tight and blam! it's done! yes, but then the tongue hanging out, the horrible face? no – the knife? or a sabre, a long sabre? zap! in the heart...yes, but then the blood flows out in torrents, streaming. – Ugh! what a devil of a.... Poison? a tiny little vial, quaff it and then...yes! then the cramps, the runs, the pains, the tortures, ah! how awful (it would be discovered, anyway). Of course, there's the gun, bam! but bam! would be heard. – Nothing, I can think of nothing. (He paces gravely back and forth, deep in thought. By

accident, he trips.) Ow! that hurts! (He strokes his foot). Oof! that
hurts! It's not serious, it's better already. (He keeps on stroking and
tickling his foot). Ha! ha! that's funny! Ha! Ha! No, it makes me
laugh. Ah! (He abruptly lets go of his foot. He slaps himself on the
head.) I've got it! (Slyly:) I've got it! I'm going to tickle my wife
to death. There![1]

Man's relationships to his God, his love of God? God is love, and He is
cruel. God's love of man, man's love of woman. Perhaps it all comes back to a
question of origins? Freud says that identity is formed through the Oedipal contest for
a mother's love, a contest no woman can win. In his description of an ontological,
"already always" inscribed biological possibility of knowing and being, men come to
consciousness, but women come to nothing. This is why we don't amount to much.
Lacan puts out the I's of this theory, reconciling the patient to permanent discord and
disunity. Derrida uses the mysteries of initiation for his Gothic theology believing, like
the medieval alchemists, that the word is not sufficient to communicate magical,
arcane knowledge. His work is not unlike that of the Christian mystic Meister Eckhart,
who distinguished between the Godhead, which is undefinable, and God, which is a
human image and a way of talking about the Godhead. This abstracts from the
"maialogical perspective" of Robbie Pfeufer Kahn (1989) which sees the maternal
body as the matrix, the body-in-relation, through which the unworded young enter
social relations and language.[2] For speaking does *articulate*: link to others. What does
deconstruction disarticulate? Derrida parades his receptivity to *différance*, writing
of the hymen. *Sexual* difference is not Derrida's concern; indeterminacy and
hermeneutics are his focus and woman is his style. Or, as he says in "Becoming
Woman":

The title for this lecture was to have been *the question of style*. However, it is woman who will
be my subject. Still, one might wonder whether that doesn't really amount to the same thing –
or is it to the other (1978a, p. 128).

Woman's value is she represents textual difference. Certainly, the theological origins
of the interpretation of texts in wars of religion and scriptural struggles should be
remembered when reading Derrida. It is the use of the feminine that is at issue here,
but in order to take this up we must return to origin, and the Word of God.[3]

---

1. Paul Margueritte, *Pierrot Murderer of his Wife*, published by Calmann-Lévy, 1886 and quoted by
   Jacques Derrida (1981a) "The Double Session", in *Dissemination*, pp. 200-201, in his discussion of
   Mallarmé's *Mimique*.
2. Kahn (1989) also questions the model of the "androgynists" Chodorow and Dinnerstein, and the
   Freudian notion of the ineluctable trauma of separation.
3. I capitalize God only in order to ironize the theology of the supposedly anti-ontotheological
   deconstructionist approach. Of course, I am also pretending that irony is still possible in these
   circumstances.

Good, or evil? God, or feminine pleasure? The sacred, or the profane? Who is sacred, and who profane? It was Lévi-Strauss who was the first to raise the question of the sacred, of the being of myth and ritual, in a twilight of the gods where patriarchal man aspired to be reborn as a god of mythic structure. Lévi-Strauss was also original when he included cultural experience in a theory of communication. His structures sought the Other, in an Oedipal quest for self (same) subjectivity, by positing Man as a tool in harmony with language and the voice of god. The question of the sacred in the writing of Lévi-Strauss is continued in postmodernism's messianic quest for Superman. Does the sacred include evil? Is evil sacred, or shall we leave the question of demonology to the Dionysian philosophers of desire? How did the notion of evil enter postmodernism? Lacan raised theological questions that would preoccupy Derrida one summer: of the Commandments, an elected people, and the God who said, *"I am that I am, and You shall have no other Gods before me."* Derrida was preoccupied with the evil genius of God and his vengeance. His questions follow the biblical section Lacan uses in *L'éthique de la psychanalyse* (1986, p. 101), namely, Chapter 7, verses 7 to 14 of St. Paul, Epistle to the Romans:

Wherefore the law is holy, and the commandment holy, and just, and good. Was then that which is good made death unto me? God forbid. But sin, that it might appear sin, working death in me by that which is good; that sin by the commandment might become exceedingly sinful. For we know that the law is spiritual: but I am carnal, sold under sin.

It is the evil of God that prompts Derrida, while Lacan's theory of cognition poses the evil of desire. Descartes' radical doubting of all things culminates in Derridean deconstruction. This musing on the diabolical nature of God resonates with the Gnostic belief of late antiquity in an evil creator. According to Proverbs, "Fear of God is the beginning of knowledge" (Proverbs, 7). What has not been recognized is that Derrida is suggesting that the fear of God is the beginning of writing. No less phallic than Lacan, Derrida elects the penis as God's text, circumcision His mark, and thus, the mark of Man. The mystery of iniquity here is really the mystification of Derridean inequity.

In "The Political Theology of Language,"[4] Derrida (1987a) raised questions about the signature of revenge, asking: "What is revenge when it is not human?" In other words: what if the true God is not "supremely Good and a fountain of truth" (Descartes: 1958, p. 181)? He spoke of the unfolding of vengeance through that which calls itself a nation. In phrases which defer meaning, in a radical scepticism where no meaning is meant, and summary is a violence, if not an impossibility, it is difficult to fix Derrida's signification without transgressing his law against interpretation.

Derrida used nationalism as a means of understanding the structure of language. By noting that vengeance is necessarily transgenerational, he focuses on the difference

---

4. Course given by Jacques Derrida June 1-26, 1987, Ninth International Institute for Semiotic and Structural Studies, University of Toronto.

between private revenge, and the revenge of heroes, which is part of the founding of states. The appeal to national consciousness always presupposes the expected return of a ghost, a founder. The relation to a spectral dimension, the lost body of a founding king or mythic hero means superiority to those without access to universal meaning. Derrida introduced the notion of writing in the form of a prescriptive language. The three significations of language are corruption, revenge, and the ghost, which come together in the experience of national affirmation. He discussed the debate between Spinoza and St. Paul on circumcision, where Spinoza idealizes circumcision not as a literal mark but a disposition of spirit with respect to law. Circumcision is a spiritual and not a physical mark, and the circumcised is he who obeys the precepts of the law. The sublimation of the mark of circumcision universalizes election. National, like literal circumcision is extrinsic, temporal to the covenants of man with gods and governments. Circumcision of the prepuce leaves God's mark on man, the trace of God's spur, a question of His style.

The origin of the law, and the covenant, is in the first corruption. The Jewish people had begun to transgress. Theocracy, then, is founded on the corruption of language; the empowerment of the prophet to interpret signs; transgression and the need for a recognizable word. God as absence, and Spinoza's astonishment that God wants vengeance, is a continuing theme. Woman as God or as divine revenge is not openly considered by Derrida. That God should want revenge is an impossibility which God's essence should make impossible. Is God's love for the being he created not infinite? What Spinoza glimpses with astonishment requires that he rethink God and revenge: is revenge infinite? Is God finite enough to feel and give way to revenge and hatred? These are the questions posed in "The Political Theology of Language" (1987a).

Derrida has brought together three texts (Spinoza, Heidegger, Scholem), and the theme which connects them is revenge, a non-verbal and diachronic interpretation of time. In fact, time appears and becomes diachronic when it is given birth by revenge. In all three texts examined by Derrida, the power of reprisals is evoked, a power which has no human dimension and which cannot be described. This power reveals a dimension in which God's revenge is all too human. Revenge is related to the origin of law, love, language and history. Public and private revenge meet at the foundation of the state.

According to Derrida, God wanted to destroy the Jewish people so that they would know that he is: know his name, *sham*, know that he is, *ergo sum*, and that he is Jehovah. But His children rebelled, and the revenge of God was the election of the Levites. Jealousy, and the destruction of the state, followed the moment of terror of the Jews and their request for mediation. What fascinates and terrifies Spinoza is that a God who should be infinite is susceptible to evil passions. It is in the name of his Name that God gives bad laws to the people so that they may know his Name, without any possibility of knowing his Name (1987a). (Something like Rumpelstiltskin, who would take the maid's child unless she could guess his name?) Thus, the institution of laws by God in the name of God can be evil. But Derrida's fascination with the messianic idea of Judaism and the sacredness of language, the role of the apocalypse in the sacred language, admits that deconstruction cannot do without the sacred. This is really not a very surprising revelation. In spite of the emphasis on structure rather than history which is the source of the sacred for some Marxists, and in spite of consciousness, which is sacred to the existentialists, Derrida's epistemology is based on an interpellation by divine law of the circumcised.

Derrida was, with Julia Kristeva and her husband Philippe Sollers, part of the circle that produced or wrote for *Tel Quel*, the Maoist, structuralist literary avant-garde publication of 1968 Paris.[5] His work at that time focused on Husserl's theory of meaning. In *Speech and Phenomena* (1967/1973), Derrida critiques what he sees as the metaphysical underpinnings of Husserl's phenomenology. He reproaches Husserl for separating language and experience, and for maintaining a belief in a pre-linguistic kind of meaning and presence. For Derrida, there is no presence which lives in the world, only difference which lives in language. J. Rassam exposes this modern form of nominalism, and the belief that only what can be said is real: "only the living word preserves the ideality and presence, because the voice continues to speak and to hear itself in the absence of the world" (1975, p. 2). Clearly, the God of Genesis is the most famous nominalist... voice creates things by naming them. Generally, a nominalist position is characterized by a strong empiricism and the belief that without language, rational thought is not possible. Hence, they emphasize the role of language in consciousness, even to the extent of arguing that the manipulation of signs is the major activity of thought and signs are said to have meaning only within a context and a relation of signification.

J. Rassam argues that Derrida's deconstruction of the ontological in *Speech and Phenomena* was a return to the highest nominalism of the Middle Ages, specifically the work of Abelard and Occam who first investigated the question of ontology using the logic of language. Rassam reminds us of Abelard's dictum: "*Significare autem vel monstrare vocum est, significari vero rerum*"[6] (1975, p. 2). The *res-vox* relationship in Derrida's work is one where matter is spoken, and the sign is material. The sound of its voice to the self may be the primary sense of the patriarchal prophets.[7] After all, in the beginning was the Word. Meaning comes to being only through the process of signification. Derrida's theory of *différance* (substitution) thus reminds Rassam of Occam who argued that universals are those terms which take the place of things. Rassam finds that the inspiration and conclusions of the Middle Age and postmodern nominalists are the same: all use the logic of language for their metaphysical inquiries.

---

5. See Mary Caws, (1973, Spring) Tel Quel: Text and Revolution. *Diacritics, 3*, (i), pp. 2-8; and George Alexander (1976), The Group TEL QUEL. *Working Papers in Sex, Science and Culture, 1* (2), pp. 3-11.
6. It is the task of speech to indicate and demonstrate, but of things, to be dictated.
7. The Sybils and other female oracles acted as conduits in the dialogue between the spirit and human worlds. Delphi, Greece's oldest oracle, dedicated to the Great Mother, is from *delphos*, womb (1983, p. 1092). In Rome, in the second century B.C., the priestess' pronouncements guided the emperor's decree (Walker: 1983, p. 1092)

If only the structure of meaning is considered, meaning can exist independently of that which it signifies. Derrida's originality as a nominalist is the priority he gives the written over the spoken word.

Deconstruction may be even more unoriginal than Rassam suggests. Midrash is Judaic exegetical process. Its three dimensions are: *"(1) the principles or processes of exegesis; (2) the purposes of exegesis accomplished in a given interpretation of a single verse, and (3) the formal program of collecting and arranging exegesis into complications"* (Neusner: 1986, p. 39, Italics in original). Jacob Neusner explains how the predominant form of Midrash, Rabbinic Midrash of *"parable or allegory* – reading one thing in terms of another" (1986, p. 3; italics in original) emerged in late antiquity. It is distinct from earlier, purely written hermeneutical processes of reading scripture. This Rabbinic Midrash, or Judaism of the dual Torah, oral and written, stems from the belief that God's revelation of the Torah to Moses at Sinai "came forth in two media: one written, the other formulated and transmitted only through memory" (1986, p. 3). Rabbinic Midrash "appeals to some other set of values or considerations than those contained within the verse or topic at hand" and "reads Scripture within the principle that things are never what they seem" (1986, p. 44). Neusner also indicates that this method and attitude is similar to the doctrine of Pharisaism, of "hermeneutic pretense" (1986, p. 3) and metamorphosis: things are not what they seem and one behaves as if they were other. Deconstruction modifies Rabbinic Midrash but retains its hermeneutic pretense for pure masculine reading: signification and resignation, palimpsests without end.[8]

Foucault called Derrida the last classicist. Classicism, for Foucault, was the *episteme* between the Renaissance and the modern period ordered by a relationship to the word that was under the law of representation; the being of language was absolute, raw and meaningful. In "Mon corps, ce papier, ce feu,"[9] a fiery twenty-page rejoinder to Derrida's "Cogito and the History of Madness," Foucault (1972) took up Derrida's critique of the role of madness and dreaming in the Cartesian development of doubt. This dispute between Derrida and Foucault centers on Descartes' discussion of madness in the first pages of *The Meditations*. Each accuses the other of being "metaphysical" in interpreting the rationality or irrationality of the relationship of knowledge to being. Ironically, theirs is a contest over the *grounding* of anti-foundationalism. They debate the grounds of philosophical discourse, and the nature of the "nothingness of unreason" (Foucault: 1973a, p. 285). What emerges as of interest for us here is the theme of the *origin* of meaning and its relationship to Nietzsche's sense of and mastery of "feminine" formlessness. What is the matrix after the death of the Creator? *Pudenda origo*[10] warn Foucault (1972, p. 584) and Nietzsche

---

8. Christine Froula (1988) indicates Derrida's father-son genealogy and line of authority.
9. This is the appendix to the 1972 Gallimard edition of *L'historie de la folie*. It is only found in this edition. English translation by Geoff Bennington, "My Body, This Paper, This Fire," *The Oxford Literary Review*, Autumn, 1979, 4, (1) pp. 9-28. Translations here are my own.
10. One's descent must be a source of shame.

(1978, p. 148) whenever they claim "Life is will to power" (Nietzsche: 1978, p. 148). Aristotle postulated a "First Cause" and the Christian Fathers – notably St. Thomas Aquinas – built their systems upon his account of the Unmoved Mover of all things. Aristotle's concern with the conjunction of matter and form led him to postulate four types of causes: material, formal, efficient and final. Matter is the material cause, and form the cause which produces new entities. The efficient cause, the motive force behind production, becomes Foucault's discursive practices. The final cause, which determines the course of development, is ostensibly negated by both Foucault and Derrida. Platonism's only reality was the Idea. Derrida and Foucault debate the First Cause of the Word: formal or efficient? In *De Generatione Animalium*, Aristotle maintained that women contribute simple material to the child, whereas the sperm contains form, essence and soul.[11]

In "Cogito and the History of Madness," Derrida (1978b) argued that the essence of Foucault's 673-page treatise on *Madness and Civilization* could be reduced to the three-page discussion of Descartes and the Cartesian cogito, where Foucault's misunderstanding of the materiality of the sign was most evident. Specifically, Derrida noted that Foucault does not find this question of prior philosophical or methodological importance: how can the history of madness be written in the language of reason, for whom and by whom? He also questions Foucault's "strict structuralism" (1978b, p. 44), and his resolute rejection of all etiological questions. Derrida begins his essay with a meditation on the unhappiness of the disciple, for he studied "under Michel Foucault" (1978b, p. 31). He feels that he must realize that the Master is absent, like real life. Derrida challenges himself to break the glass, and cease the infantile game with his reflection in the mirror, in order to start to speak. Surrounded by absence and shattered glass, Derrida speaks of madness and the Cartesian cogito.

Derrida refers to Foucault's project of writing a history of madness itself, letting madness be the *subject* of the book. He is disturbed that Foucault attempts to write this history of madness, an archaeology of a silence, in the language of reason. He argues:

If the *Order* of which we are speaking is so powerful, if its power is unique of its kind, this is so precisely by virtue of the universal, structural, universal and infinite complicity in which it compromises all those who understand it in its own language, even when this language provides them with the form of their own denunciation. Order is then denounced within order (1978b, p. 35).

Liberation from the language of reason and the writing of the history of madness would only be possible in madness or silence. "*Either* do not mention a certain silence... *or* follow the madman down the road of his exile" (1978b, p. 36). Derrida reminds Foucault of the Hegelian law of the dialectic, to point out that the revolution against logos could only be made within it. And a history of madness against reason is

---

11. Aristotle, *De Generatione Animalium* (1912), Oxford, II.737a.25. For feminist critiques of Aristotle, see Elizabeth Spelman (1983), Arlene Saxonhouse (1991) and Prudence Allen, R.S.M. (1985).

not possible since history itself is a rational concept. Derrida orients Foucault: "It is the meaning of 'history' or *archai* that should have been questioned first, perhaps. A writing that exceeds, by questioning them, the values 'origin,' 'reason,' and 'history,' could not be contained within the metaphysical closure of an archaeology" (1978b, p. 36). According to Derrida, Foucault's hypothesis is that the two monologues, madness and reason, can be liberated, their determination and point of rupture can be spoken and understood. But Derrida asks if Foucault's book could be written: "Who wrote and who is to understand, in what language and from what historical situation of logos, who wrote and who is to understand this history of madness?" (1978b, p. 38). Derrida seems to take the same position as Sartre to Foucault's previous work: the book is successful because it is not original. Psychiatry and psychoanalytic theory have dislocated, however minimally, the perception of madness as simply unreason and created an opening for Foucault's critique. Foucault's book was to be expected.

Derrida is particularly disturbed that Foucault does not acknowledge serious and prior methodological and philosophical questions of language. The issue for him is the history of the dissension within the original logos that separated into reason and madness. "It thus seems that the project of convoking the first dissension of logos against itself is quite another project than the archaeology of silence, and raises different questions" (1978b, p. 39). Derrida prefers to find the origin of this division internally, rather than in what Foucault terms The Decision, division by external command. Derrida sees this internal revolution against the self as occurring during the Middle Ages and altering the Greek tradition. He is concerned that Foucault has hidden the "true historical grounds" (1978b, p. 39) of this decision by not investigating its semiology. Derrida accuses Foucault of metaphysics: "The attempt to write the history of the decision, division, difference runs the risk of construing the division as an event or a structure subsequent to the unity of an original presence, thereby confirming metaphysics in its fundamental operation" (1978b, p. 40).

Derrida also faults Foucault for proceeding as if he "*knew* what 'madness' means" (1978b, p. 41) through a previous and already given understanding of the concept in spite of reason's language and use: all that is negative is madness. He is also disturbed by the similar treatment of the concept of truth. Derrida's second concern with Foucault's omission of the history of pre-classical logos relates to the methodology and historicity of reason. The Great Internment is not studied as a sign, it is not determined to be cause or symptom. Derrida points to Foucault's structuralism:

This kind of question could appear exterior to a method that presents itself precisely as structuralist, that is, a method for which everything within the structural totality is interdependent and circular in such a way that the classical problems of causality themselves would appear to stem from a misunderstanding. Perhaps. But I wonder whether, when one is concerned with history (and Foucault wants to write a history), a strict structuralism is possible, and, especially, whether, if only for the sake of order and within the order of its own descriptions, such a study can avoid all etiological questions, all questions bearing, shall we say, on the centre of gravity of the structure (1978b, p. 44).

Foucault does not say whether Descartes' expulsion of reason from thought in *The Meditations* is "a symptom, a cause, a language" (1978b, p. 44). Nor are the structural links to the entire drama of The Confinement elucidated. For Derrida, what is necessary is a study of the intention and content of philosophical discourse, which he then proceeds to give of the passage putting Descartes and Foucault in dialogue.

What emerges here is Derrida's critique of the proposition that philosophy can call up madness with language, which is itself a carrier and enforcer of normality. This is the "essential and universal necessity from which no discourse can escape, for it belongs to the meaning of meaning" (1978b, p. 53). Derrida insists that his own critique is "strictly Foucauldian" (1978b, p. 54). Writing is logos, is reason, it carries meaning and normality and sense: madness is silence, absence, and the source of writing. "Within the dimension of historicity in general, which is to be confused neither with some ahistorical eternity, nor with an empirically determined moment of the history of facts, silence plays the irreducible role of that which bears and haunts language" (1978b, p. 54). Silence gives birth to language, which is separated from madness by itself. Language is born of "a nothing that neutralizes everything..." (1978b, p. 55). According to Derrida, Foucault defines madness as negativity, and then reconfines it. No subversion of reason is possible with language. "The misfortune of the mad, the interminable misfortune of their silence, is that their best spokesmen are those who betray them best;" (1978b, p. 36). Derrida claims that Foucault's work is "a powerful gesture of protection and internment. A Cartesian gesture for the twentieth century" (1978b, p. 55). Aiming to intern Classical reason, Foucault misses the etiological question of the very possibility of meaning. Descartes, at least, did not intern madness, he did not exclude it from the cogito as Foucault has done, madness was within thought for most stages of doubt for the Cartesian cogito. Foucault's reduction of the Cartesian project "risks erasing the excess by which every philosophy (of meaning) is related, in some region of its discourse, to the nonfoundation of unmeaning" (1978b, p. 309, endnote).

Derrida's Descartes strives to exceed the totality of that which can be thought – to exceed history – in the direction of Nothingness and Infinity. Foucault does violence to this project by enclosing it within a historical structure: "a violence of a totalitarian and historicist style which eludes meaning and the origin of meaning" (1978b, p. 57). Structuralism and political totalitarianism "beckon each other historically," and Foucault "runs the risk of being totalitarian" (1978b, p. 57). Derrida's greatest indictment of the Foucauldian project is: "Structuralist totalitarianism here would be responsible for an internment of the Cogito similar to the violences of the Classical age" (1978b, p. 57). Derrida refers to the epigraph *compelle intrare*, from Foucault's chapter on The Great Internment, to argue that forcing the entry of madness into the world, and this emphasis on intraworldliness, calling back and containing that which is supposed by the world, is the very essence of violence. Yet in advancing this argument Derrida insists that he is not referring to an other world, or to transcendence, for that would also be a violence similar to the flaw he sees in Foucault's argument.

Foucault responds to this "remarkable critique" (1972, p. 9) by quoting and questioning at length Derrida's reading of Descartes. Foucault argues that Descartes uses madness to formulate epistemological questions, and does not proceed through an exclusion or silencing of it. It is Derrida, he retorts, who arranges the debate to ask whether or not there is something anterior or exterior to philosophical discourse, and it is Derrida who passionately rejects the notion that philosophical discourse has its condition of being in an act of rejection or refusal. Foucault hurls back the epithet of "Cartesian", it is Derrida who is "continuing the Cartesian exclusion" (1972, p. 599). Descartes found that the philosopher excluded madness in order to establish himself as sane. But, Foucault points out, Derrida rejects this as meaning the disqualification of the philosopher and a distinction between philosophical discourse and madness. Any exteriority, separation, and determination of philosophical discourse is counter to Derrida's project to exceed totalities. "This Cartesian exclusion must then be excluded because it is determining" (1972, p. 599). Foucault then details how Derrida proceeds to negate the notion that philosophical discourse excludes madness.

The essential difference between Foucault and Derrida is this: Derrida is preoccupied with the textual energy of philosophy, and the organization of texts, while Foucault focuses on discursive practices. As Foucault says of their rupture:

[Derrida]... refers less to the organization of meaning in the text than to the series of events (acts, effects, qualifications) which carry with it the discursive practise of thinking: it is a question of the modification of the subject through the exercise of discourse. And it is my impression that a reader as remarkably assiduous as Derrida could only have missed so many thematic, literary and textual differences because he misunderstands those that form the principle, that is, "discursive differences" (1972, p. 593).

Foucault's denunciation of Derrida is worth quoting at length:[12]

I am in agreement on one fact at least: it is in no way due to inattention that the classical interpreters, before and like Derrida, erased this passage from Descartes. It is systematic. A system of which Derrida is today the most influential representative, in its final glory: the reduction of discursive practises to textual traces; the elision of events in order to retain only traces for a reading; the invention of voices behind texts in order to avoid analyzing the modes of implication of the subject in discourse; the designation of the origin as said and not said in the text in order not to reinstate discursive practices in the field of transformations where they are effectuated.

I will not say that it is a metaphysics, *the* metaphysic or its closure that is hidden in this "textualization" of discursive practices. I will go much further: I will say that it is a very historically determined little pedagogy which is manifesting itself very visibly. A pedagogy which teaches the student that there is nothing outside the text, but that inside it, in its interstices, in its spaces and unspoken areas, reigns the reserve of the origin; that it is therefore not at all necessary to search elsewhere, but only here, not at all in the words, certainly, but in

---

12. Gayatri Chakravorty Spivak provides a Derridean perspective on this difference in her "Translator's Preface" to Jacques Derrida, *Of Grammatology* (1976), especially 1x-1xii.

words as erasures, in their *grill* "the meaning of being" speaks itself. A pedagogy which conversely gives to the voice of the masters this sovereignty without limit which permits them to indefinitely repeat the text (1972, p. 602).

Derrida's nominalist philosophy does indeed search in the erasure of words, in the absences and empty spaces, the being of language, hidden in the "reserve of the origin" (1972, p. 602). For Foucault, this isolation of the text from the strategies of power which produce it is consistent with the Classical ideology of knowledge. But their debate also reflects the struggle over whether deconstruction or social construction, grammatology or archaeology, will be the most famous French philosophy. But can we take their word for the meaning of this debate over logos, silence and the signifier? Or can such madness only be passed over in silence? Perhaps we should address the origin of the matter: *pudenda origo*.

Maat was the Egyptian goddess of truth, and justice, the original lawgiver, primordial Mother and measurer. She was also the judge of the dead, whose hearts had to be lighter than one of Maat's feathers in the Hall of Judgement. But her rituals were distorted in the process of patriarchal usurpation. Barbara Walker writes that "Egyptian priests drew the Feather of Maat on their tongues in green dye, to give their words a Logos-like power of Truth so their verbal magic could create reality" (1983, p. 562). Derrida also seeks origin in the Word and sacrifices the (female) Flesh to it. *Couvade* is practiced in many forms, historically, in the formation of a body politic, as well as in more primitive rituals (like postmodernism). Christian prophets have also heard the word of god: their prophecy *matters*, as they aspire to imitate their God's act of creation. But this claimed ability to speak reality into being does not extend to women. We only hear the Word of God, and if we hear it in our left ear, we become pregnant! This ability of course, is the only thing about women that matters in patriarchal ideology, and it has not been a philosophical matter, as Mary O'Brien has pointed out. The three wise men at the birth of structuralist and poststructuralist philosophy have a cumulative message for women: Lévi-Strauss tried to convince women we are spoken, exchanged like words; Lacan tried to teach women we can't speak, because the phallus is the original signifier; and then Derrida says that it doesn't matter, it's just talk. Women are still used as the raw material for poststructuralist analyses, exchanged in their words like tokens or fetishes. In "Becoming Woman,"[13] Derrida uses woman as a "name for that untruth of truth" (1978a, p. 129), uses the hymen and woman as slippery metaphors for his stylish play with meaning. Truth is a woman, for Nietzsche, and for Derrida, life is a woman:

But perhaps this is the greatest charm of life: it puts a golden-embroidered veil of lovely potentialities over itself, promising, resisting, modest, mocking, sympathetic, seductive. Yes, life is a woman! (1978a, p. 128).

---

13. "The Question of Style" (1977) is a revised edition, although it was published earlier.

Like Nietzsche, he believes that only men should speak of woman. Derrida holds that "femininity or female sexuality" (1978a, p. 129, italics in original) are the "essentializing fetishes" of the "dogmatic philosopher" (1978a, p. 129):

For it is the man who believes in the truth of woman, in woman – truth. And in truth, they too are men, those women feminists so derided by Nietzsche. Feminism is nothing but the operation of a woman who aspires to be like a man. And in order to resemble the masculine dogmatic philosopher this woman lays claim – just as much claim as he – to truth, science and objectivity in all their castrated delusions of virility. Feminism too seeks to castrate. It wants a castrated woman (1978a, p. 130).

Derrida then claims to speak our truth, women's true truth which is: woman has no truth, no essence. To search for woman, to search for truth, is to seek an essence, a fixity, an ontology and a metaphysics. Woman should not believe in herself:

There is no such thing as the essence of woman because woman averts, she is averted of herself. Out of the depths, endless and unfathomable, she engulfs and distorts all vestige of essentiality, of identity, of property. And the philosophical discourse, blinded, founders on these shoals and is hurled down these depthless depths to its ruin. There is no such thing as the truth of woman, but it is because of that abyssal divergence of the truth, because that untruth is "truth." Woman is but one name for that untruth of truth (1978a, p. 128).

This textual practice is similar to Derrida's silencing of feminist questions at the ISISS symposium: the eternal return of Nietzsche's maxim? The young woman in the gallery who pointed out Derrida's phallic aspects was told she was "too quick on the draw", "a little premature" (1987a). He wanted to preside over our infinite witness of his punning in the space of meaning. The young woman was also rebuked for lack of generosity: had he not written of difference?[14] The audience was silent. Frances Bartkowski[15] first raised some warnings about Derrida's deconstruction: "Derrida speaks (for) the feminine while not seeming to hear or read that (sic: what) women, not woman, wish to say" (1980, p. 77). Nietzsche is Derrida's metaphor:

We men wish that woman should not go on compromising herself through enlightenment – just as it was man's thoughtfulness and consideration for woman that found expression in the church decree: *mulier taceat in ecclesia*! It was for woman's good when Napoleon gave the all too eloquent Madame de Staël to understand: *mulier taceat in politicis*! And I think it is a real friend of women that counsels them today: *mulier taceat de muliere*! (Nietzsche: 1987, p. 145).

---

14. This concurs with Kathleen Barry's (1990) sociological study of the Tootsie syndrome: "an extremely unhealthy *hatred* of real women, particularly real women who do not concur that the Tootsies are more of women than they are" (1990, p. 492, italics in original). Barry ironizes: "Tootsie feminist theorists are also astute in being able to detect 'Rhetoric' in merely-only-women feminist theorists, who it is clear speak from their bias and not from real feminist truths" (1990, p. 491).
15. See also Linda Kintz's critique (1989) "In-different Criticism, The Deconstructive 'parole'," in Jeffner Allen and Iris Young, Eds., *The Thinking Muse;* and Kathleen Barry, "Deconstructing Deconstructionism (or, Whatever Happened to Feminist Studies?)" *Ms.* 1, 4, (Jan/feb, 1991), pp. 83-85.

Thus, the "true friends" of women tell us that we should be silent about women and woman, feminine sexuality, for our own good, silent about the emancipation of women, and let men speak of the feminine.[16] Aphasiac, absent, without speech, we should be the source of their writing. Does not Lacan also say of women speaking of women/woman "they don't know what they are saying, which is all the difference between them and me"[17] (1985a, p. 144)? But what if *this* truth was a little dressed-up lie, the truth of a man becoming his idea of a woman?[18] Suppose Derrida/Nietzsche/Lacan was a man, what then?

Derrida takes up Nietzsche's femininity with style. In the revision of "Becoming Woman" in *The New Nietzsche*, Derrida dresses not only himself in drag, but also Nietzsche, Freud, and Abraham; part of the process of promotion for the choirboy is to robe the priest. Of *Spurs*[19] (Derrida: 1981b) Jane Gallop remarks: "Being antiphallic becomes the new phallus, which women come up lacking once again" (1988, p. 100). Women not being impotent, I would add.

Here is Derrida, being charming:

The title for this discussion will be the question of style. But my subject shall be woman.

The question of style – it is always the question of a pointed object. Sometimes only a pen, but just as well a stylet, or even a dagger. With their help, to be sure, we can resolutely attack all that philosophy calls forth under the name of matter or matrix, so as to stave a mark in it, leave an impression or form; but these implements also help us to repel a threatening force, to keep it at bay, to repress and guard against it – all the while bending back or doubling up, in flight, keeping us hidden, veiled (1977, p. 176).

Derrida lingers over Nietzsche's approach to *woman*, presenting him as a feminine saviour whose grip on truth and woman spurned presence for distance. And Derrida,

---

16. Kathleen Barry describes this new "placement" over women, a revamped masculinist practice: "Tootsie men have gone far beyond the need for feminist women.... He is feminist and logically much more of a feminist than feminists – that is, women who have identified feminism as a political condition" (1990, p. 491).

17. Originally appeared in Jacques Lacan, "Dieu et la jouissance de *La femme*," Livre XX, In *Le Séminaire de Jacques Lacan, livre XX, Encore*, (pp. 61-71), Texte établi par Jacques-Alain Miller, Paris: Editions du Seuil, 1975, p. 68.

18. Nancy Jay's study of blood sacrifices and patrilineal descent seems relevant to the practices of postmodernism: "The only action that is as serious as giving birth, which can act as a counterbalance to it, is killing. This is one way to interpret the common sacrificial metaphors of birth and rebirth or birth done better, on purpose and on a more spiritual, more exalted level than mothers do it. For example, the man for whose benefit certain Vedic sacrifices were performed dramatically re-enacted being born, but he was reborn as a god, not a helpless infant. The priest, in officiating, in enabling this 'birth' to take place, performed a role analogous to that of a mother. Some of these metaphors are astonishingly literal: In the West African city of Benin, on the many occasions of human sacrifice, the priests used to masquerade as pregnant women, having sent all the real women out of the city" (1985, p. 294).

19. *Spurs* (1981b) is a lightly revised edition of Derrida's "The Question of Style" (1977).

ambiguous adventurer into the abyss, borrows the mask of the feminine, playful traveller:

> Style will jut out, then, like a *spur*…
> With its spur, style can also protect against whatever terrifying, blinding or mortal threat might present itself or be obstinately encountered: i.e., the presence, and hence, the content, of things themselves, of meaning, of truth (1977, p. 176).

What Derrida affirms here is his hope that Nietzsche has escaped the ontological grip of woman, essence, truth, and remained a bachelor. Derrida's intentions are transparent in "Force and Signification": "The structure was thus a receptive one, waiting, like a girl in love, ready for its future meaning to marry and fecundate it" (1978c, p. 18). Derrida's ambiguous "feminine" style will be his weapon as he attacks matter, matrix, meaning, presence. The fear of the vulva, the abyss, is the fear of the feminine ship, the uterus. Derrida one-ups Nietzsche's virgin male motherhood and immaculate self-conception by avoiding the O of Origin: ovum. An Aristotelian sperm in the heaven of ideal forms, he is never fixed by conception, never identified by birth, never originating and never presence/present. The closer man is to the uterus, the closer he is to death. To be present in the world is to be soon absent. If the price of identity is mortality, *différance*, indeterminateness, promises infinity. Absence/presence, anterior/exterior in Derrida and Foucault are, then, significantly linked to *pudenda origo*: how to master the matrix of meaning, solve man's materialization via the female form and win the secrets of genesis.

If Derrida deconstructs self-presence, the voice of God as thought becoming deed, and the phonetic speech form as self-authenticating truth (logocentrism), he does so to undo the primacy of speech over writing, not man over woman. "[W]riting," says Derrida in *Of Grammatology*, "the letter, the sensible inscription, has always been considered by Western tradition as the body and matter external to the spirit, to breath, to speech, and to the logos" (1976, p. 35). Body/spirit and other dualisms are traced to the letter/spirit opposition and a problem of writing. Derrida supplements the spirit with the letter of patriarchal meaning; masculine in origin and destination. Derridean mystery/mastery only appears equivocal. He collaborates. The literal *infans* disseminates. Derrida, sperm dodger, jealous narcissist, orders: there will be no getting pregnant! No more mothers! God is a satellite keeping his distanz from ova/matter/woman.

Barbara Johnson puts it differently, of course, in her introduction to *Dissemination*:

> To mean…is automatically *not* to be. As soon as there is meaning, there is difference. Derrida's word for this lag inherent in any signifying act is *différance*, from the French verb *différer*, which means both "to differ" and "to defer". What Derrida attempts to demonstrate is that this *différance* inhabits the very core of what appears to be immediate and present (italics in original, 1981a, p. ix).

The essential strategy of Derridean "undoing" of Western metaphysics and dualism is the negation of presence and in particular, that of woman and mother.[20] In his study of Rousseau's *Confessions* in *Of Grammatology*, he considers Rousseau's Mamma and Thérèse. Of the two women he says: "in what one calls the real life of these existences 'of flesh and bone'... there has never been anything but writing" (1976, p. 159). This reading of Mamma and Thérèse is the foundational moment of Derrida's new science of writing:

[T]here have never been anything but supplements, substitutive significations which could only come forth in a chain of differential references, the "real" supervening, and being added only while taking on meaning from a trace and from an invocation of the supplement, etc. And thus to infinity, for we have read, *in the text*, that the absolute present, Nature, that which words like "real mother", name, have always already escaped, have never existed; that what opens meaning and language is writing as the disappearance of natural presence (1976, p. 159; italics in original).

Différance, the dangerous supplement, and all Derrida's readings repeat as Barbara Johnson does: "our very relation to "reality' already functions like a text.... Nothing, indeed can be said to be *not* a text" (1981a, p. xiv; italics in original).

Derrida shows how writing and masturbation are both supplements for a presence, for real intercourse/discourse. Same difference as Plato's structure of desire, or Socrates debate with Agathon on the question of love in *The Symposium*. Socrates asked: "Does Love desire the thing that he is love of, or not?" "Of course he does," answered Agathon. "And does he desire and love the thing that he desires and loves when he is in possession of it or when he is not?" "Probably when he is not," Agathon replied. "If you reflect for a moment, you will see that it isn't merely probable but absolutely certain that one desires what one lacks, or rather that one does not desire what one does not lack.... Love will be love of beauty...then, if Love lacks beauty, and what is good coincides with what is beautiful, he also lacks goodness" (Plato: 1956, pp. 76, 78). The dangerous supplements, writing or masturbation, are supplements for a dangerous presence. Rousseau fears that a perfectly fulfilled heterosexual desire would annihilate him: "If I had ever in my life tasted the delights of love even once in their plenitude, I do not imagine that my frail existence would have been sufficient for them. I would have been dead in the act" (Derrida: 1976, p. 155). Rousseau's desire for a woman he called "Mamma" was threatened by her presence: "I only felt the full strength of my attachment to her when she was out of my sight."[21] Dissemination: against insemination, against the containment of male form

---

20. He also "takes on" the role of the mother: in *Glas* (1986), Derrida searches for the mother; in "The Law of Genre" he plays in a mother/daughter role. Thus, he mimics the mother as much as Nietzsche. My interpretation goes against the grain of Hélène Cixous' Derridean reading of Derrida and dualism. In "Sorties," a section of *The Newly Born Woman*, Cixous (1986) does speak very briefly of masculine dreams of motherless filiation, but she does not recognize misogyny in Derrida.

by female materiality. Male attraction to and repulsion for female flesh: the penis as artful dodger. Frances Bartkowksi wonders whether this metaphorization of deferral and delay is "an endless auto-affection? a tantric reserve? a spermatic economy of the nineteenth-century variety? where woman and feminine metaphors of undecidability are kept forever at bay/play? For there is a mastery and pleasure in play over and in the abyss" (1980, p. 77).

Is deconstruction a practice which threatens masculine authority?[22] Nietzsche's character advised Zarathustra to take whips to women; Derrida's chosen fictional Pierrot brings an inescapable signifying chain. However, it is claimed in traditional readings that deconstruction undoes binary oppositions of Cartesian self. It is said that especially in "The Double Session" in *Dissemination* (1981a), Derrida exposes a classical onto-theo-logy in theories of representation in Western literature and philosophy: speech as direct presence, the unequivocal mastery of meaning. Derrida's reading strategy is to show that both speech and writing inaugurate lack rather than presence (to speak is to be immediately lost, since language is a chain of signifiers and a structure of Saussaurian differences, rather than the transparency of things to words). In any case, the spurring/spurning of presence and meaning is central to "The Double Session," where Derrida strategizes Mallarmé's reading of "Pierrot Murderer of His Wife" to repose the form/content signification of the mimetic structure.

Let us see, since we must see, this little book...[and the scene]: In the barn of an old farm, in the midst of a crowd of workers and peasants, a mimodrama – with no entry fee – of which he gives an outline after having described the setting at length. An inebriated Pierrot, "white, long, emaciated," enters with an undertaker. "And the drama began. For it truly was a drama we attended, a brutal, bizarre drama that burned the brain like one of Hoffmann's fantastic tales, atrocious at times, making one suffer like a veritable nightmare. Pierrot, who remains alone, tells how he has killed Columbine who had been unfaithful to him. He has just buried her, and no one will ever know of his crime. He had tied her to the bed she was asleep, and he had tickled her feet until a horrible, ghastly death burst upon her amongst those atrocious bursts of laughter. Only this long white Pierrot with his cadaverous face could have come up with the idea of this torture fit for the damned. And, miming the action, he represented before us the whole scene, simulating the victim and the murderer by turns" (Derrida: 1981a, pp. 198-199). Woman/meaning is masturbated to a mimed death, and we are to be amused at the

---

21. This is Barbara Johnson's (Derrida: 1981a, p. xii) use of J.M. Cohen's translation of Rousseau's *Confessions*, Penguin, 1954. Gayatri Chakravorty Spivak translates the phrase in *Of Grammatology* as: "I only felt the full strength of my attachment when I no longer saw her" (Derrida: 1976, p. 152). This is the disgust for female presence and sexuality as discussed earlier. See also: Somer Brodribb (1991), "Discarnate Desires: Thoughts on Sexuality and Post-Structuralist Discourse," *Women's Studies International Forum, 14,* 3, pp. 135-142.

22. Gayatri Chakravorty Spivak acknowledges that a discourse of man in the metaphor of woman (1983, p. 169) is "present" in Derrida, and she recognises that the feminist deconstructionist must undo this double displacement, yet she still sees deconstruction, like Marxism, as a gift. Frances Bartkowski disagrees: "A feminization of philosophy, if we may call deconstruction that, as Gayatri Spivak has, is still fully within phallocentrism, though other centrisms – logo-, phono-, ethno-, may have been radically decentered" (1980, p. 77).

lesson (very pedagogical) that there is no language for a female presence, there is only the signifying chain to a bed/dream. We are not real, we are read/dead. Humiliated in being forced to laugh at our murder, and to be mimicked to death.

This methodology that centres on literary sensations rather than literal acts is similar to Ovid's "male narcissistic identification with the female victim" described by Amy Richlin (1987). Her reading of Ovid's *Metamorphoses* shows that Philomela is raped by her brother-in-law and her tongue is cut out so that she cannot tell her sister of her abduction and assault. Richlin's reading shows that in Ovid's story, "the act of rape is a blank: Ovid explores the sensations of the woman raped." Masculine delight in this terror and enjoyment of a certain *frisson* is related to the fear of the women. Ovid, then was the first deconstructionist. Derrida's *Metamorphoses*[23] is a mock epic of satire and degradation which maintains the authority of disorder and proposes the death of the reader. There is no escape from the dictionary, from texts, from this *lit* of reflected, refracted, fractured meanings, with mirrors. In this, Derrida agrees with Lacan's theory of the eternity of the signifying chain to hysterical death. There was a murder but no one significant died. Jacques the Riddler? Foucault depoliticized sexual relations between men and women, and Derrida supplements this: there can be no escape from male textual or sexual relations. At the trial, form represents matter. Derrida claims woman: we must remain the unwritten page, the hymen, the membranes of his metaphor, writhing, not subjects of our own writing. Columbine's words are choked away by deadly stimulation/dissimulation: the Joker's misogynous confusion of female senses/meanings. Such a sophisticated murderer as Pierrot does not leave marks. This is the language of batterers when in *Dissemination* Derrida says: "It is the hymen that desire dreams of piercing, of bursting in an act of violence that is (at the same time or somewhere between) love and murder" (1981a, p. 213).

Is deconstruction a subtle displacement of the hierarchies of Western philosophy and literature with the archi-écriture of a snuff film? Is it more dissimulation, sordid clowning behind a mask which does not even reflect in the Lacanian mirror? Logos and graphos: the spoken dictat is supplemented with *it is written*. New masks for the dictator, new authority for the law, engraved, inscripted and veiled like a threat.

Fascinated with the mystery (*sic*) of his inequity, he feigns neutrality: *nothing matters* moves to *everything is permitted*. There is presence: masculine dominance. Big Brother is a deconstructionist, working at the Ministry of Dissemination. He erases evidence, and absents the murdered woman. Where there is God, there is no justice for women. Derrida's lesson is that *we* must imitate *him*. If there is nothing outside the text, it is impossible to go beyond it: we can only mime Derrida. But in truth, feminist knowledge is creative, not mimetic

---

23. To pursue this parallel, refer to Amy Richlin (1983) Chapter 6, "Catullus, Ovid, and the Art of Mockery," in her *The Garden of Priapus, Sexuality and Aggression in Roman Humour*, New Haven: Yale University Press.

5

LACAN AND IRIGARAY:
ETHICAL LACK AND ETHICAL PRESENCE

The most subtly necessary guardian of my life being the other's flesh. Approaching and speaking to me with his hands. Bringing me back to life more intimately than any regenerative nourishment, the other's hands, these palms with which he approaches without going through me, give me back the borders of my body and call me back to the remembrance of the most profound intimacy. As he caresses me, he bids me neither to disappear nor to forget but rather, to remember the place where, for me, the most intimate life holds itself in reserve. Searching for what has not yet come into being, for himself, he invites me to become what I have not yet become. To realize a birth still in the future. Plunging me back into the maternal womb and, beyond that, conception, awakening me to another – amorous – birth (Irigaray: 1986, p. 232-233).

In other words – for the moment, I am not fucking, I am talking to you. Well! I can have exactly the same satisfaction as if I were fucking. That's what it means. Indeed, it raises the question of whether in fact I am not fucking at this moment (Lacan: 1977, p. 165-166).

If henceforth there is nothing but lack, the Other falters, and the signifier is that of his death (Lacan: 1986, p. 227).

According to Lacan, the unconscious is structured like a language. In fact, language governs everything: "I don't want to put myself in the position here of elaborating a theory of consciousness, but it is quite clear that the things of the human world are things of a universe structured in speech, that language, which is dominated by symbolical processes, governs everything" (1986, p. 57). Never mind the sun:[1] without the Phallus there is no human life at all!

Lacan's *Écrits* is his best known work, where he elaborates his theory of how the word creates mind. His theory of the symbolic is a theory of the *structure* of ontology and epistemology. Lacan stated in a 1969 interview that the notion of intersubjectivity had come up between the two World Wars as a sort of smokescreen for Freud's real problem, "the structure of intrasubjectivity" (Caruso: 1969, p. 143). But even this term sets up an opposition, he argues, between inter- and intrasubjectivity and leads us into the error of considering the units of these structures (ego, super ego, ideal ego) as autonomous units, functioning in the common ground of a self or a subject. What is really at issue here is an infinitely more complex structure which permits us to take into account the discoveries of analysis. Lacan rejects the phenomenologists' concept of totality: "nothing is more contrary to the analytical experience" (Caruso: 1969, p. 144). For Lacan, "The relation of object poses itself not at the level of inter-subjectivity, but at that of subjective structures, which in any case would lead us to problems of *intrasubjectivity*" (Caruso: 1969, p. 144, italics in original). The subject originates in a division and separation, and the formal system of the duplication and dimensions of the subject is what Lacan is dedicated to theorizing; its topological structure.

...the *subject* is that which a signifier represents for another signifier. Here we have the root, the inauguration of the foundation of subjectivity, as much as it can be deduced from the necessity *of an unconscious which is insurmountable because of its very nature, of an unconscious that could not be lived in any case on the level of conscience* (Caruso: 1969, p. 160, italics in original).

Thus, it is the unconscious which requires further exploration and analysis, in order to discover the basis of a pre-subjective logos. I want to suggest that Lacan's theory of cognition can only be understood in relationship to his early work on desire, discord

---

1. Freud's *Moses and Monotheism* traced original reason from the religion of Akhenaton, the fourteenth century B.C. Egyptian pharaoh who according to Freud was the rationalist precursor of Moses. The cult of the sun god was the first attempt at monotheism and reason. The God of both Akhenaton and Moses was the god of light, "His attributes are those of a thought which regulates the nature of reality," says Lacan (1986, p. 212). The fertility rituals related to Goddesses and the female cycle of generation are negated by Lacan: he interprets the rites of the Pharaohs around the clay of the Nile as an instance of the essential link between man and meaning. These rituals were important for man's support of language: in Lacan's theory of cognition they signify male memory and not nature's fertility. If man did not remember the Nile, the natural order could not continue. A delusional disorder? Like Lévi-Strauss, Lacan is fascinated by sunsets, which require man's witness: "What relation can there be between man and the return of the sunrise? If it is not that, as a speaking man, he sustains himself in a direct relationship to the signifier?" (1986, p. 264). Lacan's structuralist interpretation of the origin of the real and symbolic worlds is in the best patriarchal tradition. He worships the Son, the logos whose thoughts and symbolic order regulate the nature of reality. All these suns! There are novas in Lévi-Strauss, apocalyptic twilights and lightning flashes in Foucault, Nietzsche's *Thus Spoke Zarathustra* opens with the sun; atomic erasures with no memory of solar warmth and fertility?

and *das Ding*,[2] such that cognition is a desire for death. He builds on Freud and de Sade who saw death and desire as the true link to the other. Thanatos is the logos of desire. Lacan ties the nature of *logos* to death in the desire for the other as the *form*ula for language.

This articulation of ethics and desire in *L'éthique de la psychanalyse* is the basis of his theory of cognition. Published in 1986, it is the collection[3] of Lacan's university seminars from the 1959-60 period. *L'éthique* has not been the object of significant critique, but Lacan cherished these seminars and hoped to edit them himself. Instead, they are his first posthumous work, and unlike the primarily exegetical studies of the early fifties, they are his first original interpretation of Freud's theory. Philippe Julien, author of *Le Retour à Freud de Jacques Lacan* (1986) argues that Lacan never again went as far as he did in this seventh seminar (Gentis: 1986, p. 20). This was a time of excess and exaltation: the heroic quest to define pure desire, a law of the unconscious with no conscience. A tragic tone was central to the seminar and Lacan at one point remarked: "Ah, my students, if they knew where I was taking them, they would be terrified" (Gentis: 1986, p. 20). This was the world of the hero of experimental literature, the *nouveau roman*. Julien admires this style: "Lacan proposes a new path – without comfort, without landmarks, without railings. And that is the ethics of psychoanalysis, that is where desire leads" (Gentis: 1986, p. 20). To an empty space and Sadean temporality.

According to Lacan, analytical experience has discovered the circle of obligation and guilt in desire, a circle which is imposed on us. *L'éthique de la psychanalyse* plunges us into a consideration of ethics and the morbid as early as the second page. A particularly morbid desire is accentuated. He searches for this terrible face of desire in Freud's work:

Is it sin that designates the Freudian oeuvre from the start, the murder of the father, this great myth placed by Freud at the origin of the development of culture? Or is it a sin still more obscure and more original that he formulates at the end of his work, the death instinct in other words, inasmuch as man is anchored, in the most profound part of himself, to its fearsome dialectic? (1986, pp. 10-11).

These are the *entre-deux-morts* between which we are pulled for the rest of the book: the murder of the father, and *thanatos*, a desire for death. This ontology is the individual psycho-social version of Foucault's *rerum concordia discors*.[4] But it would be a mistake to expect to find in Lacan this cloth of death and desire fully woven. It

---

2. Very little has been written specifically on the concept of *das Ding* in Lacan. Ellie Ragland-Sullivan understands it as follows: "For Lacan, 'It' was *das Ding*, truth hiding in the unconscious Other (A)... [which is]...the discourse of the mother, father, culture and of language itself, which has been repressed and is subsequently displaced into concrete language and relationships and onto other substitute objects" (Ragland-Sullivan: 1987, p. 190-191).
3. An English edition is under preparation with W.W. Norton.
4. Nature's harmony in discord.

threads his reflections, it is in remnants in chapters which are themselves juxtaposed like a *jeu de mots*. Meaning is inferred but never clearly assembled. Meaning is never arrived at, it never comes to anything, even with a great deal of manipulation, for Lacan's meaning is never so spontaneous as the literature suggests.

The three ethical heritages which Lacan puts forward are the Aristotelian, the Christian and the Kantian: sovereign good, brotherly love, and the categorical imperative, all of which operate according to moral combinations of the Good and the Law. Freud redrew moral mythology in *Totem and Taboo* with an original murder of the father; the source of repression lurks within the energy of desire. For Lacan, Freud's mythology is a happy discovery because it indicates not simply a structure which imposes itself upon us, but the condition of civilization. Lacan's lectures on psychoanalysis and ethics attempt to legislate this process in civil and criminal codes, through a discussion of the law of discourse, and the relationship to the signifier. Lacan turns to Freud's *Civilization and its Discontents*, written after his discovery of a death instinct, in order to elaborate his own view of individual and culture. Lacan is more interested in the synchronic use of the signifier rather than the diachronic, etymological concerns that preoccupied Freud (1986, p. 56) who believed in meaning across the generations of language. For Lacan, moral experience is not limited to the paradoxes of the individual superego. Desire remains always in the jurisdiction (juris/diction) of the law of discourse, founded on the exigencies of *das Ding*. Ethics is not the social chain of obligation, it is also that which underwrites the elementary structures of kinship studied by Claude Lévi-Strauss. Man makes himself an object of the sign, in an unconscious and reliable process. Man submits to the law of the unconscious and to that which presides over the supernatural structure. "That which, across the generations, presides over this new supernatural order of structures is exactly that which gives reason to man's submission to the law of the unconscious" (Lacan: 1986, p. 92). But ethics is beyond even this level of structure; ethics "begins the moment when the subject asks the question of this good which he had searched for unconsciously in social structures and where, at the same time, he is led to discover the profound link by which that which presents itself to him as law is closely tied to the very structure of desire" (1986, p. 92). The *I* of the superego is none other than the I which asks itself what it wants.

Central to his discussion is Freud's horror of the Commandment *Thou shalt love thy neighbour as thyself*. Lacan links such fear to the law of desire, and the imaging of self-image. "If something, at the summit of this ethical commandment, ends in a manner which some find so strange, so scandalous...that is because it is of the law of the relation of the human subject to himself that he makes himself, in his relation to his desire, his own neighbour" (1986, p. 92). Self, other, desire and death reflect each other and not themselves. Lacan sees a murderer in the mirror, or Roman Polanski's *The Tenant*.

The late eighteenth century was marked by Kant's *Critique of Practical Reason* and de Sade's *Philosophy of the Bedroom*.[5] "Men of pleasure" proposed the liberation of desire but this philosophy has failed, according to Lacan, because the libertine is the man most burdened by law and duty (1986, p. 12). Mirabeau, de Sade, Diderot, the writers of excessive libertinage, present the ideal of natural pleasure and all write in defiance of God:

God, as the author of nature, is summoned to give an explanation for the most extreme anomalies that de Sade, Mirabeau, Diderot, or anyone else requires of us. This challenge, this summons, this ordeal must not permit any other outcome than that which finds itself actually realized in history. He who submits to the ordeal finds there, in the last instance, its premises, that is to say, the Other before whom this ordeal is presented, its final Judge (Lacan: 1986, p. 12).

The "erotic" ordeal is an interpellation of Divine Judgment. Even in medieval times, ordeals were known as the Judgment of God. The pleas for divine patriarchal presence became hysterical with de Sade's yearning to touch divinity, to be divinity, in the control and desecration of tempting women. In the twilight of the gods, he finds Him, the Other and the Judge, a faithful defiance of the god of Moses within the circle of masculine obligation, guilt and desire.

Freud found the roots of morality in desire itself, its censure, negation, and sentiment of guilt and obligation. What Lacan introduces is a terrifying aspect of desire, by building on the work of Freud and de Sade. Both Kant and de Sade eliminate sentiment from morality, Lacan notes, and liberate the entire horizon of desire from all sentiments save one: pain. Sade inverts Kant, so that Desire dominates the Law.

In summary, Kant is of de Sade's opinion. For, in order to attain *das Ding* absolutely, to open all the floodgates of desire, what is it that de Sade shows us on the horizon? Essentially, pain. The pain of others, and also the subject's own pain, for they are on occasions, but one and the same thing (Lacan: 1986, p. 97).

Sadism expects to glimpse its own and the face of God in another's pain. Millett describes this as "the death fuck" (1971, p. 292). Lacan is drawn to the death fuck as a theory of cognition, a law of discourse, or an ethics of desire: "*jouissance* is an evil... because it involves harm to the other" (1986, p. 217).

Lacan considers the law which forbids men to desire their neighbour's cattle, wife, or donkey. The value of all these objects relates to:

that on which the human being can rely as being *das Trude*, *das Ding*, not in the sense of being his good, but the good where he resides. I would add, *das Ding* as the correlation even of the law of the word in its most primitive origin, in the sense that *das Ding* was there in the beginning, that it was the first thing that could separate itself from what the subject began to name and to

_____

5. Emmanuel Kant, *Critique de la raison pratique*, 1788; Marquis de Sade, *La Philosophie dans le boudoir*, 1795.

articulate, that the lust of which it is a question here addresses itself, not to anything that I desire, but to a thing to the extent that it is the Thing of my neighbour (1986, p. 100).

The commandment against covetousness keeps a distance from the Thing. "The value of this commandment is found in the distance it preserves from the Thing in as much as it is founded on the word itself" (1986, pp. 100-101). Survival is a Nietzschean distance from the Thing created in the original separation within self. Distance, commandment and the Thing are all fundamentally created by the word, *phallus*. And, I should note, that internal voice which came from God, now comes from pre-subjective logos. Freud's originality was to locate the voice of the conscience in the Other. The Lacanian mirror shows that the fundamental cruelty (formerly, original sin) of the Other is also that of oneself. Freud demonstrated that the true link to the Other is death and desire. Now, we have entered *das Ding*, the place of emptiness and the origin of desire. It resonates with the Hegelian Master/Slave dialectic, where the desire of the subject is to have the desire of the Other. Lacan does not look at this dynamic intersubjectively, but refers to that field behind the subject, the field of *das Ding*. It is a dark place, being anti-Enlightenment. *Das Ding* is beside the subject when a small group of men are able to suspend the life of a planet with a nuclear satellite (1986, p. 125).

What is this mysterious Thing calling desire? Lacan repeats early Christian concerns: if a reasonable/perfect being created the world, why is there evil? (1986, p. 146). Lacan's transposition of this Biblical passage reveals his meaning: the toils of desire. The original chapter 7, verse 7 to 14 of St. Paul, Epistle to the Romans in the St. James version of the Bible reads:

Is the law sin? God forbid. Nay, I had not known sin, but by the law: for I had not known lust, except the law had said, Thou shalt not covet. But sin, taking occasion by the commandment, wrought in me all manner of concupiscence. For without the law sin was dead. For I was alive without the law once: but when the commandment came, sin revived, and I died. And the commandment, which was ordained to life, I found to be unto death. For sin, taking occasion by the commandment, deceived me, and by it slew me.

Lacan replaces *sin* with *la Chose*:

Is the Law the Thing? God forbid. Nay, I had not known the Thing, but by the Law: for I had not known lust, except the Law had said, Thou shalt not covet. But the Thing, taking occasion by the commandment, wrought in me all manner of concupiscence. For without the Law the Thing was dead. For I was alive without the Law once: but when the commandment came, the Thing revived, and I died. And the commandment, which was ordained to life, I found to be unto death. For the Thing, taking occasion by the commandment, seduced me, and made me desire death (1986, p. 101).[6]

---

6. I have used the Biblical English, rather than complicate the comparison by translating Lacan's modern French version of St. Paul. However, I have kept Lacan's use of "made me desire death" ("m'a fait désir de mort") instead of "slew me", and his choice of "m'a séduit" instead of "deceived me".

This substitution shows the knot of law, desire and death in Lacan's ontology. Or, as he states, "The dialectical relation between desire and Law makes our desire burn only in relation to the Law, through which it becomes a desire for death" (1986, p. 101).

But that's his Thing. Lacan refutes the work of Melanie Klein on the centrality of the mother in theories of symbol and sublimation and replaces her mother with his Phallus. The centrality of the mother as *imago* appears in the work of Irigaray and Klein. Lacan regretted that the father of psychoanalysis left it in the hands of women, who "are beings full of promise, at least to the extent that they have never kept any yet" (1986, p. 214). Lacan sees his own work as a critique of the Kleinian group who put the mythic body of the mother in the rightful place of *das Ding* (1986, p. 127). It is the phallus that Lacan wants to put in the minds and hands of women. He finds Freud correct in exposing a knot of sin, desire and law as the foundation of moral law, but he cuts himself off from Freud's belief that the mother is *das Ding*.

And so, the step taken by Freud, at the level of the pleasure principle, is to show us that there is no Sovereign Good, that the Sovereign Good is *das Ding*, which is the mother, the object of incest, is a forbidden Good, and there is no other Good. That is the foundation, reversed in Freud, of moral law (1986, p. 85).

Lacan wants the *imago* for the phallus.[7] The mother must be the phallus, since that is the only Thing that can be desired. Lacan applies the contemporary science of linguistics to Freud's theory of the field of the unconscious to argue that the phallus is the primordial signifier. In a 1958 presentation, "The Meaning of the Phallus," Lacan claimed that the phallus was most symbolic: it is naturally the privileged signifier. (But what does the phallus mean? it means death. Whose? the mother's.)

The phallus is the privileged signifier of that mark where the share of the logos is wedded to the advent of desire. One might say that this signifier is chosen as what stands out as most easily seized upon in the real of sexual copulation, and also as the most symbolic in the literal (typographical) sense of the term, since it is the equivalent in that relation of the (logical) copula. One might also say that by virtue of its turgidity, it is the image of the vital flow as it is transmitted in generation (1985b, p. 82).

Lacan claims origin, action, generation and matrix for the phallus. The phallus is naturally the signifier because there is one libido and that One is male. Women can only come to culture and language by wearing the phallus, and then always inadequately and incompletely. This rejection of women, material and abstract, is nowhere more evident than in Lacan's view of *vulva*. First, he suggests that the name derives from the universal sound men make during intercourse. The vulva is a void and void of meaning. All it signifies is being empty of a penis:

---

7. Was it in this seminar that Luce Irigaray recognized the absorption of the maternal and the feminine by *das Ding*, and is that the insight that led to her expulsion from the Lacanian school?

It is in as much as the feminine sexual organ, or more exactly, the form of openness and emptiness, is at the centre of all of these metaphors, that the article has interest, and a value for centering reflection, for it is clear that there is a gaping opening, a lapse of the expected reference (1986, p. 199).

Man is prior as structure or sex, and the desire for death is the foundation for all mind and all ethics. For what does the privileged signifier, the phallus, mean? It means death. Lacan is another Eros who lives in Erebus, in darkness, avoiding Psyche's lamp and gaze.

The death of God in a monotheistic ideology might herald the return of the Titans, a panoply of deities; from a supreme totem to the stated anarchy of postmodernism. If God is dead, it is both structure and desire which now say, *I am that I am*. Dionysus is especially well favoured by the philosophers of desire, and let the women beware Agave's fate, she who refused to recognize the story of his divine birth from the thigh of Zeus. No-name women who don't have a language should not talk back. "Ah, my students, if they only knew where I was taking them," mused Lacan. Did Irigaray see the particular and not "universal" man who was taking God's place?

Clearly among the angels (who have no sex), Kristeva claims to have transcended the category of women: "I have never experienced that 'slave' mentality, that feeling of being excluded or repressed...the sulking slave-like position that is still fairly widespread [in France]: 'they took this, they stole that, my way is barred, I am not appreciated...etc.'" (1977/1987, p. 114). Her notion of the semiotic is meant to supplement Lacan's theory of the symbolic order. The feminine must be a practice of the semiotic, eternally provoking the phallic symbolic, but never moving into signif-ication. Kristeva adheres to Lacan's notion of the symbolic order as the exclusive domain/prerogative of the phallus; a place where the feminine/female cannot be represented. It must vibrate, shock, energize, spark the phallic symbolic, but the feminine semiotic must never speak a female word/world.

Never strident, never complaining, Kristeva suspects those who are interested in women as a group, in female collectivity, community, politics, of avoiding their neuroses: "I am convinced that those who engage in issues concerning women not in order to examine their own singularity but in order to be reunited with 'all women' do so primarily in order to avoid looking at their own particular situation..." (1977/1987, p. 114). Thus does she misrepresent the intensely personal/political origin of women's movements. "These are the same women who today are bitterly or perversely opposed" (1977/1987, p. 114) to Freud and psychoanalytic theory. Antagonism to Freudian analysis becomes another neurotic episode. Resistance is impossible in the Foucauldian universe; for Kristeva it is quite simply *perverse*. She accuses feminists of fantasizing that their sex, language and psyche have been "betrayed by a knowledge that is neutral or masculine" (1977/1987, p. 115). In other words, they are hysterical and the Fathers of psychoanalysis (and semiotics) are innocent.

A little has been said about Lacan's misogyny (Gallop: 1982). Sarah Kofman defended Nietzsche, and now Catherine Clément enters the field on Lacan's behalf. Even in the early 1960s, Clément was among the audience in Lacan's seminars. Clément's *Life and Legends of Jacques Lacan* is dedicated to Jacques-Alain Miller, Lacan's son-in-law, supporter, designated interpreter and posthumous editor. Given her attachment to the inner circle, it is not surprising that Lacan's "problems with women" such as Françoise Dolto and Luce Irigaray receive little attention from Clément. Ellie Ragland-Sullivan also protects Lacan from feminist accusations. She argues that he has been misunderstood by Irigaray who, for some reason, takes his theory of phallic signification as prescriptive rather than descriptive (1987, p. 273). She charges that the Derridean feminists Jane Gallop, Alice Jardine, Luce Irigaray and Hélène Cixous mistakenly find Lacan's work less relevant to a concern with sexual difference (1989, p. 63). Ragland-Sullivan argues that "the post-structuralist American Lacan is not the Lacan known in France or other countries where Lacan's texts have been studied for two and three decades" (1989, p. 34). She finds that his contribution to current cultural critique has been neglected, and that his work has been ignored, misunderstood, and neglected – or copied and used without credit. "Americans are still not aware of the degree to which Lacan influenced post-structuralist thinkers and writers who never credit him" (1989, pp. 38, 39). She mentions Derrida, Barthes, Deleuze in this context and Lyotard as well. Well before Lyotard's critique of metanarratives, Lacan had shown "*there is no metalanguage*" (1989, p. 58, italics in original). Loyal to a man she believes is virtuous, rather than stimulated by one she knows to be a prick (Gallop: 1982, p. 37), Ragland-Sullivan is more compelling in terms of intellectual honesty. Fortunately, it is not necessary to choose between these two ways of relating to Lacan.

It is not unusual that someone so phallic-centred as Lacan should be so well defended. Lacan, Sade, Nietzsche and Derrida speak of nothing but women, and yet it is said they all speak ironically. Women are told we must be patient, sympathetic, and amused, we must be humble in our approach to capricious genius. Clément tells us that Lacan was inspired by the style of paranoid madwomen, the objects of his earliest studies. Descriptions of Lacan as a "phoenix", "shaman," "prophet" and "witch" appear repeatedly in her book. Was the image in Lacan's mirror an hysteric? "Transvestite, he found in the fantasies of women a passion for language that constantly obsessed him. He identified with their tortures, their anguish" (1983, p. 49). Clément notes Lacan's "incoherent, disturbed" (1983, p. 56) writing style derived from his studies of "inspired madwomen" (1983, p. 56). Actually, he made a calculated use of feminine delirium and panic, which he determined to be incommunicable and strange: inhuman? It was with feminine *jouissance* that Lacan sought to identify himself, presenting himself as a mystic (1983, p. 67). Lacan never stopped talking of women.[8] Clément claims that feminine *jouissance* is the core of Lacan's thought, and she focuses on "God and the *Jouissance* of The Woman" to prove, uncritically, that he was a real Ladies' man. Certainly, Lacan appropriates the style of a madwoman possessed

---

8. See *Feminine Sexuality*.

by desire, and then says that only a man can speak of it. O magical, detachable, disappearing phallus! What is this hysteria to be a possessed female body but a male fantasy of possessing female bodies and wombs?

Juliet Mitchell and Jacqueline Rose (Lacan: 1985a) are utterly loyal to this deadly game in their introductions to *Feminine Sexuality, Jacques Lacan and the école freudienne*.

When Lacan himself did refer to biology, it was in order to remind us of the paradox inherent in reproduction itself, which, as Freud pointed out, represents a victory of the species over the individual. The "fact' of sexed reproduction marks the subject as *"subject to"* death (Rose in Lacan: 1985a, p. 35).

In contrast, Page duBois (1988) criticizes the Lacanian feminists Juliet Mitchell and Jane Gallop for failing to historicize the concept of gender and thereby perpetuating the notion of the castrated female as human destiny. In similar reference to Jane Gallop's *Reading Lacan*, duBois charges:

To continue to consider the phallus as the transcendent signifier, to accept the inevitability of the "idea" of transcendence, to accept the fantasy of the subject who is supposed to know, to believe that the phallus, and language, control us but that somehow our escape lies in knowing that male privilege is an imposture, even though based on an acceptance of the centrality of the phallus – all this seems to me only to perpetuate a metaphysics of wholeness, presence, deism, and worship of the symbolic father (1988, p. 188).

According to Lacan, women stubbornly jeopardize their access to phallic *jouissance* by foolishly celebrating an anti-phallic nature even after he has told us there is only a phallic unconscious.[9] Male narcissism is outraged by otherness and female autonomy. Written on the dissolution (ultimate structuralist achievement?) of his school in the winter of 1980, a *querelle des femmes* closed his work:

It is only on condition of not losing themselves in an anti-phallic nature, of which there is no trace in the unconscious, that they can hear that of this unconscious which does not tend to speak itself, but reaches what is being elaborated from it, as though procuring for them truly phallic *jouissance* [orgasm] (Lacan: 1980, p. 12).

We are warned that women will only achieve phallic *jouissance* if we remain silent. Thus did Lacan close the circle of his phallogocentricism: there is only a phallic unconscious, the phallus is the most significant of all signifiers. The Master's success is to make this convincing and to render the *female* uncertain, aphasiac and amnesiac, to disqualify all woman-centred views of the imago, the symbolic and the real. Phallocracy is always in place: we can imagine with nothing else. There is only penetration, or lack of penetration, says the Master. Macciocchi remembers Lacan's

---

9. Jacques Lacan, "L'Autre manque," pp. 11-12 in "Dissolution", pp. 9-20, *Ornicar?* 1980, no. 20-21.

dissolution of his School, and his words "Le pére sevère persévere"[10] (1983, p. 487). Jacques-Alain Miller, Lacan's son-in-law, wrote of the school: "Elle lui résistait, il l'a étrangleé"[11] (Macciocchi: 1983, p. 487). Thus does the phallus insist on being the original, seeking to silence the *querelle des femmes* when women participate.

Sheila Jeffreys (1985) (1990) and Margaret Jackson (1984a) (1984b) have both argued that certain nineteenth- and twentieth-century theories of sexuality were elaborated in the face of feminist gains, and served to organize hostility to women who were autonomous socially and sexually. The work of Havelock Ellis in particular can be seen as a response to growing feminist campaigns against male sexual violence. Sexology was elaborated to reinforce and restabilize masculine supremacy. Flight from the masculine paradigm was labelled sick and deviant, now it is simply called essentialist. Margaret Jackson argues:

Ellis' 'science' of sex constitutes above all an apology for and justification of precisely that form of male sexuality which contemporary feminists were challenging: a sexuality based on 'uncontrollable urges', power and violence. By claiming that this form of male sexuality was biologically determined, and therefore inevitable, the feminist challenge was undermined and male domination legitimated (1984a, p. 53).

We could substitute "Lacan" for "Ellis" to see what this new French sexology corresponds to, and how it responds to our contemporary feminist campaigns against sexism in the media and in language, and writings on feminine pleasure. Lacan tells us that women are biologically incapable of representing the phallus, are eternally secondary citizens in the symbolic order, and can only come through the phallus. Heterosexuality remains natural and institutionalized in the theories of both Ellis and Lacan. Neither were amused by female autonomy. In discussing the body-image, Lacan asserts:

All the phenomenon we are discussing seem to exhibit the laws of *gestalt*: the fact that the penis is dominant in the shaping of the body-image is evidence of this. Though this may shock the champions of the autonomy of female sexuality, such dominance is a fact and one moreover which cannot be put down to cultural influences alone (Lacan: 1953, p. 13).

The phallus as original signifier is constructed on the belief in the *nothing of women's sex*. Lacanian psychoanalysis is the theory that women *must* do what men want and be silent. His domination is biologically and symbolically determined by his socio-linguistic laws of development. Or as Nietzsche hoped: "The man's happiness is: I will. The woman's happiness is: He will" (1986a, p. 92). Dale Spender points to a historical feminist awareness of a central masculine fear: the independence of women and the irrelevance of men (1983, p. 144). In a way that recalls the fate of feminism under Ellis and his followers, Liz Stanley illustrates how the work of Foucault and Lacan was taken up in 1980s England as the only sexual theory. The history of

---

10. The severe father perseveres.
11. She resisted him, he strangled her.

feminist thought and practice is distorted and ridiculed in order to consolidate a sexual theory purged of feminist politics and independent women (1984, p. 61). Only feminist accounts which fit in with these projects are acceptable as sexual theory to the male-stream representatives of the French school. Stanley charges:

The underlying "project" in all of this seems fairly clear. It is one which promotes men's liberationism by taking over "sexual politics" and the right to define what this is and what analyses of it exist…. It does; partly by using sexual theory and the parody of "feminism" to drive a wedge between feminism and a theory of sexual politics. And it does so partly by producing a construction of "sexual politics" which omits most of what feminism associates with it, and in particular its analysis of male sexual power and women's oppression (1984, p. 61).

Good French philosophy proceeds in the manner of the immanent critique, playing off sections of the text to reveal internal contradictions, demonstrating the hidden reliance on repudiated beliefs, and the consequences of a text's actions.[12] If this were good French philosophy, then, or the time of the sophists, we would now proceed through a close examination of how the Lacanian text contradicts its psycho-ethical suppositions, and perhaps argue that Lacan's universe *entre-deux-morts* still depends on a bourgeois sense of happiness. The partiality of the immanent critique is that rationality is seen as culminating in the most recent immanent critique: the unreason of reason, the reason of unreason. Yet there is a critical position that is not that of the discipline or the disciples: a critique by those who do not learn from the Master to what they may object. We might try something else then, and show how Lacan complicates Freud's question "What do women want?" with his own argument that men want death. Our ironic reversal might not be acceptable no matter how immanent.

The feminist and psychoanalyst, Luce Irigaray, was expelled from the Lacanian school in 1974, because as the back cover says, *Speculum of the Other Woman* (Irigaray: 1974/1985c) "provoked the wrath of the Lacanian faction, leading to her expulsion from the Freudian School and from her teaching position at Vincennes." Her originality and resistance certainly indicate courage. *Speculum of the Other Woman* (1974/1985c) and *This Sex Which Is Not One* (1977/1985d) review Western philosophy from the position of female morphology and difference.[13] Her reversal of

---

12. A witty critique of critique appears in Vincent Descombes' (1986) "Introduction: Analytical versus Continental Philosophy?" in *Objects of All Sorts, A Philosophical Grammar*, (pp. 1-14), Lorna Scott-Fox and Jeremy Harding, Trans. Baltimore: Johns Hopkins University Press.
13. For a clear presentation of Irigaray's representation of difference and how it has been misunderstood as anatomical determinism, see Margaret Whitford (1988) (1989). Diana Fuss's *Essentially Speaking, Feminism, Nature and Difference* (1989) contains summaries of anti-essentialist positions and chronicles the essentialist/constructionist opposition which she characterizes as central to contemporary feminist debates. As an "anti-essentialist who wants to preserve…the category of essence" (1989 p. xiv), she attempts to show that essentialism is not necessarily reactionary. This work contrasts with Judith Butler's (1990) *Gender Trouble* which argues that the foundational categories of nonpoststructuralist feminism are oppressive and exclusionary. An excellent discussion is Angela Miles's chapter "Anti-essentialist reductionisms: Equality versus specificity" in *Transformative Feminisms: Integrative Global Perspectives*, New York: Routledge, forthcoming 1993.

Nietzsche supposes: what if women were a language, what then? Irigaray's *Parler n'est jamais neutre* (1985b) shows how all language is sexed, how discourse is not neutral. "L'ordre sexuel du discours" (1987d) is a close grammatical cataloguing of texts, deciphered according to hysterical or obsessive compulsive characteristics. Such attention to grammar and psychology, and belief in the primacy of language and sexuality in culture is post-Lacanian.

Irigaray's ethical premises and approaches to Desire and the Law were, like Lacan's *L'éthique de la psychanalyse*, produced as a series of university seminars. Hers were delivered in 1982 in Rotterdam. In *Éthique* Irigaray takes up Plato's *Symposium*, Aristotle's *Physics #V*, Descartes on the passions of the soul, Spinoza's lecture on ethics, Hegel's *Phenomenology of Spirit*, Merleau-Ponty on the visible and invisible, and Levinas on totality and infinity. These commentaries return to the main essay on sexual difference, with passages on love of the self, the same, and the other.[14] She invokes, transgresses and revokes much of Derrida and Lacan by insisting on sexual difference. Contrary to Derrida's critique of onto-theo-logy, she proposes a feminine divine. Unlike Lacan, she argues that women have a sex, a language – and an ethics. *Éthique de la différence sexuelle* (1984) argues that sexual difference is the question of "our" philosophical epoch. Psychoanalytic theory, art, and the women's movement have not yet realized a revolutionary conceptualization of sexual difference. The women's movement has achieved change by wringing concessions from those in dominance, but new values have not been put in place (1984, p. 14). The fertile meeting of the two sexes has not yet occured at a political, poetic level. A revolution in thought and ethics is required so that the work of sexual difference can take place, a labour that will reconsider the "subject and discourse...the world...the cosmos" (1984, p. 14). The universal has been masculine (1984, p. 14), subjectivity of the Father; the masculine paternal. But the coming of sexual difference will bring our salvation:

Sexual difference will constitute the horizon of worlds of yet unknown fertility. At least in the West, and in not reducing fertility to the reproduction of bodies, of flesh. A fertility of birth and regeneration for amorous couples, but also the production of a new epoch of thought, art, poetry, language...the Creation of a new *poietics* (1984, p. 13, italics in original).

Irigaray is proposing a differently sexed rather than neutral Word, its plural rather than singular incarnation. In formulations such as this, Irigaray indicates her belief in linguistic and divine salvation. She offers us a strangely erotic thaumaturgy and insists on a feminine divine, and the centrality and mystery of the heterosexual caress.

Irigaray's formula for new epochal changes involves the following categories: space-time, the habitation of places, and envelopes of identity: "Each epoch inscribes a limit to this trinitary configuration: *matter*, *form*, *interval*, or *power*, *act*, *interval*-

---

14. The other is not the child of Sara Ruddick's (1989) ethical paradigm, or the other woman, as in Janice Raymond's *A Passion for Friends* (1986), but man.

intermediary" (1984, p. 15, italics in original). A new epoch would signify a different relationship between: "man and god*s*, man and man, man and the world, man and woman" (1984, pp. 15-16). Irigaray finds that traditionally, woman has signified *place* for man as the maternal feminine, she has been an object which he uses to limit space, an envelope of identity against which man defines himself. Man cannot escape the master-slave dialectic because he does not permit women's subjective life, there is no dynamic inter-subjectivity where he changes places and becomes her place. Instead, he becomes a slave to a God he endows with absolute power, although he is secretly a slave to the maternal feminine he seeks to obliterate. Without a place of her own, woman becomes threatening to man, who cannot leave her place.

A reconsideration of the economy of space and time is central to Irigaray's focus on sexual difference: "the feminine is lived as space, but often with the connotations of abyss and night (God being illuminated space?), the masculine is lived as time" (Irigaray: 1984, p. 15). Irigaray accepts sexual difference in feminine depth/darkness and shining masculine temporality, in contrast to the feminine temporal consciousness theorized by O'Brien (1981; 1989a). What is at issue here is a concept of the space and time of patriarchy as the corruption of sexual difference by Gods, versus the theory of the appropriation of the dialectics of reproduction by an ideologizing masculine consciousness. Irigaray maintains that ethical and moral questions must consider the law of the couple, and the family. Here she introduces divine law, which she sees as historically of feminine origin, and based in gynocratic societies where religious and civic realms were once one. A maternal genealogy of a feminine sacerdotal order was replaced with the mother-son culture by the people of man: "in the beginning, divine truth was communicated to women and transmitted from mother to daughter" (1987b, p. 422). Yet Irigaray's political and cultural solution to this primacy of man is simply representation of the mother-daughter bond in aesthetics and language (1987a). Here she remains Lacanian and perhaps Cathartic: her idealization of the mother-daughter relationship omits actual birth. Perhaps this is a fear of the charge of "biological determinism," or a common prejudice that reproductive consciousness cannot be put into words. Certainly, Irigaray is more interested in the divine phenomenology of relationships between the mother-child or male-female lovers than with reproductive consciousness, which Mary O'Brien (1981) has elaborated as historical, materialist and dialectical. Because Irigaray agrees with Lacan that the subject is constituted strictly in and through language, she can only return to the mother and the maternal through language. Now the production of *language* and not *things* is central to the formation of subjectivity.

Irigaray considers the temporal and spatial implications of the mucous differently than Sartre's vision of women as holes and slime, although Irigaray's use of the *in itself* and the *for itself* reveals a partial existential heritage. She contests de Beauvoir's and Sartre's hostile consciousness, but returns to a religious existentialism, via a celebratory, divine, loving consciousness. Irigaray reintroduces the notion of the feminine dialectical divine: "In other words, this mucous in its touch, its properties, would hinder the transcendence of a God foreign to flesh, of a God of stable and immutable truth" and represents "the overthrow or perhaps the fulfilment of dialectics" (1984, pp. 107,108). The mucous is never simply material to be worked on, transformed: it cannot be negated, its traces remain. Love, song, breathing are the mucous, it cannot be reduced to consumption, or "to the production of any child" (1984, p. 108).

It is through a reading of Aristotle's *Physics IV* that Irigaray introduces the matrice, the place and the interval. She considers at length in what ways the woman is a place for the child or the man, and never for herself. Morphologically, how can the man become a reciprocal place for the woman, become the maternal feminine nostalgia of original matrice, a receptacle for that which is given? "For a meeting to be possible between man and woman, it is necessary that each one become a place, both appropriated for and to the other, and towards which he or she would be transported" (1984, p. 46). This is crucial for a *rapprochement*, and an ethics of sexual difference, in her gravitational economy of desire. The archaic relationship with the maternal feminine must be transcended by a love of the same which can hold the same outside of itself and recognize its difference (1984, pp. 97, 98). The Homeric importance of the body as the doorway to self has been forgotten. Instead, a turning inward to the maternal-material-natural has dominated dialogue with God. The love of the same has become teleological, exterior. The creation of symbolic and economic systems of exchange has replaced the natural economy and the rhythms of the cosmic order (1984, p. 99).

Morphologically, woman is two lips, and Irigaray's work proclaims the power of women's sex to speak. But in order to enact this morphology she "must retain the *spatial* and the *fetal*" (1984, p. 18, italics in original) which have historically been appropriated by man as he constructs the maternal feminine in nostalgia for his first space, the womb, "Taking, again and again, the tissue or the texture of spatiality from the feminine" (1984, p. 18). Irigaray emphasizes matter and materiality as the essence of woman's meaning to man but laments the non-reciprocity of it; man incarcerates woman, envelops her in the house as the housewife, while he envelops himself and his objects with her flesh. Irigaray concludes that a new conceptualization of place is required in order to inaugurate a new epoch, and to build an ethic of passions: "It is necessary to modify the relations between form, matter, interval, limit. This has never been posed in a manner that permits a relation between two loving subjects of opposite sexes" (1984, p. 19).

Only the male has been mobile between the enveloping and the enveloped body, for that which arouses desire gives transport to the other. Maternity, Irigaray states, cannot really be considered a transport (1984, p. 19).[15] She does not return to the question of mobility or action or psychic charge and the maternal. Irigaray instantly engages the

---

15. Of course, few find ecstasy in labour, but Judy Chicago's Birth Project reveals its movements and catharsis.

devouring apparition which becomes a danger if there is not a third term, and not only a term in the sense of limitation. Again, this is not a coming to terms with/of someone in her last term. This third term is that which surrounds, and could act as the relation of the enveloping body to its limits, "relation to the divine, to death, to the social, to the cosmic" (1984, p. 19). Otherwise, the enveloping body becomes all powerful, for there is no interval, no between. An entrance and exit to that which surrounds for both sexes is crucial. Stasis without closure, and freedom of liberty would then be possible for both lovers. It is through "a return to Descartes' first passion: *admiration*" (1984, p. 19) that this can be achieved. This is a passion that has been appropriated for Gods and objects of art, but stolen from sexual difference (1984, p. 20). Admiration has no opposite, it is the opening of a still free subjectivity to the unknowable, the different, that which is seen for the first time. It holds open a space which makes separation and alliance possible. According to Irigaray, this look of the first encounter is an interval which can never be closed. There can be no consummation: there is always a difference that remains (1984, p. 20). What has remained has until now been given to God, the neutral, or the child (1984, p. 21). The interval is silenced in a deferred future, separated from the present by a no-man's land, or it is annihilated immediately. This is an interval which never has been, but must be celebrated (1984, p. 21).

What must be discovered is why our sexual difference has been cheated of its empirical and transcendental moment, why it has missed "its ethic, aesthetic, logic, religion...its destiny" (1984, p. 21). Certainly, the separation of soul and body, the sexual and the spiritual, the inside and the outside by a dualist oppositional culture has contributed to this, Irigaray argues. Everything possible intervenes so that these realities do not join, do not marry, and are devalued by a transcendental that has cut off the sensible. The potential of generation must be welcomed within sexual difference and within ethics, as in eastern religions which speak of "the vital, aesthetic, religious fecundity of the sexual act. The two sexes giving to one another the seed of life and eternity, the progress of the generation of one and of the other, between one and another" (1984, p. 21).

Consummation is never accomplished, and the consequence of this, to mention only the most beautiful is: the angel (1984, p. 22). "He" circulates, "destroys the monstrous...announces the new morning, the new birth" (1984, p. 22). The angel is a virgin body of light, a divine gesture. This destiny and work of love is God's destiny for the body. Gesture and not speech is their nature: angels communicate between the envelopes of God and the body, promising another incarnation of the body, messengers of an ethic like art (1984, p. 23). But the question Irigaray poses is: "can the angel and the body find themselves together in the same place?" (1984, p. 23). Traditionally, theologians have responded negatively, while for Irigaray "a sexual or carnal ethics demands that the angel and the body can find themselves together" (1984, p. 23). Then a world can be created where man and woman can meet and sometimes live in the same *place* (1984, p. 23).

Like the binary oppositions in the work of Lévi-Strauss, Irigaray has discovered in the alliance of the masculine and the feminine, the elementary structure of erotic ethics, a spiritual genealogy. Masculine and feminine must, like the mortal and the divine, the earth and the sky, the horizontal and the vertical, be celebrated, but not under the eye of God the Father, who stands guard at the doorways of the infinite and absolute; His vigilance that has brought destruction (1984, pp. 23, 24). Irigaray argues that only sexual difference can delimit this place. Through a rejection of mirrored symmetry, each body, sex and flesh can inhabit this place and a new sexual ethic be created. It is the feminine sex which holds the mystery to this new being and becoming:

A recasting of immanence and transcendence, notably through this *threshold* which is never considered as one: the female sex. Threshold of access to the *mucous*. Beyond classical oppositions of love and hate, of absolute fluid and ice – a threshold always *half open*. Threshold of *lips*, strangers to dichotomized oppositions. Gathered one against the other, but with no suture possible. At least real. And the assimilation of the world by them or through them without reducing them abusively to an apparatus of consumption. They welcome, shape the welcome but do not absorb or reduce or incorporate. A sort of door of voluptuous pleasure? Useless, except as that which designates a *place*: the place itself of uselessness, at least usually. Serving neither conception nor *jouissance* strictly. Mystery of feminine identity? (1984, p. 24, italics in original).

Like the cross, the archetype of Between, the feminine lips, two vertical, two horizontal, permit going beyond limits without risking the abyss. Because of the fertility of the porous, "each finds himself [*sic*] in that which cannot be said but which makes the suppleness of the soil of life, and of language" (1984, p. 25) where a communion subtly crosses the intimacy of the mucous. Where the alliance is not symbolized by a child, but by the life or death that lovers give to one another. Irigaray asks:

And if the divine is there as the mystery of that which animates this copula, the *is* and *to be* in sexual difference, can the force of desire overcome the avatars of genealogical destiny? How would it accommodate that? With what power? Remaining nevertheless incarnated. Between the idealistic fluidity of the unborn body, unfaithful to its birth, and genetic determinism, how can we find the measure of a love that will make us pass from the condition of mortals to immortals? Certain figures of gods become man, of God made man, and the doubly-born, indicate one path of love (1984, p. 25).

As *une grande amoureuse*, Irigaray is part of the mystic tradition criticized by de Beauvoir in *The Second Sex*. The feminine sex is an aporia, a mystery, a miracle which is yet to come. The Father, Son and the Holy Ghost are in the shadows of Irigaray's mystery, as is Dionysus, the doubly-born one. This erotic symbolism of the divine bypasses the procreativity of the body, and sees love as an angelic dialectic. Love points the way to delirium, rapture, the way out of the cage of heredity, the body, and history.

Irigaray's rejection of procreation is again articulated in her essay on Plato's *Symposium*. Here she applauds Diotima's lecture on love to Socrates, and especially the "original" theory of the dialectic. According to Irigaray, Diotima's dialectic has at least four terms: the two poles of the here (the below), love (the intermediary) is the pathway and the conductor, the mediator par excellence, to the there: the above, the divine. "Never completed, always evolving" (1984/1989, p. 33), love as mediation is never absorbed in a synthesis, but it permits a meeting, and a transvaluation of two, which returns to a greater perfection in love. Diotima "presents, uncovers, unveils the existence of a third that is always there and that permits progression: from poverty to wealth, from ignorance to wisdom, from mortality to immortality" (1984/1989, p. 32).

Irigaray makes central Diotima's answer to the question of love's existence: "This action is engendering in beauty, with relations both to body and to soul…. The union of a man and a woman is, in fact, a generation; this is a thing divine; in a living creature that is mortal, it is an element of immortality, this fecundity and generation" (1984/1989, p. 37). According to Irigaray, this pronouncement has never been understood, and even Diotima disappoints Irigaray, as we shall see. But first, in Irigaray's interpretation, love is originally a divine conduit between the mortal and the immortal; it is creation. It assures a living immortality to each love, it is a fertile intermediary, it is the presence of the immortal within the living flesh. "Love is fecund before all procreation" (1984/1989, p. 37), insists Irigaray. Diotima "miscarries" (1984/1989, p. 38) when she makes the end of love the child, when "she seeks a cause of love in the animal world: *procreation*" (1984/1989, p. 38, italics in original French). When love thus loses its demonic and intermediary mediation, a schism is opened between the mortal and the immortal. This she sees as the "founding act of the meta-physical" (1984/1989, p. 38). There will be lovers of the body and of the spirit, and the place of movement of love will be occupied by the child as mediation, and the passage to immortality which lovers bestow on one another is closed. "Love loses its divinity, its mediumlike alchemical qualities between couples of opposites" (1984/1989, p. 38). This methodological error of Diotima has fixed it on the time-space plane, and lost a vital conduit from living beings to the transcendental. The quest for immortality is postponed until after death, when it is in fact the one transmutation that requires our attention in the present. Irigaray rejects both teleologies for love: the child and future immortality, for love is not a means, it has no purpose other than incessant becoming.

In "L'Amour de soi [Self-Love]" (1984), Irigaray argues that love has been annihilated in the One when Two are necessary. In order to discover the two, the maternal and paternal functions must no longer be hierarchized. Love and eroticism should not be separated, there must be many aspects of the feminine, and a feminine divine must exist. This section of *Éthique de la différence sexuelle* presents the tradition of God the Father engendering his son through a virgin mother (1984, p. 70). The maternal feminine mediates the father-son genealogy which occults the mother-daughter relationship. Traditional interpretations of the Gospel underemphasize the feminine social celebration of the evangel, the ties between Mary and Elizabeth, Mary and Anna, and the attention Christ paid to women (1984, p. 71). The centrality of the glory of God in traditional interpretations is disrespectful of the Scriptures and is founded on the masculine nostalgia for the original One (the matrice of the womb) usurped by God the Father. All bridges to the transcendental have been taken away from women, and it is no longer a horizon that corresponds to woman's morphology, of the mucous and the porous.

In "L'amour du même, l'amour de l'Autre [Love of the same, love of the Other]" (1984, pp. 97-111) Irigaray argues that the love of the same stems from the sense of indifferentiation with the first place, the matrice, the womb that nourished, the earth – mother (1984, p. 97). (Men and women must get over the *same* matter? where is Irigaray's sexual difference?) Lacan returned incessantly to Freud's horror before the maxim, *Love thy neighbour as thyself*. Irigaray's same is the fluid, blood and matter of the original, the maternal other. Forgotten, unrecognized, assimilated, indifferentiated, yet it has constituted the living subject. "This priceless same, and the Other in his relationship to the same, is without doubt that which menaces us with the greatest peril today" (Irigaray: 1984, p. 98), *Das Ding* with a (sexual) difference? Irigaray seems to be putting forward a *das Ding* theory of the Original matt(t)er, a female *this Ding* which menaces us all. And yet she claims to take the position that the relationship of the people of man to this Same is menacing us all – women and men. So it is not quite the Same Thing as Lacan is speaking about, this perilous matter. Or *is* it parallel to *das Ding*? Like heaven to hell, these angelic and demonic ethics?

Irigaray refers us to *Speculum of the Other Woman* (1985c) and her critique of Freud's imperative: women must renounce the maternal and enter the law of desire for the father. She was also critical of Hegel's argument that this dimension must be suppressed for the good of the family and the state. In *Éthique* she states that women's fusion with the maternal feminine, and their competition for it, precludes the alliance of different feminine selves. What Irigaray suggests is a new symbolism so that love among women can take place: instead of the collaboration "in their own annihilation, reducing themselves to a same which is not *their* same" (1984, p. 102, italics in original). At present, women are the gateway between the exteriority and interiority of men. In order to be this gateway for themselves, women need a feminine language, for "without a feminine sexed language, they are used for the elaboration of a so-called neutral language where they are forbidden to speak" (1984, p. 105). Irigaray argues that Antigone has been forbidden an ethical act of her own, in the same way that the ethical world of women is paralysed in its becoming. Women have only been the horizontal, the soil and ground for man's vertical erection and transcendence. "Always mediators of the incarnation, the body and the world of men, women had never produced the singularity of their own world" (1984, p. 106). Everything women need to accomplish their own acts is outlawed by the civil order as well as the symbolic order. Antigone is put outside the city, she is forbidden "language, marriage and maternity" (Irigaray: 1984, p. 105). She can only kill herself, all other action is forbidden. "Life, blood, air, water, fire" must be returned to her (1984, p. 106) and the cult of dead individuals and laws, and obedience to a state founded on the suppression of feminine ethical action must end (1984, p. 106). An ethical feminine world must be realized among women, with vertical and horizontal dimensions, between mothers and daughters and between sisters. Vertical B/being has always been denied to feminine becoming, but Irigaray insists it is required for a "female people with its own symbols, laws and gods" (1984, p. 106). Women may make a world from that which has always been latent, potential, hidden: the mucous. An infinite openness to pleasure is a feminine body extending in infinite space-time, insatiably:

There where man painfully lives and experiences as impossible the break of or in *space* (being born, leaving the body of the mother), the woman lives as a suffering or even as an impossibility the break of or in *time* (this is their empirico-transcendental chiasm?). Man is separated from this first space which will be, for him, everything. He lives a sort of exile between the *never again there* and the *not yet* there. Woman can go to the place of spatiality. If she comes to her desire, she must confront the finitude of time, the limit of time. She is assisted in this by her relationship to the cyclical (Irigaray: 1984, p. 67, italics in original).

In order to comprehend the other in a non-egotistical fashion, one must have either the "infinite intuition" (1984, p. 108) of a god or a subject who remains open and unfinished, with an attitude towards the becoming of the other which is neither active nor passive. Otherwise, hate becomes the single dimension of the Infinite. In the Western tradition, "the *Other* often manifests as a *product of the hatred* of the *other*" (1984, p. 109). This hatred of the other is mystified, and the Other, constituted as love of the same, becomes a transcendental guardian of cohesion with power over language, sign and symbol. This transcendental, intangible God of unity is both man's language and the maternal feminine he has swallowed. This God has assimilated the love of the maternal feminine, the love of the other, to the love of a same which has been elevated to complete power. Here, Irigaray elaborates an excellent critique of the replacement of voice in discourse (1984, p. 133); how language becomes nonsense when it is emptied of sense (1984, p. 109). She analyzes the reasons for man's (and clearly Derrida's) fierce attachment to discourse as *teknè* without voice or presence (1984, pp. 108-111).

Irigaray wants to transform the divine into a tangible enchanting, singing presence of the O/other. She calls for the end of a transcendental discourse held by one sex, the end of masculine truth. There will be a new meeting, the rapprochement of the sexes, when men and women will speak for the first time since the garden was lost and their voices were covered with the Law. This motif of the erotic revelation of the divine is repeated in the final chapter of *Éthique de la différence sexuelle*.[16] It is her new, Marian and mystical Song of Songs. She returns to the "amorous matrix" where human flesh can be celebrated by the lovers through the tactile co-creation of the world.

If we were to proceed using Irigaray's linguistic methodology in *Sexes et parentés*, it would be necessary to count word categories. Repetitions of "that first house of the

---

16. This final chapter appears as "The Fecundity of the Caress: A Reading of Levinas, *Totality and Infinity* section IV, B, 'The Phenomology of Eros'" in Richard A. Cohen, ed. *Face to Face with Levinas*. New York: State University of New York Press, 1986, pp. 231-256.

flesh," "birth," "cradle," "due date," "born," "fecundity," "womb," "mucous," "interuterine," "maternal," seem to suggest that she is discussing procreation, but this is not the case. "The evanescence of the caress" heralds a future of mutual fecundity "prior to any procreation" (1986, p. 234). The lovers give each other life in this birth of ethics through touch:

The most subtly necessary guardian of my life being the other's flesh. Approaching and speaking to me with his hands. Bringing me back to life more intimately than any regenerative nourishment, the other's hands, these palms with which he approaches without going through me, give me back the borders of my body and call me back to the remembrance of the most profound intimacy. As he caresses me, he bids me neither to disappear nor to forget but rather, to remember the place where, for me, the most intimate life holds itself in reserve. Searching for what has not yet come into being, for himself, he invites me to become what I have not yet become. To realize a birth still in the future. Plunging me back into the maternal womb and, beyond that, conception, awakening me to another – amorous – birth (1986, pp. 232-233).

Irigaray argues that the female body has been lost somewhere between the mother and the male lover in a territory that admires neither "the one who gave me my body" nor "the one who gives it back to me in his amorous awakening" (1986, p. 233). The caress leads to the mystery of the other through a "moment of ultimate sympathy" and a return to "the deepest level of elemental flux, where birth is not yet sealed up in identity" (1986, p. 234). This fluid consciousness is an opening, a possibility, mystery, infinity and immortality. "Prior to any procreation, the lovers bestow on each other – life. Love fecundates each of them in turn, through the genesis of their immortality. Reborn each for the other, in the assumption and absolution of a definitive conception" (1986, p. 235). Irigaray's mystery is unlike the fatality that is domination, sameness and the obliteration of difference.

The gesture of the caress opens a "future coming, which is not measured by the transcendence of death but by the call to birth of the self and the other" (1986, p. 232). And a son is born. But, "the son does not resolve the enigma of the most irreducible otherness. Of course, he is not engendered without having had his place in the crypt of the loved one's womb. Where the lover falters, and whence he returns without any possible recognition or vision of this terrain" (1986, p. 234-235). The woman after lovemaking is "regenerated by having gone back, with him, beyond the fixed, deadly due date of her birth? Returned to the acceptance of her life by the lover and accompanied on this side of, and beyond, a given day of reckoning" (1986, p. 235). The male lover faces the Thing and rescues woman from the "crypt" of her womb, that Same thing.

Irigaray agrees with Lacan that the unconscious is structured like a language. But which one, she asks, the male or female language? To give women their differently sexed language is her project. It is a difference between an ethics of demonic lack and death; and an ethics of angelic presence and rebirth. Lacan's unconscious, *das Ding*, his lack and language, are of death: "if henceforth there is nothing but lack, the Other falters, and the signifier is that of his death" (Lacan: 1986, p. 227). Irigaray's language is the language of a redeeming, spiritual, heterosexual love, which rescues woman from her body and her time, and delivers man from his space and woman's body. Men and women must help one another in finding a way out of the labyrinth of mat(t)er.

The essence of Irigaray's feminist critique is a rejection of the Same/One which is masculine. But where is this difference that women's two lips would speak (1985d)? What are women's values in Irigaray's work, or what would they be? Are they only alive in the new dawn, the new garden, once the heterosexual caress has inaugurated the new epoch? Cultural representation of a female genealogy is her political project for women's liberation, the heterosexual creation of the world is her ethics. This is very much in contrast to Sarah Lucia Hoagland's (1988) *Lesbian Ethics, Toward New Value*. While working on her reading of Levinas (the subject also of this section of *Éthique de la différence sexuelle*), Irigaray was interviewed by two Dutch activists. She responded to some questions surrounding lesbian sexuality that had come about with the publication of "When Our Lips Speak Together" in *This Sex Which Is Not One* (1977/1985d). In this interview, Irigaray asserts: "What I think is the most important to reveal now is the discovery of the woman as lover, and of the couple as a loving couple. The couple that shapes the world" (1983, p. 199). When asked: "When you refer to a loving couple, do you mean particularly a man and a woman?" she responded: "I think that man and woman is the most mysterious and creative couple. That isn't to say other couples may not also have a lot in them, but man and woman is the most mysterious and creative" (1983, p. 199). Clearly, Irigaray is saying that the heterosexual encounter is most potentially creative of new ethics and values. But this encounter cannot take place until women love themselves and other women (1983, p. 199). Irigaray has certainly spurned Lacan's deadly unconscious at great personal and political cost. Yet she believes in grammar, in these new gods, and in the new man. This is her Bridal chant of lyrical exchange between two sexes and between the human and the divine. It is closet hysteria. She has forgotten the *politics* of sexual difference. Reader, she married him.

But I feel I must pause in my exasperation with Irigaray's perfumed reconciliation, healing the domination of women with that old magic: sorcerer love. Let us compare Cixous' project to transmute the worlds of love and war. Her couples are Achilles and Penthesileia (Queen of the Amazons), and Anthony and Cleopatra: all warriors who fall in love brutally. They betrayed one another – either by devouring the other or inhaling last breaths – until a final ecstatic merger in the selfsame. "Achilles is Penthesileia is Achilles" (Clément and Cixous: 1986, p. 112). This is very far from the tender moments of Irigarayan sexual difference where caress, not injury, transforms. Cixous' "Sorties" in *The Newly Born Woman* does not exit the male fantasy of female power because it is bound to a Lacanian conceit of the fatal, in a Dionysian theatre where all stars must be crossed. Cixous' heroines are truly heroic: they replicate a masculine ideal of tragedy, glory and quest. Irigaray's actions now appear more radical, yet neither she nor Cixous are newly born women, except in as much as they may be doubly-born: Dionysian.

Écriture féminine, launched by Cixous' (1976) manifesto "The Laugh of the Medusa," claims to access another writing/being and is open to men as well as women.[17] I argue that Cixous should take a Women's Studies course, and some anglophone feminists should resolve their colonial mentalities. In Cixous' own work, two men, Kleist and Achilles, are sometimes the Queen of the Amazons. A Cixousian feminine text may have male or female authors. Indeed, it is virtually only male authors who fascinate Cixous in *The Newly Born Woman*: Kleist, Shakespeare, Mallarmé, not de Staël, de Pisan, Stein. Cixous searches for a text to read "the many-lifed being that I am" (1975/1986, p. 98) and finds it in the "elsewheres opened by men who are capable of becoming woman" (1975/1986, p. 98). Bisexuality for Cixous is being a thousand beings: "Bisexuality – that is to say the location within oneself of the presence of both sexes, evident and insistent in different ways according to the individual, the nonexclusion of difference or of a sex, and starting with this 'permission' one gives oneself the multiplication of the effects of desire's inscription on every part of the body and the other body" (1975/1986, p. 85). Cixous' bisexuality is not Irigaray's (1977/1985d) woman-to-women sexuality of "When Our Lips Speak Together." Instead, Cixous' many-sidedness will allow her to take up all positions, to inhabit and to be both inquisitor and sorceress, hysteric and psychoanalyst. What she loves is the *story* of Dora, the outrageous young woman who obsessed Freud throughout his career. Dora was traded to Mr. K. by her father who wanted more freedom to pursue his affair with Mrs. K. Dora resisted and broke off therapy with Freud as well. But Cixous says, "I don't give a damn about Dora; I don't fetishize her. She is the name of a certain force, which makes the little circus not work anymore" (1975/1986, p. 157). Cixous does give a damn however about Dora as Story, as dizzying space in which it is possible to fragment, expand and side "frenetically with the different characters" (1975/1986, p.

---

17. A note on the pedagogy of *l'écriture féminine*. In "Le 'comment-don'," Rosi, a foreign student attends Hélène Cixous' doctoral seminar on *l'écriture féminine* at the university from which Luce Irigaray was expelled. Rosi is taught that detailed readings of Virgil and Ovid elucidate the logic of masculine writing and demonstrate the space for another, feminine voice. This soon leads to the notion that Ovid, Virgil and women's bulletins are part of the same combat. Indeed, the textual practices elaborated from a reading of Virgil and Ovid are then used to examine feminist slogans and to conclude that feminists, whom Cixous denounces for lacking an understanding of the unconscious and psychoanalysis, suffer from "unilinear, anal thinking" and "absolute imbecility". Particularly offensive to her is the feminist slogan, "The ayatollah dumps Iran, Lacan dumps the Unconscious." This slogan, according to Cixous, clearly indicates poetic inadequacy and a lack of polyvalence. The seminar continues as follows: "The French women students are silent. Two or three of the foreign women students, perhaps whose libidinal economy has escaped the 'feminine' discursive schema of the seminar, dare to speak. They say that there are, among the feminists called imbeciles, those who are working on psychoanalysis and women's liberation, and that, really, the one doesn't stir without the other, right? [A reference to Irigaray's work.] The reaction is frankly bad: "If they work on the unconscious, the unconscious will work them too!" Again asked for her reasons for this hatred of feminists, Mme. Cixous explains that she has difficulty explaining to foreigners, such as American feminists, who come out of a cultural context lacking in class struggle and psychoanalysis, the theoretical importance of this division of women into two camps. These students must therefore do some catch-up work because the others cannot wait for them" (Rosi: 1980, p. 10).

148) in a hallucinating, masturbatory mimicry; as text that can be entered by the polyvalent Cixous experimenting her thousand selves:

As Dora, I have been all the characters she played, the ones who killed her, the ones who got shivers when she ran through them, and in the end I got away, having been Freud one day, Mrs. Freud another, also Mr. K..., Mrs. K... – and the wound Dora inflicted on them. In 1900, I was stifled desire, its rage, its turbulent effects (1975/1986, p. 99).

Cixous is bi- even multilingual. Contrary to Andrea Nye's (1989, p. 202) assertion, Cixous' *l'écriture féminine* is decidedly not the practice of Irigaray's *parler entre elles*. Cixous asserts: "It is not because a man [Freud] discovered it that I am going to be afraid it will be a bearded unconscious. Women have not made discoveries...that must be changed. But that which has been discovered is valid for the universe" (Conley: 1984, p. 147). In *Speculum of the Other Woman* (1985c) Irigaray brilliantly demonstrated how that which has been discovered as valid for the universe is bearded.

Psychoanalysts Lacan and Irigaray believe in the primacy of language, but indeed they do not speak the same one. If Lacan's genre is Gothic, Irigaray is a Harlequin writer. Tania Modleski describes the two faces of literate love, gothics and harlequins:

Both deal with women's fears of and confusion about masculine behaviour in a world in which men learn to devalue women. Harlequins enable women to believe that devaluation is only apparent, a mask, as it were, hiding the man's intense and ferocious love for the woman.... In Gothic novels, the woman often suspects her husband or lover of trying to drive her insane or trying to murder her or both. Clearly, even the most disturbed reader would have difficulty attributing this bizarre behaviour on the part of the male to a suppressed though nearly uncontrollable passion for the heroine. Another way of expressing the difference between the two types of narrative is to say that the Harlequin heroine's feelings undergo a transformation from fear into love, whereas for the Gothic heroine, the transformation is from love into fear (1982, p. 60).

Socratic Lacan, the Ladies' man, who desires nothing always, has said our desire and disobedience are rooted in an electricity, a raging passion for the phallus – *pas drôle*. But then, "any woman who does not let herself be raped or attacked placidly by pretending not to be aware of anything, especially the identity of the rapist, can paradoxically be accused of a secret, interior, hidden complicity. That is sufficient to absolve the aggressor. He simply acted as that which reveals the hidden desire of this woman" (Dardigna: 1981, p. 156). We must point to his direction of female desire and reveal that the Word of Father Lacan is a lie: "Thy desire shall be to thy husband, and he shall rule over thee." Love as rape is Lacan's Gothic moment; masculine Eros lives in Erebus, in darkness.

In the final section of *L'éthique de la psychanalyse* on Antigone, Lacan discusses the essential links between ethics and aesthetics. We should note however that this is achieved through Antigone's transition to a Dionysian death. In Sophocles and the seminar of Lacan, the cathartic moment comes at the point of her death: she is *entre-deux-morts*. This cathartic "birth" comes when the heroine finds beauty/desire in/and death. And language, which is the chorus, the witness and the heroic entry of the tragedy into time points to the limit which must be crossed so that desire may be lived. For the law of desire is death. Desire is suspended *entre-deux-morts*. At the critical moment the play's chorus invokes the god Dionysus three times, for Antigone here represents pure desire, pure desire for death. In *Éthique de la différence sexuelle*, Irigaray refers without acknowledgement to Lacan's work on Antigone. Irigaray is discussing the love of self, and the generically different possibilities for its creation. Feminine desire does not speak the same currency as the masculine, does not run the risk of erection. Woman can take pleasure indefinitely with and through touching, and this coming again is not pathological. Irigaray counters Lacan, "As Antigone says: her desire wants everything immediately or to die. Not *and* die. *Or*: die. The everything now of the feminine is not the equivalent of to die" (1984, p. 67, italics in original). Woman can be induced to the economy of desire of God the Father, but not of love for God the Father, for that is not possible without a place of self-love, says Irigaray, and new gods can create such a place. Is that what is lacking?

"'God' is necessary, or at least a love so attentive it is divine" (Irigaray: 1984, p. 25). Do women need Gods and men? Will they give her back her body (Irigaray: 1986, p. 233)? He will not, and indeed, he cannot. Imagine what life and desire are like, with dates who are melancholy and fascinated, who claim to have had a great many illusions and to have lost them all, and say to women, like Mr. Rochester to Antoinette "I'll trust you if you'll trust me. Is that a bargain?" (Rhys: 1985, p, 504). What presides in this masculine desire is the fascination for the omnipotence of God the Father. Irigaray should beware the sacrificial nature of divine love. Now they claim He is dead, but it is themselves they set before us in his place. Which is not the place of our desire. I argue that we must reinterpret Psyche's search, to see that she seeks reconciliation with Aphrodite, not Eros; she desires her own self and creativity. Then the phallus falls away as the signifier of and in our writing, the reference point of our self-realization, that which must be touched for legitimation. Otherwise, the restriction of/to our sexuality is complicit with the diminishment of women's thought and political originality, the constriction of our creativity and male direction of our desire. Psyche, as primordial outcast, anarchist, "nobody's darling" (Alice Walker: 1983, p. 39) must disrupt and disintegrate all repressive, restraining patriarchal categories and forms, uproot and burn the Laws of the Father. She must continue in search of her mother's garden, redefine the relationships of individual and community, self and other, and find Sophia. It is this desire, this sense, which is at (the) stake: *psycho-sophia*.

Now let's be patient/s! some insist. And a number of recent American collections point to the entry of women into the empty space between feminism and psychoanalysis, a place of feminine invisibility where the dominant look remains masculine. What these new texts chart is not their stated "wary absorption of feminism and psychoanalysis with one another" (Feldstein and Roof: 1989, p. 1), but a movement away from sexual politics, past a more acceptable focus on gendered subjects to the creation of a psychoanalytic theory called feminist and the membership of the female psycho-analytic critic in the profession. It is this standardization which is being negotiated in these collections: a very political process.

"The antagonism between feminism and psychoanalysis is well known," according to the collection edited by Marleen Barr and Richard Feldstein (1989, p. 1). And it is the antagonism that is problematized as requiring resolution, intercession, mediation – compromise. The position claimed in the editorial is one of "mediation" because "the disruptive relationship between the two disciplines" (1989, p. 1) poses a problem for the feminist psychoanalytic critic. The book is modelled in admiration and response to Jane Gallop's (1982) *The Daughter's Seduction*: "Gallop, a mediator between French feminism and French psychoanalysis, sets up textual interventions to create 'exchanges' between these opposing discourses" (1989, p. 1). The American umpire; but what has become known as French feminism *is* largely psychoanalytic, so the opposition is already…"mediated".[18] Discontent requiring appeasement: a pluralist equalization of desires, contexts, is to be healed by a textual intervention – discourse. Textual play, textual surgery and operations – but who is the patient? Whose body is being cured, what language must it learn? The pretext of feminist psychoanalytic theory has shifted from using Freud's theory of sexuality to look at gender, to a practice of positions until the right methodology for feminist psychoanalytic theory can be announced, an experiment in relationship, mood, attitude, style, appearance, and packaging. The feminist psychoanalytic profession: What form will it take? How can it succeed the Father? Standing before the closet, not a Thing to wear. Self-situated on the fence between a discourse of "dissatisfied" feminism and patriarchy defined as melancholic discourse, it awaits discursive silence while practicing the organization of consent, and the dispersion of dissent.

Discontented Discourses: where does the misery come from? Who's unhappy with what? Feminist psychoanalytic critics want to be happy with the path they have chosen, content with the course of psychoanalytic theory's history and future. Of course, the original feminist content and method of sexual politics will have to change for this to be realized. This is the education to deference which is part of the professionalization of women (Brodribb: 1988a); woman being a career now open to men. Edited by Marleen Barr and Richard Feldstein, *Discontented Discourses* is organized as follows: "In each of the essays presented here, feminism and psychoanalysis intercede to mediate between a patriarchal discourse (named by each chapter's title) and a feminist discourse (named by each chapter's subtitle)" (Barr and

---

18. In "Woman's liberation: the tenth year," Christine Delphy (Duchen: 1987) documents the anti-feminist theory and practice of the group *Psychanalyse et politique* which copyrighted the name of the women's liberation movement in France. Collette Guillamin (Duchen: 1987)) takes issue with the psychoanalytic writing by Luce Irigaray, Hélène Cixous and Julia Kristeva in "The question of difference." What has been published and translated of French feminist texts is largely psychoanalytic, unlike the work of Delphy and Guillamin.

Feldstein: 1989, p. 1). Such a traditional police version of a "dysfunctional family" or domestic dispute is wilfully ignorant of the history of feminist thought (Spender, p. 1983) and the masculine practice of abuse. This domestic dispute is then to be judged by the "synthesis" of this abuse, feminist psychoanalytic theory or the Athena that claimed to be father born.

Feminism and Psychoanalysis (1989), co-edited by Richard Feldstein and Judith Roof, poses feminism and psychoanalysis as symmetrical Mother/Father discourses. If female psychoanalytic critics do not always question the role of men, is it because they do not deeply question their own role in psychoanalytic theory? To question the role of men would be to question their own professionalization as women, and to suspect their own phallocentric tendencies. The series of "feminism and psychoanalysis" books, begun by Juliet Mitchell's (1975) *Psychoanalysis and Feminism*, consents to psychoanalysis for feminism and argues that with a little manipulation it can satisfy. The appearance is created of psychoanalytic theory as imperfect but modifiable, malleable – the best and only source of knowledge of self and other. Some women workers (critics) are thus co-opted by management (Freudian/Lacanian theory) into providing expertise and energy about how women/feminism can be managed to fit into this workplace.

The "feminism and psychoanalysis" series is speaking to the Father, not to other "sisters" who approach psychoanalytic theory differently.[19] Elizabeth Grosz makes this paternal choice in *Jacques Lacan, a feminist introduction*:

to the question of which feminisms to use to highlight the interaction of feminist and psychoanalytic theory, I intend to focus only on those feminist accounts that maintain some sort of positive, even if critical, relation to Lacanian psychoanalysis. This means that pre- or anti-psychoanalytic feminism will be avoided (1990, p. 23).

Catabute, the thirteenth fairy, is now uninvited to the ball by the King and Sleeping Beauty herself! Instead, this is a daughter-Father orientation, rather than a daughter-mother or sister-sister encounter. What marks the mainstream framings within the "feminism and psychoanalysis" paradigm is an inability to acknowledge context and content. Ironically, they admonish feminism for what, in fact, rude feminism knows and feminist psychoanalytic theory only partially recalls: the politics of "sexual polarity" (Millett: 1971, p. 311). In contrast, their asexual politics is the strategy for successful compliance.

---

19. One exception is: Toril Moi, "Patriarchal thought and the drive for knowledge," (pp. 189-205) in Teresa Brennan, ed., *Between Feminism and Psychoanalysis*. London: Routledge, 1989. Toril Moi does touch very briefly on Nancy Chodorow, the mother-child bond and object relations theory. But as Brennan states, "Chodorow's appropriation of psychoanalysis is not represented in this book" (p. 20, note 5). One would like to say that the Brennan collection is the most thoughtful and the least sexist – certainly the introduction is the most useful. However, it is oriented to Lacanian psychoanalysis and to the notion that a female symbolic is lacking. It rereads Freud and Lacan for a theory of knowledge. Again, the belief that methodology is distinct from ideology is pure science (fiction).

This idealization of feminism as discourse or ideology serves to deny the political context of women vis à vis psychoanalytic practice; it wishes to evade the force of feminism's confrontation with misogynistic theory and practice. Instead of permitting women to disengage, disentangle, escape from the Father, it enforces relation and response, it demands that women pay attention to psychoanalysis. At the same time, it is clear that neither Freud, Lacan, the French nor the American Psychoanalytic Associations, were or are in dialogue with feminism. The male-stream associations are not giving centre stage to rebellious and radical critiques. Posing this context as a dialogue is misleading; the Father is as usual absent but well represented and defended, even here at the margins. It is claimed that feminism is present, or at least represented, but it is in fact distorted, especially that of Friedan, Greer, Millett and de Beauvoir, "plaintiff feminists" responsible for that "early, adversarial characterization of a perceived masculine bias in psychoanalysis" (Feldstein and Roof: 1989, p. 1).

Feldstein and Roof (1989) find that feminism uses the family model to stay in a safe [sic] place, the private realm, because it is afraid of and uncertain about the Lacanian category of the symbolic, and because it wants to avoid appeal to third terms such as law which it suspects of being sexually biased. Therefore, feminism omits or is missing a third term and lacks a concept of the symbolic. Can't think abstractly? Or cannot accept the "tyranny of the abstract" (O'Brien: 1989b, p. 45)? Only very recently, they argue, has feminist criticism addressed "theory, philosophy, history, language and law" (Feldstein and Roof: 1989, p. 3) – apparently not the purview of de Beauvoir, Greer or Millett, also critiqued in the previous collection co-edited by Richard Feldstein.

Richard Feldstein and Judith Roof (1989) reproach feminist critics for using familial and harlequin models to frame the "encounter" (their neutral formulation) with psychoanalysis. Any pointing to the law of the Father over the daughter is "misleading", because it puts the drama in "the sexualized, emotionalized, personalized, privatized, erratic sphere of the home and bedchamber rather than in the structured, impersonal, public realm" (1989, p. 2). Feldstein and Roof reproduce the public/private, family/culture dualism, and have no sense of the development or practices of these forms. In sociology, this is known as the family-as-an-independent-system approach. Profoundly conservative, the functional/dysfunctional family is not related to theory, philosophy, history, language, law! What is central to all of this is that Lacan is reread as a symbol which feminism must use if it wants to be serious-minded. According to Feldstein and Roof, feminist psychoanalytic theory is only now emerging from the haven of the safe, familial metaphor, from the swamp of the non-political, the simple, and the binary. Only now perhaps emerging from the "problematic bond" with the mother? The purported dyadic mother-child arrangement must give way to a third term, the phallus, and this trinity is the pluralism which funds poststructuralism's *appearance* of heterogeneity.

Jane Flax[20] very briefly raises the concern that in fact, "To a large extent even 'post-modern' culture and philosophy are still constituted by bonding of fathers and sons against the return of the repressed 'mother-world'" (1986, p. 343).

Feminist critiques of the family, of sexual politics, were not critiques of culture, of domination? It is precisely this discontented editorial voice which has not understood the feminist critique of the public/private split: the family does not exist independently from culture or language.[21] It is the foundation of patriarchy and its expression. And the barrier between public and private life is the foundation of male supremacy. The "third term" is in fact the male supremacist notion of the necessity of this split; it is also called "second nature" in political theory. Feminist critiques of the Law of the Father do not replicate this binary opposition, they unmask it, they do not use the mask as their third term, their symbolic. In contrast, they make visible the violence of Lévi-Straussian binary rule and theories of kinship. But *Feminism and Psychoanalysis* mistakes Lévi-Strauss for a feminist and feminists for nature.[22]

These gender-and-psychoanalysis books also produce the notion that feminism is a codependent of psychoanalysis. Their use of the addiction to pain model is apolitical family systems theory where codependency is used as an apologetics for child sexual abuse. What their analysis depends on is sexism. For example: "As suitable parables for what is perceived by some feminist psychoanalytic critics to be a problematic and evasive drama of love, hate and incompatibility, metaphors of romantic ambivalence reflect the wary absorption of feminism and psychoanalysis with one another" (Feldstein and Roof: 1989, p. 1). Thus, feminism is in a codependency relationship with psychoanalysis and Feldstein and Roof suggest a three-point recovery plan: emerging from the domestic haven in a heartless world, overcoming binary opposition, and opening to a third term: the Lacanian symbolic. Leaving behind earlier questions of gendered subjects and sexual difference (which themselves replace the sexual politics orientation), feminist psychoanalytic critics can now take up advanced, post-graduate issues (theory, philosophy, history, language, law)! This speaks to the misreading of and low esteem for "purely" feminist endeavours, and is revealed in such slips as "Lou Andreas-Salomé, Nietzsche's mistress and a friend and student of Freud's" (1989, p. 6-7). This is the arrogant new man defining women and feminism against the standard of masculinity: same difference.

For a moment, Judith Roof considers the "unintended" moments of rebellion against masculine psychoanalytic theory by some of the participants at the 1986

---

20. An essay by Isaac D. Balbus attempts to show that the feminist psychoanalytic theories of Jane Flax, Nancy Chodorow and Dorothy Dinnerstein indicate that "the Foucauldian deconstruction of True Discourse betrays assumptions that can only be characterized as a classically male flight from maternal foundations" (1987, p. 110).
21. See also Nancy Chodorow's (1989) critique of Lacanian theory in *Feminism and Psychoanalytic Theory*, "Psychoanalytic Feminism and the Psychoanalytic Psychology of Women."
22. Kinship is a system for men's insertion into culture, as Mary O'Brien (1981) and Geraldine Finn (1989) have argued.

conference held in Normal. She concludes that there is simply no escape from the phallic signifier, "And such is the frustration of feminism in the context of psycho-analysis" (1989, p. 343). As though psychoanalysis were magic and not ideology! Feminism is still the castrated woman here, and the "critics" cannot conceive of a symbolic order that is not patriarchal.

Jane Gallop raises questions about the poststructuralist feminist identification with the masculine: "In 1978, Elaine Showalter saw feminist critics as Annie Hall, women in 'men's ill-fitting hand-me-downs.' In 1983, she saw male feminists as Tootsie, men in women's clothing. But what about the post-structural feminist who is wearing the hand-me-downs of men-in-drag, writing a feminine which has become a male transvestite style.... What is the position of the woman who identifies with men who identify with women?" (Gallop: 1988, p. 100).[23]

According to Roof, then, "When Paul Smith asks why no one has questioned the role of men as presenters at this conference – questions, in effect, the role of men in feminism – it seems in some way the feminist psychoanalytic critics, male and female, are almost all men in feminism who simultaneously resist the contradictions inherent in that role" (1989, p. 348). While I do not wish to interrupt this tentative self-critique, I do want to indicate that even this is a gloss on sexism, a sexist gloss. A woman raising Paul Smith's question in this group would risk being labelled "plaintiff" and "domestic", while Smith is likely to gain (feminist) credibility. Nor are women phallic signifiers just by holding membership: the contradictions are not the same, the sexes are not interchangeable, even in the practice of feminist psychoanalytic theory. Women may act in a phallocratic sexist manner, but they do not symbolize patriarchal power, they do not have the authority. The narcissistic relation to the Father is not identical for both sexes. How to write psychoanalytic critiques without authority: this is her dilemma in the empty space between feminism and (in) psychoanalysis, where the only role for the bearded woman is to criticize hysterics.

---

23. See Modleski (1991, pp. 3-6) for an account of Showalter's recent turn-around.

6

OUT OF OBLIVION

Philosophy, both ideal and material, has not found women's praxis in giving birth interesting; rather, it has sustained a nagging death fetish, a preoccupation with finitude. Death without birth is not only abstract and unrealistic, but signals an odd unwillingness to give meaning to species persistence as the material substructure of temporality. I want to suggest that such an elision is possible only where thought is masculine (O'Brien: 1989b, p. 84).

In masculine philosophy, the question of being has always been related to the structure of language. The notion that symbols are more real than that which they symbolize is Platonic. In Genesis, essences are ideas which God possesses for all eternity, and existence is simply the actualization of these essences which only acquire being through the act of creation, which is an act of speaking: "Let there be light, dark, heaven, earth." This is creation *ex nihilo*: "In the beginning God created the heaven and the earth, and the earth was without form, and void".[1] God – spirit, value, creativity, consciousness – is idealized, not materialized. As Rosemary Radford Ruether (1975, p. 14) points out, "Creation is seen as initiated by a fiat from above, from an immaterial principle beyond visible reality." *Ex nihilo* is viable only if you can imagine a nothing that *is*.

God has his theologians: Jacques the Divine, Reb Derrida.[2] The Word of God is an action which must be received in faith and in self-abnegation. This Word is manifest in the Holy Scriptures, in nature, and in the minds and hearts of the faithful. Being communicated and being received are key aspects of the mystery of Christ. The Son of God is the Light of the World, and his Coming was as the Word out of silence. In John

---

1. Genesis, Chapter 1, verses 1 and 2, King James version of the Bible.
2. In *Writing and Difference* Derrida ends the chapter "Ellipsis" with "Reb Derissa" (1978d, p. 300) after a passage in which imaginary rabbis consider: "God succeeds God and the Book succeeds the Book" (1978d, p. 294).

1, 1-14, *Logos* is the second person of the Trinity, incarnate as Jesus Christ. The prophets of the Old Testament believed God's word, *Logos*, had a virtually independent existence as well as original creative power. "In the beginning was the Word, and the Word was with God, and the Word was God. The same was in the beginning with God. All things were made by him; and without him was not any thing made that was made."[3] God creates *ex nihilo*. The Word creates everything out of nothing. Matter does not make matter. Everything rests upon the absolute and ineffable word. Only words matter.[4] Nothing matters.

God forbid, we are of woman born! say the men. Yet our matter is not of her form; ours must come from elsewhere. Descartes denies the obvious: "I ask: therefore: from what do I derive my existence?" (1953, p. 207). God must have created me and my conception of his existence proves it is so (Descartes: 1953, p. 207). Mind over matter. The anti-matter formulation which is the heart of patriarchal dualism has many styles and appearances, of which the latest is postmodernism. Descartes' preoccupation with the relationship to matter is carried over in *Les Immatériaux* and solved through technoscience, which is "a sort of intelligent prosthesis offered to reality so that it may know itself" (Album, *Les Immatériaux*, 1985, p. 26). The material and the immaterial, the body and the spirit and their splitting is the impossible wet dream of first (religious) philosophy and its secular derivations. The energy of matter's creativity, to what can it be appended? How to elaborate masculine creativity and power in the face of matter's forming potential is the practical and theoretical enterprise of patriarchy. The strategies are various, but repetitive.

The French tradition, which we address here, is essentially Gnostic. Not for nothing, then, did Deleuze point to the Cathars as key to Foucault's ontology. A medieval sect sometimes referred to as Manichaeans, they inhabited southern France from the eleventh to the thirteenth centuries and were at the origins of dualism in Europe. But Gnostic theology has earlier traditions. The Gnosticism of late antiquity had a formative influence on early Christianity. While it has variously Judaic, oriental and Hellenistic versions and origins, it is a more severely dualistic and transmundane religion of salvation than Christianity. Oriental Gnosticism is represented by the Zoroastrian doctrine, that is, the doctrine of Zarathustra. Nietzsche introduces his *Thus Spoke Zarathustra* with extensive praise for the Gnostic cosmogony (1986a, pp. 30-31). However, Nietzsche's personal interpretation and Christian pietism turns the transmigration of souls which is an abomination in Gnostic theology into an eternal return that can be affirmed. The Orphic cults of Dionysus, the other god of the philosophers of desire, were also influenced by Gnostic theology (Rudolph: 1983, p. 286).

---

3. The Gospel according to Saint John, New Testament, Chapter 1, verses 1, 2, 3, King James version of the Bible.
4. For the fantasies of French reproductive technologists who dream of male pregnancy, see the interviews with Jacques Testart and Réné Frydman (Breen: 1984). The mouth cavity is considered to be the most logical cavity for gestation in men!

Gnostic cosmology is anti-mundane and holds that an Evil Creator (Archon or Demiurge) created the world which is an abomination, and entrapped in man particles of the light, the Good One, the utterly Alien God. Evil is incarnation: this mixed state, of the flesh and the divine spark or spirit (indeed, all material existence) is corruption and illusion; the body is the grave, not the temple of the soul. The chaotic slime of matter and darkness is utterly unlike the Good One, who for that reason is absolutely unknowable, ineffable and alien. Only the Messenger of Light, whose call to the soul to know its origins and know itself as nothingness[5] and as a stranger to the world will allow the divine light to gather up the particles of all its luminosity and destroy forever all Matter, all World, all Cosmos, evil and darkness. The purpose of redemption is to liberate the pneumatic spirit through the realization of the transmundane nature of God and the state of illusion and alienation which is life in the world. From the Nag-Hammadi 1945 discoveries of *The Gospel of Truth*, the writings of Coptic-gnosticism: "What liberates is the knowledge of who we were, what we became, where we were, whereinto we have been thrown; whereto we speed, wherefrom we are redeemed; what birth is, and what rebirth."[6]

The Good One has decreed that matter (known as the Hyle) must be destroyed, so that all light and divine particles will be liberated. Thus, Gnostics must "abstain from marriage, the delights of love and the begetting of children, so that the divine Power may not through the succession of generations remain longer in the Hyle" (Jonas: 1967, p. 232). It is not lust but reproduction which makes sexuality a contamination, in contrast to the Christian Church's opposite formulation, whereby reproduction is the only justification for sexuality. Gnostic theology is fundamentally anti-reproduction: "the souls are lost parts of the godhead to be retrieved – in that case reproduction prolongs divine captivity and by further dispersal makes more difficult the work of salvation as one of gathering-in" (Jonas: 1967, p. 145). Again, "the reproductive scheme is an ingenious archontic [evil] device for the indefinite retention of souls in the world" (Jonas: 1967, p. 145).

The study by Hans Jonas, *The Gnostic Religion, The message of the alien God and the beginnings of Christianity* delineates two types of Gnostic revolts against the cosmos and the world: extreme asceticism and extreme libertinism. There is either the withdrawal from the luxuries and pleasures of the senses, or a spiting of the norms of nature, a transgression of balance and natural law which defies nature and mundane norms through excess. Certainly, there is no moral perfectibility possible or desirable in a view which sees the cosmos and its order as constraints on the incorruptible but entrapped spirit's return to Alien Light. Jonas points to the obligation of gnostic

---

5. See especially Hans Jonas (1967, pp. 280-281) for a contrast between Greek and Gnostic precepts to "know thyself" or "flee thyself".
6. Exc. Theod. 78.2 in Jonas (1967, p. 45). See Jonas (1967, pp. 42-47) for a summary of Gnostic thought. Thanks to Larry Hurtado, Department of Religion, University of Manitoba, for discussions on Gnosis and Midrash.

libertinism "to perform every kind of action, with the idea of rendering to nature its own and thereby exhausting its powers" (1967, p. 272). Sin, excess and transgression are the pathways to transcendence and release from worldly immanence. Jonas provides gnostic doctrines of libertinism reported by Irenaeus:

Not otherwise can one be saved than by passing through every action, as also Carpocrates taught.... At every sinful and infamous deed an angel is present, and he who commits it...addresses him by his name and says, "O, thou angel, I use thy work! O thou Power such-and-such, I perform thy deed!" And this is the perfect knowledge, unafraid to stray into such actions whose very names are unmentionable (1967, p. 274).

Ex-tase (standing outside) is an other strategy to escape the body. Perhaps the Dionysian tearing apart of animals and the delirium of the maenads reaches towards such an out of body state: the ecstatic nihilism of religious existentialism?[7] This Gnostic hymn, then, seems to praise deconstruction's hermetic negative theology[8] and knowledge of the unknowable:

O thou beyond all things
    what else can it be meet to call thee?
How can speech praise thee?
    for thou art not expressible by any speech.
How can reason gather thee?
    for thou art not comprehensible by any mind.
Thou that art alone ineffable
    while thou engenderest all that is open to speech.
Thou that alone art unknowable
    while thou engenderest all that is open to thought...
End of all things art thou
    and one and all and none,
Not being one nor all, claiming all names
    how shall I call thee?[9]

What this means is that postmodernism is neither original nor unusual. Gnostic Jean-François Lyotard also aspires to join electric immateriality and be freed from matter by technoscience, the new Messenger of Light: "And since one day we must really emigrate from earth..." (Lyotard and Théofilakis: 1985, p. 14). Francis Bacon

---

7. See Jonas (1967, pp. 284-289) for a description of "Ecstatic Illumination" and gnosis as "knowledge of the unknowable": "It involves an extinction of the natural faculties, filling the vacuum with a surpassingly positive and at the same time in its ineffability negative content. Annihilation and deification of the person are fused in the spiritual ecstasies which purports to experience the immediate presence of the cosmic essence" (1967, p. 284).

8. For an application of *ayin* (nothingness) and *alef* (the ineffable), see Daniel C. Matt (1990), "The Concept of Nothingness in Jewish Mysticism." In Robert K.C. Forman (Ed.), *The Problem of Pure Consciousness, Mysticism and Philosophy*, New York: Oxford University Press.

9. Opening lines of a hymn by Gregorius the Theologian, cited in Jonas (1967, p. 289).

authored *The Masculine Birth of Time*; Lyotard's exhibition of *Les Immatériaux* was *The Masculine Birth of Space*. But the body is heavy, it resists its dispossession, dematerialization and deconstruction, or so Lyotard laments:

...the body is the region of resistance to certain severe postmodern tendencies: it resists at the level of aesthetic perception but also from its habitat, etc. Will there be a cleavage between what is of the body and which is not very modifiable, and the rest. I don't know (Lyotard and Théofilakis: 1985, p. 14).

Lyotard's 1985 Paris exhibition at the Centre Georges Pompidou took place six years after the publication of *La condition postmoderne*. Ihab Hassan describes the "eerie, ingenious" (1987, p. 228) exhibition as a scene of slippage where senses dissolve:

Walking through this (almost) dematerialized electronic environment – a space of invisible codes, artistic concepts, inaudible whispers   the visitor senses himself also disappear into disembodied sensations, states of mind. The semiotic model replaces the model of matter and/or spirit. We are left only with forms of energy and their flux of energy and their flux of transactions, with *les immatériaux* (1987, p. 228).

Figure 1: Egyptian bas-relief – goddess offering the sign of life to King Nectanebo II, last independent Pharaoh of Egypt – presented in a dark area. Sound of breathing, and a long corridor with a mirror at the entrance area.

"Bas-relief, Fragment of Temple wall of Karnak-North." Museum of Grenoble, Egyptian Collection. Photo: Peter Willi. Printed by CCI (Centre de Création Industrielle, Centre Georges Pompidou, Paris).

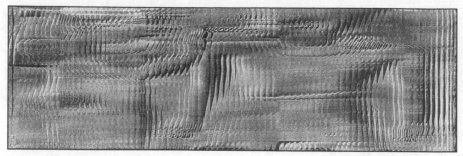

Figure 2: Fragment of the temple wall of Karnak-North. Same bas-relief as in the entrance hall, but projected in a wavy image. The matter-effect is absent. Silence on the tape.

Montage by M. Peltzer after a process developed by Jiri Kölar, Centre de Création Industrielle.

What is in mind is a disruption and displacement of what is perceived to be destiny. The somber entrance hall, filled with the sound of breathing, contains an Egyptian bas-relief, a fragment of temple wall from Karnak which depicts: "Goddess offering the sign of life to Nectanebo II". The exit area, which is silent, no longer breathing, presents the same temple fragment, but in a speeded, wavy image such that "the matter-effect is absent" (Inventory).[10] The organizing concept, according to the presentation dossier, is mât: "For memory, in Sanskrit *mâtram*: matter and measure (from the root *mât*: to make with the hand, measure, construct" (Album, 17). Maat is also the goddess of life, unnamed and unidentified throughout the exhibit. Barbara Walker (1983, p. 618) defines mater: "Aryan root word for both 'Mother' and 'Measurement,' giving rise to such English derivatives as matrix, matter, metric, material, maternal, matron, etc". Isis, the Karnak temple representation, is one form of Maat (1983, p. 562), the Egyptian name for Ma, the "basic mother-syllable of Indo-European languages" (1983, p. 560) for the "material force that bound elements together to create forms at the beginning of the world" (1983, p. 560). And the voice of the mother is really the first sound.[11]

One enters *Les Immatériaux* through Beckett's Theatre of the Non-body, which stages "absence in the world, absence of the world. The body exhausts itself" (Inventory). Five paths are indicated, each one leads to the Labyrinth of Language. "The model of language replaces that of matter": this is the *parti pris* of *Les Immatériaux* (Album, 17). The pathways are: *matériau* (materials); *matrice* (matrix); *matériel* (material); *matière* (matter); *maternité* (maternity). Each path corresponds to its sequence: not-body, not-speech, not-other, not-history, not-me.

---

10. The following citations will be from either the *Inventory* which contains photos of the exhibition site, from the *Album*, which is a written documentation record, or the *Épreuves d'écriture*, which is the third section of the catalogue produced on *Les Immatériaux* held from March 28 to July 15, 1985 at the Centre Georges Pompidou, presented by the Centre de Création Industrielle. Page numbers are not always available for citations.

11. Kahn (1989, p. 29) introduces the notion of a "maialogical perspective" into the theory of the language of birth. Consider also how Derrida reacts so strongly against speech and the presence of the mother that it evokes: the origin(al) presence.

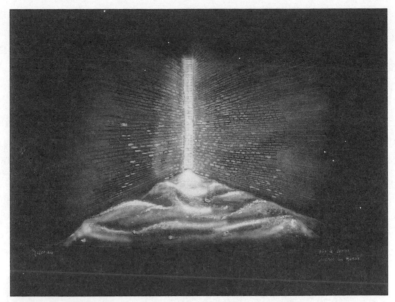

Figure 3: Materials. Not-body. Absence of the World.

Diorama by Jean-Claude Fall and Gérard Didier. Photo Gérard Didier – printed by Centre de Création Industrielle. Artwork designed by Gérard Didier. Fall Diorama.

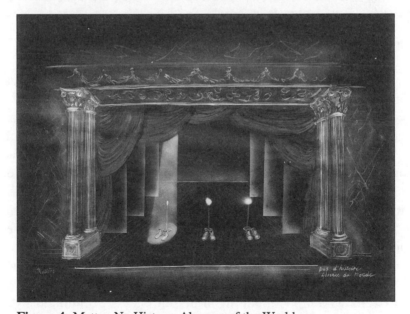

Figure 4: Matter. No History. Absence of the World.

Fall Diorama. Printed by CCI (Centre de Création Industrielle). Artwork designed by Gérard Didier. Photo Gérard Didier. Diorama by Gérard Didier and Jean-Claude Fall.

These two photos appeared in *Les Immatériaux*, at the Georges Pompidou Centre, 1985, Paris, in the section called "Theatre du non-corps" [Theatre of the Non-Body] with the captions indicated here.

In Lyotard's language game, everything is a message. Mother is the jealous origin of all messages. In the section *matériau* Lyotard shows how you (male) can escape (or reverse?) one of her games: "Sex: masculine. Now, it happens that you detest being a man. Biochemistry and surgery can make you the body of a woman. Make this material, this sex of birth, in conformity with your desire. Escape the destiny that was traced for you" (Inventory). *Matériau*, says Lyotard, is that which resists and on which human labor inscribes a message (making a table, for example). Now, the message can do without the material, cease to struggle with it. And all material resistance will be overcome! New materials can be conceived and simulated, according to the nature of the project. No longer forced to struggle with and dominate nature, man will simulate and invent it – thus disrupting his natural destiny. He can give birth to mommy! Under *matière*, Lyotard claims that reality is not independent of the message which signals it to us. The question of things is defined by Lyotard in terms of crimes and conviction: "Nothing exists, not even the worst of crimes, if there is no trace of it. The matter of an object only exists through its traces" (Inventory). Our only relationship to reality is analogy. As for *maternité*, it is:

the source of the message, that which gives the message its existence and gives the author authority. The sender imprints its destination on the message and on the recipient his destiny.... Whether the message is a sentence, a visible image, a building, a child, a richness, a meal, an article of clothing, – we, postmoderns, renounce attributing to it an origin, a first cause. We do not believe that it was predestined to us by a mother and we do not assume paternity. Freedom of the orphans (Inventory).

Or, as the site of reproductive engineering exalts: "The child who comes from no-where" (Inventory).

Lyotard's game of language represents the postmodern universe of dematerialized knowledge. In postmodern genesis, the word of creation is absolute through *teknè*. Its matrix is the indeterminacy of life and death, the exchangeability of subjects, the casual commercialization of human material and its rigid scientific control. None of postmodernism's commentators have recognized how reproductive and genetic engineering is its spermatic economy and "male-stream" culture, its regimes of accumulation and signification. It originates in a masculinist crisis to relegitimate patriarchal power, filiation and articulation. It pretends a brave new world which will find new materials to eternalize patriarchal power in a postmortem culture where life is simply the time which is not yet death: halflives of the immaterial. These are the phallic de-signs which postmodernism disseminates. Stimulated by death, not energized by life, the eternal clone always waits. Never generative of new forms, always dreaming of filiation, and immaterial genealogies.

What emerges from this analysis of nothingness and matter is an account in which an anti-matter consciousness *ex nihilo* assures transcendence. Lévi-Strauss, Sartre and Foucault are preoccupied with the precarious nature of being, an opposition of life and death, and choose annihilation as the foundation of their masculine metaphysics. This is their ontology and epistemology. Sartre's formulation "existence precedes essence," is post-Gnostic then,[12] and perhaps Lévi-Strauss is neo-Aristotelian. What is central, however, is that in each case *things* are known ideally and dualistically, form is prior to superior to matter. This originates in a masculine reproductive experience which denies birth and the maternal body (O'Brien: 1981). Is there, then, a masculinist continuum? Marianne DeKoven (1989) points to the repression of the mother's body at the origins of modernist form, and how its recovery was the project of female modernists, such as H.D. Perhaps postmodernism is the insignia of paranoid semiosis, a self-righteous fear of the mother/world and revenge?[13] Postmodernism, eclectically Platonic and Gnostic but essentially masculinist and contra-mundane, posits a system of matter and form, material and force. The nature of knowledge in this system is the certainty of death. A re-idealized and ungrounded dialectic sees destruction and power's corruption as *Reason in History*: a search for annihilation and loss of mass as natural, as *The Order of Things*.

Foucault and Derrida are heralded as major writers on the body and différance, but the body is male: same difference. The emphasis on the *lived* body protests too much. This alienated theory is a defunct body of work: Lacan's fatal truth, Derrida's mortal truth, Sartre's truth of death, Foucault's nihilistic pleasure. Is death the primordial murder of the father for the mother, she who is the object of desire as Freud first argued? Or is it the knot of desire and law, the fundamental horror of Lacan's *entre-deux-morts*? The thanatic, phallic consciousness of violence and sexuality is the politics of this fixation. But whose death is it? The female body is sometimes the sacrifice, sometimes the great crime which brings art into the world, the body on which men such as de Sade act like gods, or like Nietzsche's Superman. Who is being murdered? In the *nouveaux romans* of Hubert Aquin and Alain Robbe-Grillet, the victim is always feminine, female (Dardigna: 1981). What I want to emphasize here is the false heterogeneity of Derrida, Foucault, Lacan, and Sartre. Their only truth of life is death: *Nascentes morimur, finisque ab origine pendet*.[14] A preoccupation with lack is central to Sartre's thought on need and scarcity. Lacan's image is absence. For Lacan there is no truth except fragmentation, disunity and discord, and there is no will to any other truth save this; the will to certainty is a denial of Castration. There is only a phallic unconscious. Phallocracy is always in place: we can remember and imagine

---

12. The existential anguish of Primal Man who has sunk into nature, who is conscious now but will know death: this is both the *Poimandres* of Hermes Trismegistus (Jonas: 1967, Chapter 7 and "Epilogue: Gnosticism, Existentialism and Nihilism") and *Being and Nothingness* (Sartre: 1978).

13. "Mary, Maia, Miriam, Mut, Madre, Mere, Mother, pray for us... This is Gaia, this is the beginning. This is the end. Under every shrine to Zeus, to Jupiter, to Zeus-pater or Theus-pater or God-the-Father... there is an earlier altar. There is, beneath the carved superstructure of every temple to God-the-father, the dark cave or grotto or inner hall or cellar to Mary, Mere, Mut, mutter, pray for us" (H.D., *The Gift*, typescript, Collection of American Literature, The Beinecke Rare Book and Manuscript Library, Yale University, p. 10. In Kloepfer: 1984, p. 27).

14. Manilius: From the moment of our birth we begin to die, and the end of our life is closely allied to the beginning of it. Each moment of existence is a step towards the grave.

nothing, we can remember and imagine with nothing else, nothing or else. There is only penetration, or lack of penetration. Derrida's search is for the immaterial, secret and unsayable one hundredth name of the Phallus. Rousseau's maxim, "man was born free, but is everywhere in chains" turns into a signifying chain of death for women. With the philosophers of desire, man finally comes to fill his empty void of femininity, in that mastery of matter and sense that is their "erotic". The failure and unworthiness of being resonates in the work of Foucault and Lévi-Strauss. Nietzsche as eter*nul* return asserted the death of God, Lévi-Strauss as high priest arranged for the dissolution of man. Foucault followed up with the death of man, and Derrida's wizardry never comes to mean more than the infinite intercourse of Eros and Thanatos, repetitions of *né, n'est*.[15] The punning of masculine and feminine in meaning is presided over by this male alchemist[16] who has arrogated and fetishized powers of female creation and source. Like Dionysus, who fetishizes by adding female potentiality to a male will power, Nietzsche, Derrida and Lacan disguise themselves as women,[17] to face life (death). To face woman, it is necessary to wear a mask. For woman masks death, woman is a mask, a mask who nevertheless threatens to destroy the disguise. She is what is the matter, the non-/Being who has the power to annihilate masculine logos and b/Being.

Nietzsche and de Sade were major influences on the work of Foucault and Derrida. Lacan also turned to de Sade's *Système du pape Pie VI* in *Juliette*, where Sade elaborates the theory of man's participation in natural creation through crime (1986, p. 248). De Sade is not simply the cover art for *L'éthique de la psychanalyse*. In the key sections of *Juliette* and *The Philosophy of the Bedroom*, the murder of the mother is necessary to male creativity. The section attributed to the fictional Pope Pious VI which Lacan quotes at length and makes central to his theory of ethics and desire appears in the English edition[18] as follows:

No destruction, no fodder for the earth, and consequently man deprived of the possibility to reproduce man. Fatal truth, this, since it contains inescapable proof that the virtues and vices of our social system are nought, and that what we characterize as vices are more beneficial, more necessary than our virtues, since these vices are creative and these virtues merely created; or, if you prefer, these vices are causes, these virtues only effects; proof that a too perfect harmony would have more disadvantages than has disorder; and proof that if war, discord, and crime were suddenly to be banished from the world, the three kingdoms, all checks upon them removed, would so flourish as to unsettle and soon destroy all the other laws of Nature. Celestial bodies would come all to a halt, their influences would be suspended because of the

---

15. *Né* means born, and *n'est* is not.
16. See Burfoot (1989) for a discussion of medieval alchemists and contemporary reproductive engineers.
17. See Janice Raymond (1979) *The Transsexual Empire, The Making of the She-Male*, for a critique of the contemporary medical version, and the analysis of men who become "women". Raymond argues that men seem to want to procreate but actually wish for that which is truly creative: women's Be-ing.
18. Lacan uses the edition of *Juliette* published by Jean-Jacques Pauvert, IV(78). The quote appears on page 248 of *L'éthique de la psychanalyse*.

overly great empire of one of their number; gravitation would be no more, and motion none. It is then the crimes of man which, stemming the rise of the three kingdoms, counteracting their tendency to preponderate, prevent their importance from becoming such as must disrupt all else, and maintains in universal affairs that perfect equilibrium Horace called *rerum concordia discors*. Therefore is crime necessary in the world. But the most useful crimes are without doubt those which most disrupt, such as *refusal to propagate* and *destruction*; all the others are petty mischief, they are less even than that, or rather only those two merit the name of crime: and thus you see these crimes essential to the laws of the kingdoms, and essential to the laws of Nature. An ancient philosopher called war the mother of all things. The existence of murderers is as necessary as that bane; but for them, all would be disturbed in the order of things. *It is therefore absurd to blame or punish them, more ridiculous still to fret over the very natural inclinations which lead us to commit this act in spite of ourselves, for never will too many or enough murders be committed on earth, considering the burning thirst nature has for them. Ah! unhappy mortal! boast not that thou art able to destroy, it is something far beyond thy forces; thou canst alter forms, thou art helpless to annihilate them; of the substance of Nature, not by one grain canst thou lessen its mass how wouldst thou destroy since all that is, is eternal? Thou changest the forms of things, vary those forms thou may, but*[19] this dissolution benefits Nature, since 'tis these disassembled parts she recomposes. Thus does all change effected by man upon organized matter far more serve Nature than it displeases her. What is this I say? Alas! to render her true service would require destructions more thorough, vaster than any it is in our power to operate; 'tis atrocity, 'tis scope she wants in crimes; the more our destroying is of a broad and atrocious kind, the more agreeable it is to her. To serve her better yet, one would have to be able to prevent the regeneration resultant from the corpses we bury. Only of his first life does murder deprive the individual we smite; one would have to be able to wrest away his second, if one were to be more useful to Nature; for 'tis annihilation she seeks, by less she is not fully satisfied, it is not within our power to extend our murders to the point she desires[20] (Sade: 1968, pp. 771-772).

In this section of *L'éthique de la psychanalyse* on "The Death Instinct," Lacan uses Sade's *Juliette* (1797/1968) to rework Freud's theory into a chain which links memory, destruction and history. The last sentence of this passage brings us, according to Lacan, to the heart of the death instinct. Lacan dismisses other interpretations of Freud's death instinct which view it as a return to Nirvana, equilibrium, nothingness, balance. He argues that it is not "a tendency to return to the inanimate...[but]...a will to direct destruction" (1986, p. 251). It is "equally a will to creation from nothing" (1986, p. 251). What is this creativity? Destruction and recreation: Sadeian leisure. Freud's death instinct is of the "same principle" as Sade's system, it is "creative sublimation" Lacan argues (1986, p. 251), a creativity tied to a structural element, the relationship to nature, such that all within this world touched by the chain of signifiers is linked to the *ex nihilo* which orders and pronounces it as such. Lacan introduces this section on the registry of human experience by way of a reference to Marxism. He argues that desire and the function of desire in the human libidinal economy can in no

---

19. The italicized section of this passage was omitted by Lacan.
20. The actual loss of mass in the world was not possible before the development of nuclear technology. Nuclear fission and atomic explosions occur through the loss of mass.

way be related to the Marxist dimension of need. Freud has shown us that need and reason do not illuminate the field of human experience. The function of desire is the problem of this structure. Lacan refers to the "primitive and fundamental" hold on man by the unconscious (1986, p. 247). Language and reason are hidden within the unconscious, unknown and unmastered by the being which is their base. "It is in relation to this already structured field that man must...situate his needs" (1986, p. 247). It is also from this logical field of the unconscious that desire must be articulated. *Jouissance* is the satisfaction of a drive, not a need. Drive is a complex concept, not simply reducible to instinctual energy. It is historical and has a memory. This aspect of the psychic function of drive is also the place where destruction is registered in the mind. Nature's essential subjectivity[21] is the reduction of everything to nothing, such that recreation can be continually recommenced (1986, p. 251).

But do not suppose that Lacan will accord to even a destructive nature a direct or original relationship to meaning or form. The order of nature is destruction, but that is not the origin of the chain of signifiers. "The death instinct is to be situated within the domain of the historical, in as much as it is articulated to a level that is not definable except as a function of the chain of signifiers" (1986, p. 250). Lacan argues that if the death instinct is the scribe which writes the chain of signifiers, it is not because of nature, it is because of its historical dimension in the Freudian sense. The notion of the death instinct and creative sublimation in Freud and Lacan and all that is presented by the chain of signifiers originates in something which is definitely outside the world of nature and beyond that chain. It originates in the *ex nihilo* on which the chain of signifiers and the logos of nature is founded (1986, p. 252). Freud's theory and Sade's idea were necessary, Lacan continues, because they brought Freud to "the edge of a deeply problematic abyss" (1986, p. 252) and revealed the structure of the field which Lacan has called *das Ding*.

I am showing you the necessity of a point of creation *ex nihilo* where what is historical in drive is born. In the beginning was the Word, which is to say, the signifier. Without the signifier at the beginning, it is impossible to speak of drive as historical. And that is enough to introduce the dimension of the *ex nihilo* into the structure of the field of analysis (1986, p. 252).

Lacan has gone beyond Sade's leisurely destruction of matter, and the Baconian[22] mastery of nature to provide a theory of history where there is pure destruction and creation without matter. This is accomplished from Freudian discontent. Lacan restricts the collective to the unconscious in order to normalize individual ill will and turn the conscience into an Oedipal signifier. The irrational absorbs the real and the rational; the masculine psychotic is immune to change, and female suffering will be

---

21. After this play with words on page 248, Lacan ridicules any attribution of a relationship between consciousness and nature on page 252 of *L'éthique de la psychanalyse*.
22. See Francis Bacon, (1603) *The Masculine Birth of Time*, in Benjamin Farrington (1951), *"Temporis Partus Masculus*: An Untranslated Writing of Francis Bacon." *Centaurus*, 1, pp. 193-205.

eternal and absolute. A justification for the claimed unpredictability and uncontrollability of male violence?

Distinct from the Marxist conception of dialectical materialism, Lacan proposes that "production is an original domain, a domain of creation *ex nihilo*, in as much as it introduces into the natural world the organization of the signifier" (1986, p. 253). And thought resides in the spaces between, in the intervals of the signifier (1986, p. 253). Nature and history are separate. Consciousness comes *ex nihilo*. The immateriality of structure is realized. Matter is no longer part of history or thought. Lacan proclaims the eternal return of the *ex nihilo*. Lacan did not forget Plato's lesson and metaphysical logic, that only a lack makes it possible to think of the real world. It is from the death of mat(t)er that they seek to create. It is dead matter that they seek to create. It is the death of ma(t)er that they seek to create. Lacan provides the psychoanalytic authorization for Sade's relationship to matter, creation, procreation. The suppression of gestating women is tied to the previous annihilation of mass:

"What the devil do you plan to do with these articles?"...[Juliette]...inquired of the Grand Duke. "You shall see before very long," he replied. "I am the father of the infants they are ready to whelp, and I sired them solely for the sake of the delicious pleasure I shall have in destroying them. I know of no greater satisfaction than causing a woman I have ingravidated to miscarry, and as my seminal product is uncommonly abundant, I impregnate at least one a day to insure the wherewithal for my daily destructions" (Sade: 1797/1968, p. 618).

Standing on the threshold of the modern period, the Marquis de Sade inaugurated a new dimension in the attack on woman-mother through a forcible separation and self-domination of female sexuality and procreativity. Power is sex, not birth, he claims, and wives and mothers are defiled by anti-mother father's daughters who are insatiable for male sex. The lesson girls would learn in de Sade's "School of Love" – the final chapter to *The Philosophy of the Bedroom* (1795/1965) – is self-domination. In an ideological reversal of man's domination of woman, a daughter rapes, infects and infibulates her mother, following her father's specifications and under the Schoolmaster's gaze. She is taught that to have male sex/approval and appeal, she must negate the maternal body. This Orwellian story, full of political significance, is a misogynistic masculine metanarrative.[23] What de Sade offers women, what the male sexual libertarian movement has offered women, is a violent, dissolute and poisoned masculine sexual and reproductive consciousness. Maternal actions, authority, life and origins are the target of sadistic sexuality. Eugénie de Mistival has been enrolled by her father so that the ethical notions and world view which she learned from her mother and her mother's friends will be annihilated. For it is against the ethics and power of a female community, a body of women, that de Sade writes an eternal massacre of the body, the mother and matter. But this murder of the mother which

---

23. In "'Frenchwomen,' Stop Trying", Irigaray demystifies the pornographic scene and says of de Sade: "For he is assuredly a born legislator" (1985d, p. 198).

comes from a nothingness leaves a vision of nothingness: fertility, renewal and future are lost and there can only be a bleak, sterile present which repeats the same acts. Such nihilism traps itself in sadistic recreation but not enough to want to let feminism or women live.

Andrea Dworkin (1981) shows that Sade has appealed to Camus, Baudelaire, Bataille, Barthes and Nietzsche, and reminds us even of de Beauvoir's (1955) long, apologetic essay. Dworkin indicates that Sade's "outrage at being punished for his assaults on females never abated" (1981, p. 97). Contempt for and debasement of the mother was central to his philosophy. He repeats the trial of Orestes for matricide and Athena's judgment of absolution:

Be unafraid, Eugénie, and adopt these same sentiments; they are natural: uniquely formed of our sires' blood, we owe absolutely nothing to our mothers. What, furthermore, did they do but co-operate in the act which our fathers, on the contrary, solicited? Thus, it was the father who desired our birth, whereas the mother merely consented thereto.[24]

In Greek mythology, it is Clytemnestra's fury about Agammemnon's sacrifice of their daughter, Iphigenia, that leads her to take revenge – now, postmodern Orestes and Electras[25] still side with their father rather than with their mother and murdered sister. Kristeva takes another stab at mother, insisting that matricide is a "vital necessity" (1989, p. 27). She argues that "For man and for woman the loss of the mother is a biological and psychic necessity, the first step on the way to becoming autonomous. Matricide is our vital necessity, the *sine-qua-non* of our individuation, provided that it takes place under optimal circumstances and can be eroticized..." (1989, p. 27-28). Matricide is necessary to the survival of the self: "The lesser or greater violence of matricidal drive, depending on individuals and the milieu's tolerance, entails, when it is hindered, its inversion on the self; the maternal object having been introjected, the depressive or melancholic putting to death of the self is what follows, instead of matricide" (1989, p. 28). Women must slay the mother and rid themselves of the dead maternal "Thing"; repudiate the pre-semiotic swamp of immanence and take the path of Electra and Eugénie. Kristeva argues that "For man and for woman the loss of the mother is a biological and psychic necessity, the first step on the way to becoming

24. Sade, (1966) Justine; *Philosophy in the Bedroom; Eugénie de Franval, and Other Writings*. Translated by Richard Seaver and Austryn Wainhouse. New York: Grove Press, p. 207. Cited in Dworkin (1981, p. 97). This sentiment is repeated thoughout his works by various characters, it is a key maxim.
25. Monique Plaza (1982) describes the function and development of a female self-hatred of the Mother: "The love of a woman for her son, says Freud, is the most beautiful and pure: doesn't she realize through him what is forbidden to her as a woman? To make a 'Different' one from herself, and to live though him, her object ('the same' as herself), the thing which has eluded her – to belong through an interposed person and sex, to the class of oppressors. But also: to reach, in love for her son, the height of self-hatred; to reproduce with her daughters the class of the oppressed" (1982, p. 97). Male dominance requires the mother's self-hatred (and hatred of the mother) otherwise, "no woman could tolerate molding the oppressor" (1982, p. 97).

autonomous. Matricide is our vital necessity, the sine-qua-non of our individuation, provided that it takes place under optimal circumstances and can be eroticized" (Kristeva: 1989, pp. 27-28). Matricide is necessary to the survival of the self: "The lesser or greater violence of matricidal drive, depending on individuals and the milieu's tolerance, entails, when it is hindered, its inversion on the self; the maternal object having been introjected, the depressive or melancholic putting to death of the self is what follows, instead of matricide" (1989, p. 28).

In *The Second Sex*, de Beauvoir attempted a systematic and comprehensive critique of the ideology of male supremacy. However, she accepted the anti-physis male model of transcendence, apologizing that woman was predisposed to immanence and inauthenticity because of her lesser capacity for violence against the natural world, and her enslavement to it. De Beauvoir used de Sade's spirit to argue that woman would find authenticity in crime, in murder (Ascher: 1979, p. 2). This would be the source of genuine transcendence, unlike the immanent and disgusting biological act of birth. Any attempt to find value in matter, in the natural world, contradicts existentialism's first principle: existence precedes essence. Women's weakness is her lack of under-standing of *rerum concordia discors*. To be great is "to regard the universe as one's own, to consider oneself to blame for its faults and to glory in its progress…to regard the entire earth as [one's] territory" (De Beauvoir: 1974, p. 793). Surely a feminism which relies on a fatal theory and delusional domination becomes ideological, for what would it mean to be integrated into our own negation, except the realization of patriarchal fantasy. To pursue an anti-mat(t)er, anti-physis approach is to repeat patriarchal ideology.

De Beauvoir's existential account of the historical domination of Woman and Nature is based on a model of human consciousness which is dualistic and achieves affirmation only in opposition. In her model of human consciousness, "The category of the *Other* is as primordial as consciousness itself" (1974, p. xix). Consciousness is also not necessarily dominating, for there is "in consciousness a fundamental hostility toward every other consciousness; the subject can be posed only in being opposed – he sets himself up as the essential, as opposed to the other, the inessential, the object" (1974, p. xx). Thus, the enslavement of women is a result of the imperialism of human consciousness, seeking always to exercise its sovereignty in objective fashion. Woman lost this intersubjective struggle for domination because "the male will to power and expansion made of woman's incapacity…[giving birth]…a curse" (1974, p. 88). Weakened and disadvantaged by her reproductive function, woman has not been socially creative, has no history, and has created no values. It is man, who risked his life in hunting and warfare, who made choices and developed subjectivity and universal values. It is by risking his life and killing that man realized himself as an existent. As a warrior and a hunter:

he proved dramatically that life is not the supreme value for man, but on the contrary that it should be made to serve ends more important than itself. The worst curse that was laid upon woman was that she should be excluded from these warlike forays. For it is not in giving life but in risking life that man is raised above the animal; that is why superiority has been accorded in humanity not to the sex that brings forth but to that which kills (1974, p. 72).

De Beauvoir believes that women enviously embrace the universal values created from masculine experience and participate vicariously in male violence as an applauding audience. "He it is who opens up the future to which she also reaches out. In truth women have never set up female values in opposition to male values..." (1974, p. 73). She denies the value of female reproductive experience and endorses the premise that links self-realization to violence. A lesser female potential for self-affirmation and authenticity is linked to woman's inferior capacity for and access to violence. Woman's body "escapes her control, it betrays her..." (1974, p. 688). The distinction is between those who give life, and those who give value to life through violence, and clearly the latter are superior in de Beauvoir's existentialist model. Any attempt to combine life and transcendence, to reject the isolated conceit of the male self, contradicts the major tenet of existential philosophy: there is no value in the natural world. De Beauvoir urges women to emulate the existential despair of a dualist, imperialist consciousness and the anti-physis movement of history. It is an act of bad faith[26] when women find "more verity in a garden than a city, in a malady than in an idea, in a birth than in a revolution..." (1974, p. 688). Luce Irigaray's disappointment with reproduction is less absolute: "the maternal has become relegated to procreation and is not the place for a productive matricial function" (1987c, p. 84). In "Is the Subject of Science Sexed?" she argues that production and programming of language and discourse are sexed, and what is lacking is "the fertile ground of a sexed speech, of a sexual creation and not simply procreation" (1987c, p. 87). In *Parler n' est jamais neutre*, the production of language is the motor of history central to the formation of subjectivity. But the original matrix, reproduction, is still outside history and consciousness. Irigaray turns the mirror on the father, takes his looking glass, his monocle/manacle, and makes explicit the deformation of masculine subjectivity. Insisting on her sex, she aspires to the sexualization of culture, a mother/daughter symbolic genealogy to stop the suffocation of women's collective and individual consciousness by the people of man. For Irigaray, the body of the mother as the Other is Origin, and can be reached through language and Lacan, sex and symbol. This is the consciousness and the perspective of the infant, in contrast to O'Brien's mother-centred reproductive consciousness.

Mary O'Brien's (1981) philosophy of birth reclaims this female experience from the existentialist category of unconscious immanence. This historical, materialist[27]

---

26. *Bad faith* is the attempt to escape the existential anguish of self-definition.
27. Barbara Deming sketches another materialist view of the "Great Mother, who is Death Mother and Life Mother, both; who experiences innumerable transformations and who remains eternally the same, able always to engender all things over again. In The Mother, all things exist. The words 'matter' and 'mater' (mother) are of course very close. Something for materialists to muse about I think. Beyond all contradiction, female and male are matter and are also mater, flesh of their mother's flesh – the male as a fetus in the beginning female, too; then becoming a variation of the female. Until this truth is accepted, the so-called materialist is not really a materialist" (1977, pp. 73-74).

and dialectical approach grounds patriarchy and the hegemony of masculine values in the social relations of reproduction. O'Brien's work is original in that she sees male domination as stemming not from the control of women's sexuality, but from male reproductive experience – not sexual politics, but the politics of reproduction.[28] Public/private, mind/body, subject/object: these are the dualisms that spring from the brotherhood's war against and alienation from nature. *The Politics of Reproduction* discusses the potency principle and ideologies of male supremacy, with specific reference to the work of Plato, Hegel, Marx and Freud. Mary O'Brien's reading of *The Second Sex* illuminates the question of masculine and feminine values.

Gestation, for de Beauvoir, is woman eternally in thrall to contingency. Her analysis suggests that the denial of this contention, the assertion by woman of creative pride and satisfaction in the birth of her child, or an understanding of nurture and child-rearing as authentic project, are simply evasions. They are defensive contentions, at best merely sentimental, perhaps rationalization of necessity, at worst an act of bad faith.... The implication of de Beauvoir's model of human development is not only that parturition is non-creative labour, but that the product, the human child, *has no value*, that the value of children must wait to be awarded by the makers of value, men...

It is man, de Beauvoir insists, who turns his productive labour to the creative praxis whose product is value in the normative sense. She does not note that those who create values can also negate values. The low value of reproductive labour is not necessarily immanent in that form of human labour, but may well be assigned to it by those who are excluded from it.... Uncritical acceptance by women of the male deprecation of reproductive process, however garbed by the moth-eaten cloth of venerated Motherhood, becomes itself an instance of bad faith. The low social and philosophical value given to reproduction and to birth is not ontological, not immanent, but socio-historical, and the sturdiest plank in the platform of male supremacy (1981, p. 75, italics in original).G

The centrality of existentialism to de Beauvoir's work is well known. Less well understood is the significance of her reliance on structuralism, and the implications of this for subsequent French feminist philosophy. Lévi-Strauss's theory of kinship and - exogamy was the cornerstone for her section on primitive culture and the origin of the oppression of women. She accepted without question this patriarchal anthropological perspective on the power and position of women in her fatalistic view of the female without history or values (De Beauvoir: 1974, pp. 79-84). It is this oppositional, violent approach to the Other and to matter which figures in the work of de

---

28. There is interesting work to be done through a reading of Spivak and O'Brien on motherhood and the production of value. Both write from a materialist, feminist perspective and take issue with therevisionist socialist-feminism which reduces socio-symbolic and material relations of reproduction to the domestic labour debates (see Spivak: 1987, pp. 247-252, the reflection upon her translation of Mahasweta Devi's "Breast Giver" [in Spivak, 1987]; O'Brien: 1981, pp. 223-244). Spivak argues that it "is necessary to interpret reproduction within a Marxian problematic" (1987, p. 79) and remembers with pleasure O'Brien's "excellent book" (1987, p. 278). Spivak notes that O'Brien's work contrasts with the liberal-feminist object-relations theorizing of mothering.

Beauvoir,[29] Lacan, Lévi-Strauss, Sartre and other post-war French theorists examined. Only Irigaray proposes a different self-other relationship. Caroline Whitbeck (1989, p. 56) suggests that "If a mother saw the emerging person who is her child in the way that Hegel describes, human beings would not exist. The failure of Hegel's scheme to apply to the mother's experience in the primordial mother-child relation is a significant failure." In "A Different Reality: Feminist Ontology," Whitbeck (1989, p. 56) outlines an "understanding of differentiation that does not depend on opposition and a life and death struggle."

Death and matricide, or life and birth. The first is the core of postmodernism's epistemology, the other is the matrix of materialist, radical feminist theory. In postmodernism's Orwellian world, death is life, murder is recreation, love is death. Birth is not creative, has no history, no meaning. Fertility, generation, the creativity of birth, are absorbed and mastered by the emptiness of *das Ding*, which, as Heidegger and Beckett know, never comes. The confusion in masculine creativity is profoundly related to an avowed crisis of patriarchal consciousness. They claim God is dead, but the fatal truth is this consciousness is alive. Postmodernism is simply another crisis in masculine being and knowing, a clash of the Titans. The fortunes of men, Gods, theologies and theories change. Continual crises of certainty and palace revolutions are the nature of patriarchal consciousness. The King is dead, long live the King! Science, the new god, was used by Lévi-Strauss to create a Frankensteinian structure from history. Others see the Being of language as the new divinity. Lacan believes in *das Ding*, Foucault follows the implacable march of the Demiurges. None of it is really very new. In the beginning, God said he made the word flesh. With the modern alchemists, the flesh is made word. And woman remains essential(ist): their speech requires our silence, their aesthetics requires our sacrifice, their writing requires our form.

What should our reaction be to their claim that God is dead? It is not to stand at the foot of the cross singing *Stabat Mater*[30] like Julia Kristeva (1986). What should we respond to these new Gods? Wittig has a solution. She could be discussing Lacan and Lévi-Strauss, and the exchange of words on women. Her escape from Foucault's spiral is Antigone's death.

They say, Vile, vile creature for whom possession is equated with happiness, a sacred cow on the same footing as riches, power, leisure. Has he not indeed written, power and the possession of women, leisure and the enjoyment of women? He writes that you are currency, an item of exchange. He writes, barter, barter, possession and acquisition of women and merchandise.

---

29. As Elaine Marks concludes in her study of de Beauvoir's death-centred writings, a new relationship to death would be a new relationship to others (1973). It is also important to note that de Beauvoir is anxious about her own death, and does not use the annihilation of women to affirm herself, as de Sade does.

30. *Stabat mater*, "the mother was standing at the foot of the cross", opening words of a medieval Latin hymn which describes the suffering of the Virgin Mary at the foot of the cross of Jesus. See Spivak's critique (1987, pp. 134-153; pp. 308-309; 1989, p. 145).

Better for you to see your guts in the sun and utter the death-rattle than to live a life that anyone can appropriate. What belongs to you on this earth? Only death. No power on earth can take that away from you. And – consider explain tell yourself - if happiness consists in the possession of something, then hold fast to this sovereign happiness - to die (1969/1971, p. 126).

This despair and death of women would be the triumph of sadistic, nihilistic patriarchal ideology. Luce Irigaray proposes marriage. She tries to establish an ethical law from the metaphysics of heterosexual sex. In fact, she is de Beauvoir's *grande amoureuse*, mystic and narcissist. She might have remembered de Beauvoir's caveat: "One does not offer an ethics to a God," (1948, p. 10) and certainly not to a boy named Eros. For Irigaray, ethical consciousness is a fragile, mystical thing born of enraptured male and female subjectivities. Irigaray's fundamental location in psychoanalysis retains her in its paradigm. The desire of the word and the words of desire are still the Law, rippling with the echoes of the founding myth of psychoanalysis. Nefertiti, a female worshipper of the sun god of reason and rapture, joins Akhenaton. In Irigaray's future, Psyche takes her place alongside Eros in the hall of the immortal Gods. She offers us the ritual consolation of the *hieros gamos*, the sacred marriage.[31] The taming of the shrew? For Lacan, the Other stands in the place of death. For Irigaray, the Other stands in the palace of Eros. One comes to nothing, for nothing, the other comes to God. Dionysus is also the god of romantic love, and what is masculine seduction but the transgression of boundaries by the Pursuer? Daly (1978, 67) studies the male-centred confusion which aims to draw women into the romance of self-loss: another version of pious Christian self-less-ness?

To succumb to this seductive invitation is to become incorporated into the Mystical Body of Maledom, that is, to become "living" dead women, forever pumping our own blood into the Heavenly Head, giving head to the Holy Host, losing our heads. The demonic power of Dionysian deception hinges on this invitation to incorporation/assimilation, resulting in inability to draw our own lines. To accept this invitation is to become unhinged, dismembered. Refusing is essential to the process of the Self's re-membering, re-fusing (1978, p. 67).

Barbara Christian urges us to write, to remember women's writing, and to remember why we write: "I can speak only for myself. But what I write and how I write is done in order to save my own life. And I mean that literally. For me, literature is a way of knowing that I am not hallucinating, that whatever I feel/know *is*. It is an affirmation that sensuality is intelligence, that sensual language is language that makes sense" (1988, pp. 77-78).

Another solution is the rapture of irrationality. If Apollo[32] is phallogocentric and

---

31. See Carolyn Burke's (1989) discussion of Irigaray's "flings" with the philosophers, a reading of the romantic strategy as positive.

32. Mary Daly draws on research which shows that Apollo's name is derived from The Destroyer. As the King of woman-haters, he killed the dragoness "Delphyne" (from "womb"), usurped her shrine and built a temple where the maxim was engraved, "Keep woman under the rule" (1978, p. 62).

onto-theological, Dionysus is the postmodernist hero. Postmodern feminists believe Dionysus is going to smash patriarchy. However, Dionysus was also a Greek tyrant, (Elder 367 B.C., Younger 345 B.C.) Some feminists have been sold a bill of goods/gods. They become the bacchae. As Mary Daly argues, "Madness is the only ecstasy offered to women by the Dionysian 'Way'" (1978, p. 66). Do they celebrate patriarchal chaos and the death of Apollo because they are more terrified of rational than irrational man? Do they not remember that Dionysus and Apollo shared the same shrine?[33] Postmodernism is patriarchal ideology. The particular cosmogony is Dionysian *and* Apollonian: the disorder of the unconscious, the possession of all women by phallic logos, the symbol and word of God in all things, the word from nothing making all things. Unemotionality and irrationality are one, as their reason and emotion are, in fact, One. Apollo/Dionysus is just another version of what Sheila Ruth has described as a Janus-faced image of masculinity: "on the one hand, the warrior hero, a compilation of classical ideas and warrior qualities; on the other hand, the machismo syndrome, the undercurrent of mischief, composed of a predilection for violence, intemperate and exploitative sex, and recklessness" (1980, p. 49). Dionysian loss of self as liberation is another ruse of masculinist reason.[34] Faceless masks do not change a master narrative, they are the master's normative, when deceit is truth. Femininity as the textual imaginary[35] of male uncertainty is used to seduce women. Dionysus the Possessor seeks to erase women's boundaries and territories. He is an "androgynous" man who pretends to mediate between the feminine world and the world of the Father. The previous *querelle des femmes* which lasted from 1300 to 1600 was a quarrel over the question of whether woman was human. Now, humanism is passé and feminists are accused of both that and logocentricism, but woman is still the anti-human. The male definition of woman and human as without centre is posed as the way out of humanism, master narratives and logocentricism. But women can't keep up like men, can't keep up with their style.

In "The Menace of Dionysus: Sex Roles and Reversals in Euripedes' *Bacchae*," Charles Segal mentions that Dionysus and Pentheus symbolize different masculine approaches to the feminine and the chaotic. However, we can see that both are twice born, and have difficult relationships with their mothers, the sisters Semele and Agave. Pentheus's father, Echion, is a beast from the chthonic earth religions which were suppressed by Classical Greek civilization. Sometimes Pentheus claims an autochthonous birth, as one who has sprung from the earth, at other times he is the son

---

33. See also Mary Daly, (1978, pp. 64-69), "The Illusion of 'Dionysian' Freedom". She points to female annihilation, madness and confusion as the Dionysian Final Solution for women.
34. Mary O'Brien consider the laws negotiating family and polity historically, and notes that the laws of Solon, for example: were "concurrent with religious developments in which the old chthonic and fertility cults had been consciously replaced by the Olympic heavenly patriarchs, and life-process celebrations in which women participated were 'rationalized' in the all-male mathematical mysteries of Orpheus and the intoxicated liturgies of Dionysus" (1981, p. 108).
35. In her study of sadistic novelists, Dardigna concludes: "Women become textual material for the masculine imaginary: thus do we enter contemporary eroticism" (1981, p. 40).

Figure 5:
Kylix painted by Douris.
Interior with maenad.
Courtesy Royal Ontario Museum,
collection of Elie Borowski.

Figure 6:
Kylix painted by Douris.
Exterior side showing Dionysos
with satyr and maenads.
Courtesy Royal Ontari Museum.

Figure 7:
Kylix painted by Douris.
Exterior side showing the death
of Pentheus.
Courtesy Royal Ontario Museum,
collection of Elie Borowski

of his mother, Agave. The identity crises of Dionysus and Pentheus are resolved differently. Dionysus is generally seen as representing fusion, ecstasy, excess and closeness to women, while Pentheus chooses the side of the rational, the martial and symbolizes separation from women. Yet both are misogynist, restrictive and controlling of women. This is something that neither Segal (1984) nor Evans (1988), who tries to reclaim Dionysus as a feminist god, recognize. In any case, male psychological development and identity crises are of interest here only because they reveal much about the patriarchal ideology that is postmodernism. The destruction of the feminine within the masculine psyche, if such is the case, is of less importance than the assault on women. Pentheus has never been put forward as a feminine or feminist god. It is Dionysus's claims of sensual fluidity that we must demystify since it obscures his vampirization of woman.

In Euripides' play, *The Bacchae*, which means "the women possessed by Bacchus (Dionysus)", he causes the Queen, Agave, to forget her son. In her bacchic frenzy, the power of the God makes her destroy the child she does not recognize. After destroying her memory and her child, Dionysus brings her to her senses to reveal these acts to her, delight in her anguish and exile her (take his Nietzschean distance). It is because the Queen and the women of Thebes do not believe Dionysus's story of his birth that he inflicts this upon her. The story she does not believe is that he is born of a male God. The struggle in the play is not between Pentheus and Dionysus, as traditional interpretation holds, but between Agave and Dionysus, between maternal authority and male infantile sexuality. Male eros triumphs over maternal eros. This masculine way of knowing through negation, separation, amnesia confounds female *aletheia* by taking woman out of her body and her mind: this is the politics of patriarchal ecstasy.

Several aspects of the play indicate it is meant to be pedagogical. Dionysus had already been successful in appropriating sacred feminine symbols of procreation. He was also dealing with a mortalized mother, not the goddess Demeter. In fact, the *mort*alization of the mother is key to the myth of Dionysus: both his mother and lover, Ariadne, die in childbirth. According to her Cyprian cult, Ariadne died in childbirth, killed by Artemis at the order of Dionysus. It is the murder of the mother and the death of her sacredness that is the central message of the play. The triumph of Dionysian masculine philosophy is the erasure of women's memory of birth and maternity: the death of the mother and the annihilation of her consciousness. Semele, the name of Dionysus's mother, is a cognate of Selene, the horned aspect of the Moon Goddess and an incarnation of the Great Mother of the Gods, Cybele. Hecate, another aspect of the triadic Moon Goddess, had hair of live snakes and symbolized the natural processes of death for life. Both aspects were usurped and distorted by Greece's new lady Di. Semele was "made into a woman by the Thebans and called the daughter of Kadmos, though her original character as an earth goddess is transparently evident" (Guthrie, 1955, p. 56). Demeter is another earth goddess who figures prominently in the play, and who Dionysus wears for legitimacy, as we must now touch the phallus in our work in order to speak.

The alchemists of postmodernism seek what they perceive as the magic of maternity. They speak of the death of God the father in order to prepare for his resurrection as Father the god. This will be their first miracle of divine creation and mastery over the secrets of generation after dissecting women's bodies (Corea, 1985a). Philosophically and materially, woman is the *prima materia* for this alchemical transmutation of the male word into flesh and female flesh into word. And that which astounds male ideology is woman's centrality to the procreative process. These theorists repudiate totality, even comprehensibility, but they are understandable as male ideology of *ex nihilo*, of fear of woman and of man's *materialization* via the body of woman: the transmutation of the sperm into seed, the entry into the womb/ova to become seed, to become mortal. Postmodernism is the philosophy appropriate to the new reproductive technologies[36] and for the dis-articulation of feminist politics. Derrida's message for women is: *you can't produce original knowledge, I am the origin, you have to imitate me!* Lacan is telling us: *men won't change and there's nothing you can say about it anyway!* Foucault says: *don't bother to resist, à quoi bon?* All of this is an unoriginal revamping of patriarchal power.

The Master's science finds the Master's truths and untruths. As Audre Lorde has said:

For the master's tools will never dismantle the master's house. They may allow us temporarily to beat him at his own game, but they will never enable us to bring about genuine change. And this fact is only threatening to those women who still define the master's house as their only source of support (1981, p. 99, italics in original).

Some recent feminist work has exposed the ideology of male supremacy in respected works of philosophy and literary theory. Hanna Pitkin (1984) and Daphne Patai (1984b) have written two outstanding challenges to traditional interpretations of the intellectual histories of Machiavelli and Orwell. Such feminist work is often not considered respectable, but this is the fate of the incautious and unbiddable. Or it is stigmatized as "biological determinism." O'Brien (1981) points out that Marx and dialectical materialism focus on consumption, the need to eat, Freud and psychoanalysis are based on the sex-act, and death has haunted the existentialists. "The inevitability and necessity of these biological events has quite clearly not exempted them from historical force and theoretical significance" (1981, p. 20). Lacan has not been accused of biological reductionism, yet he himself claims biological foundations for his famous concept of the mirror stage:

I mean to say that if one reads my brief article entitled "The Mirror Stage," the foundation of the capturing through the mirror image, through the image of what is similar, and its character of captivating crystallization, what is called the narcissistic crystallization of man, is founded

---

36. For a discussion of how Jacques Testart, the "father" of reproductive technologies in France, viewed the in vitro fertilization and birth of "his creation", the girl Amandine, see Brodribb (1988b, pp. 33-34). He says he fantasizes being her lover: "Because what immediately comes to mind is a meeting, a meeting when this girl will enter puberty. And I'm a little afraid that she won't recognize the weight of what I did" (Breen: 1984, pp. 102-103).

on a biological fact connected to the biological facts that Bolk has described as a prematuration of birth, like saying, lateness, the keeping of the anatomical-embryonal constitution in the vertebrated being that is man.... *The "mirror" stage is to be intended as a biological meaning* (Caruso: 1969, p. 172, my italics).[37]

Lacan's man is always born too soon, or rather, he is not born until he gazes upon his image in the mirror. "The human animal can be regarded as one that is prematurely born" (1953, p. 15). Lacan's *ex nihilo* chain of signifiers is also essentially "naturalist" and "deterministic":

Before strictly human relations are established, certain relations have already been determined. They are taken from whatever nature may offer as supports, supports that are arranged in themes of opposition. Nature provides – I must use the word – signifiers, and those signifiers organize human relations in a creative way, furnishing them with structures and shaping them (1978, p. 20).[38]

Some feminist work renders homme-age to the classical canons of "male-stream thought" by speciously coaxing the Emperor to lend us his clothes. This approach does not reveal the radical inadequacy and partiality of the Master. Instead, I insist on the vitality of radical feminist writing which is already being marginalized, neutralized and negated[39] even with the participation of those who react to it with academic caution, friendly ridicule or polemical denunciation.[40] Postmodernism appeals to those who can tolerate so-called "non-sexism" better than "feminism". In the current climate of the de-positioning of women and the re-positioning of patriarchy, pluralism, the discourse of the dominant, is repeated now by the dominated as permission to be other than ourselves. Ellen Rooney (1989) has defined pluralism, "overwhelmingly a discourse of dominant groups," (1989, p. 5) as a discursive practice to mystify the exclusion of otherness.[41] Jane Marcus charges feminist pluralism with recuperation

---

37. Translation verified by Department of Italian, University of Toronto.
38. For a critique of the misogyny of Lacanian social theory, see Monique Plaza (1984b, Fall), "Psychoanalysis: Subtleties and Other Obfuscation," *Feminist Issues, 4,* (2), pp. 51-58.
39. Renate Duelli Klein analyses the dialectics of divisiveness, and how "disagreeable" women are silenced for upsetting sensitive men: Renate Duelli Klein, "The 'Men-Problem' in Women's Studies: The expert, the ignoramus and the poor dear," *Women's Studies International Forum,* 6(4), pp. 413-421. See also Dale Spender (1983, p. 148): "The modern counterpart, familiar I am sure to most feminists, takes the form of 'I agree that your argument is sound but you *spoil* it by your presentation – i.e. too emotional, irrational, man-hating, humourless.' It is an excuse for not dealing with the ideas." Dale Spender, *Women of Ideas and What Men Have Done to Them, From Aphra Behn to Adrienne Rich,* London: Ark Paperbacks.
40. Althusserian Chris Weedon (1987) and Joan Cocks's (1989) cautious post-feminism typify this reaction to radical feminism. Chris Weedon makes male ideology accessible to women in terms of giving it access to women.
41. *Seductive Reasoning* (1989) is an excellent analysis of the ideological effects of pluralist discourse which have been inscribed in alternative (Marxist, feminist, minority) discourses. Concerned with its recuperative strategies, Ellen Rooney discusses (1989, p. 236+) feminism and pluralism, represented by Kolodny (1980) and critiques of pluralism, made by Marcus (1982) and Spivak (1987, 1989).

and recolonization:

Kolodny's liberal relaxation of the tensions among us and the tensions between feminists and the academy reflects a similar relaxation on the part of historians and political activists. What this does is to isolate Marxist feminists and lesbians on the barricades while "good girl" feminists fold their tents and slip quietly into the establishment. There is a battlefield (race, class, and sexual identity) within each one of us, another battlefield where we wage these wars with our own feminist colleagues (as in *Signs*), and a third battlefield where we defend ourselves from male onslaughts both on our work and on the laws that govern our lives as women in society. It is far too early to tear down the barricades. Dancing shoes will not do. We still need our heavy boots and mine detectors (1982, p. 623).

Postmodernist theories of sexuality increasingly speak of texts without contexts, genders without sexes, and sex without politics. These theories of gender and "sexuali*ties*" (Derrida: 1978a, p. 129) construct psychoanalysed bodies without sexes. Yet power is based on sex, not gender. Without reference to sexual politics, theories of sexuality are ideological and metaphysical. What we need to freely express ourselves sexually is a realization of community among women.

Calling for a reconsideration of the "sex/gender" distinction, Denise Thompson points out how "gender" depoliticizes feminist insights about male supremacy: "The feminist concern is not with whether the sexes are 'the same' or 'different', because such a concern says nothing about male supremacy" (1989, p. 30). In fact, "the 'sex/gender' distinction is a restatement of the old 'nature/nurture', 'body/mind' dichotomy. It separates 'biology' out from 'society', and relegates it to an outer realm where it still lurks, unmediated, unsubdued, and presumably, unknown" (1989, pp. 24-25).[42] Social construction refers to how gender is shaped and reproduced culturally, how one is made and not born a woman. Usually this perspective argues that masculinity and femininity are a relational set, symmetrical, part of a system of binary oppositions – sort of a disembodied codependency.[43] The emphasis on social "gender" to the exclusion of biological difference is part of the defensiveness and coyness that Bev Thiele describes when she says (1989, p. 7): "For years we skirted around biological difference so as to avoid biological determinism." Much recent theorizing on the body and gender refuses the female body, and this is sexism not liberation. But the suspicion that the female body is too different to be equal makes social constructivism an analysis of cultural forms where only forms matter: it is functionalist and pluralist in bias, a liberal laissez-faire gender economy. Cultural exchanges are stressed over biological processes, it's culture over nature once again. The masculinist and dualist

---

42. See Gatens (1989) who traces the "gender" versus "sex" distinction to the male scientist, Robert Stoller; also Lloyd (1989) Edwards (1989) and Thiele (1989).
43. For a feminist critique of codependency theory, see Laura Brown (1990) who argues "this model is one that oppresses women under the guise of helping them, that pathologizes the political, that moves women into therapy rather than mass action" (1990, p. 4). Instead, she suggests we "need to challenge the concept of the 'dysfunctional family', raised so often in the process addictions literature, and remind ourselves and our colleagues that under patriarchy, no family functions well" (1990, p. 4).

notion of the separation and primacy of mind over body, nature over culture continues to ignore that these are processes. Nature and nurture not only interact but shape themselves continually in the interaction. Marilyn Frye makes this point: "Enculturation and socialization are, I think, misunderstood if one pictures them as processes which apply layers of cultural gloss over a biological substratum" (1983, p. 35). She points to the absurdity of separating nature and nurture: "We are animals. Learning is physical, bodily. There is not a separate, nonmaterial 'control room' where socialization, enculturation, and habit formation take place and where, since it is nonmaterial, change is independent of bodies and easier than in bodies. Socialization molds our bodies; enculturation forms our skeletons, our musculature, our central nervous system" (1983, p. 37). Sexuality and procreativity are, as Mary O'Brien (1981) has demonstrated, historical, dialectical, and materialist processes. The notion that only forms matter is the substanceless aesthetics and politics of discarnate desires.

Mary Poovey's vision is the "brave new world of the reconceptualized subject" (1988, p. 60) which she sees as afforded by deconstruction. Her masculine-biased reduction of the extraordinary work of Luce Irigaray to biological determinism and the representation of even the assiduously "bisexual" Cixous in these terms is a traditional trivialization of women's writing. Poovey then "redeems" Irigaray and Cixous by turning them into handmaidens of Derrida, he who is the excellent, impotent Deconstructor who turns and turns in his immortal, non-reproductive coils. But Deconstructor of what? Why, of the female body, the skins to which Irigaray and Cixous so primitively cling. A methodology, indeed a technology which claims to lift identity right off the skin, the body, that disruptive, contingent, uncontrollable matter whose due date is death. Mind will no longer need to make reference to body in its identity claims; unchained at last from the sensations and limitations of the flesh. Poovey is trapped in a notion that women need to be liberated from their biology. She argues that binary categories are based on anatomical categories and therefore anatomy must be abolished, deconstructed/dissected in order to achieve the "social liberation of the concept from its natural 'referent'" (1988, p. 59). It is deconstruction and the new reproductive technologies[44] which will reorganize the individual (1988, p. 60). Purged of the female procreative body by an operation of reversal (the scientist becomes genetrix), displacement (through extrauterine pregnancy) and indetermination (the manipulation and exchangeability of genetic material); freed from

---

44. In contrast, see the journal *Issues in Reproductive and Genetic Engineering Journal of International Feminist Analysis*; and the work by Rita Arditti, Gena Corea, Jalna Hanmer, Renate Klein, Janice Raymond and others active in the Feminist International Network for Resistance to Reproductive and Genetic Engineering. Their work is available in the following sources: Arditti et al., eds. (1984), Corea (1985a), Corea et al. (1985b), Hawthorne and Klein, eds., (1991), *Angels of Power and other reproductive creations*, Melbourne, Spinifex Press; Renate Klein et al., (1991) *RU 486: Misconceptions, Myths and Morals*, Melbourne, Spinifex Press.

45. In the *Épreuves d'écriture* assembled by the exhibition, *Les Immatériaux,* Derridean Philippe Lacoue-Labarthe calls maternity "the condition for the possibility of death" (1985, p. 128). Derrida simply
cont. next page

the fixed identity of our bodies,[45] "we" can float like transcendental signifiers in space ships, extraterrestrial self-made *men* at last. The fault lay in our genes! Our birth which fixed our being had ended our becoming.

The epistemological break is the recognition of the significance of reproduction, of women, and our disruption of reified patriarchal discourse with a liberatory political practice. Women can only smash a Heloise-like relationship to knowledge and philosophy, by a clear and equivocal break with the Master. Kiss Abelard goodbye. Refuse the education of our sense and senses by and to the phallus and redirect female desire away from paranoid masculine somatophobia. Beware now the hand around our wrists as we open the door, the tears and threats, the anger and accusations; the fierce, insidious, ritual humiliation, and the violence of romantic colonization working to subvert, deny and corrupt all heretical and sensual chastity, all desire for diverse, integral, collective female presence. The men in the Master's House say, "Where do you think you are going? Why are you always doing this to me?" Then, "How dare you! Manhater! What you really need is a man!" Thus are we confronted with the most formidable of opponents: Prince Charming.

The stories of Hipparchia and Crates, Elisabeth and Descartes, or Heloise and Abelard[46] are narratives of patriarchal hegemony in love and wisdom. Michèle Le Doeuff explains how women's tenuous position in the halls and tomes of learning

---

45. *cont. from previous page*

defines it as "Place of the saintly, infinite perversity. Takes its sublime onmipotence from being opposed to nothing" (1985, p. 128). Christine Buci-Glucksmann provides the Kristeva/Athena type of denunciation in her definition of maternity: "Chasm, chaos, abyss, devouring sex or paradise lost: maternity is the fantasmic origin where the sexual and the biological coincide, where the female desire is destined, to be reconquered. 'To give birth to' institutes a dual and archaic relationship, a dangerous and desired proximity, which mother and children must renounce in order to exist" (1985, p. 128). Parisian feminists Luce Irigaray, Anne-Marie de Vilaine and Suzanne Blaise were not numbered among the luminaries invited to pronounce on maternity for the exhibit.

46. The story of Abelard, the twelfth century philosopher, and his young student, Heloise, is celebrated as one of the greatest romances. Here is how Abelard understood her learning and his love, from the section "How Abelard's Love for Heloise brought about a Fall which afflicted both Body and Soul": "At at time when I considered that I was the one philosopher in the world and had nothing to fear from others, I, who up to that time had lived most chastely, began to relax the reins on my passion... there lived in Paris a maiden named Heloise, the niece of a canon named Fulbert, who from his deep love for her was eager to have her advanced in all literary pursuits possible... I considered all the qualities which usually inspire lovers and decided she was just the one for me to join in love. I felt that this would be very easy to accomplish; I then enjoyed such renown and was so outstanding for my charm of youth that I feared no repulse by any woman whom I should deign to favour with my love. And I felt that this maiden would all the more readily yield to me as I knew she possessed and cherished a knowledge of letters... [Fulbert]... put his niece entirely under my control... telling me to use pressure if I found her remiss. I was astonished at his simplicity in this matter and would have been no more astounded if he had been giving over a tender lamb to a ravenous wolf. For when he handed her over to me not only to teach but to discipline, what else was he doing but giving free reign to my designs, and opportunity, even if I were not seeking it, easily to subdue her by threats and stripes if blandishments did not work?... And the better to prevent suspicion, I sometimes struck her not through anger or vexation but from love and affection which were beyond the sweetness of every ointment" (1964, pp. 25-28). Thanks to Patricia Mills for this reference.

contributes to a "confusion of amorous and didactic relationships" (1989, p. 104), reducing the scope of our desire to know:

[T]his erotico-theoretical transference…is equivalent to an absence of any direct relationship of women to philosophy. Only through the mediation of a man could women gain access to theoretical discourse. Here we find a predicament common to the feminine condition: that of not being able to do without a protector and mediator in any part of life defined as social (1989, p. 104).

The anxiety women experience in individual relationships is duplicated in the Master's House of Theory and Philosophy. Highly eroticized didactic relationships are embedded in a system which diminishes female originality and punishes female presence and resistance. Progressive texts and teachers promise nurture but betray innocence. The cognitive confusion that Heloise experiences is the splitting of the self into two Mrs. Rochesters: the loving Jane Eyre, and the raging madwoman in the attic.[47] Rousseau's *Emile* may be read as either a Harlequin or a Gothic narrative, depending on one's belief in the good faith of the phallus.

The feminist project must yet elaborate an ethics and aesthetics that is not filtered through or returned to a masculine paradigm, but expressed creatively and symbolically by a subject that is female. Only an unflinching autonomy can challenge extortions to feminine deference and the deferment of feminist philosophy. Women's memory is annulled in the patriarchal tradition. We must resist absorption by the androgynous myth, which, as Mircea Eliade indicates, was part of the Mephistophelian tradition (Irigaray: 1987b, p. 423). Androgyny: the eternally recurrent Same. "The same was in the beginning with God." The postmodern male author is dying, imploding as subject, while women are claiming a voice, giving birth to a feminist movement and vision and remembering against dismemberment.

Our knowledge is untranslatable and inaudible in mixed forums of masculine hegemony. Yet *les hommes roses* abstract and parade a feminist language and theory made textureless, without body, without speaking, female bodies. We serve as the raw matter for an unaltered analysis which has none of our values, we do not control this speech, insidious, neutralized, dishonest recognition of the female, spoken in a sexist practice. Yet it is we who are accused of purism and intransigence when we refuse absorption/invisibility of women's experience. We reject Foucault's power, Sartre's nothingness, Lévi-Strauss's end to the world, Lacan's fatal desire, Derrida's wizardry, Sade's creation through murder, Nietzsche's eternal return of the masculine o/One. We refuse all these transvestites of travesty. It is now more than ever necessary to continue the tradition initiated by Mary Wollstonecraft, that of the woman "who will not try and gain a hearing by being agreeable to men" (Spender: 1983, p. 158). An extorted acknowledgement, and frantic search in the masculine classics for their importance to women condemns us to an unseemly subservience. It is only a feminist coming of rage

---

47. See the novel by Jean Rhys, (1985) *Wide Sargasso Sea*, first published in 1966.

which will liberate us from the containment of the patriarchal standpoint, not the careful and dutiful tinkering with masculine constructed and male-referent categories. We must halt the deferential deformation of our experience that Pygmalion's Galatea, and Pygmalion as Galatea, have undertaken. We must open the door and leave the Masters' House of theories of subjectivity and consciousness, ideology and power, ethics and desire.

It is extraordinary and completely bizarre that we are accused of alterity, binarity when we refuse to return to what this all means for men strategically, for what they can say, what they can do. What is necessary now is feminist thinking that does not take on the masculine construction of a question, and begins a more complex way of conceptualizing, says goodbye to all that, in a disruption of the framework posed by a masculinist methodology concerned with and concealing its subjectivity, reducing the breath and breadth of female impulse and desire. We need women's work that rejects integration into the Manichaean world view, sees the incongruity of seeking in masculine paradigms a process that is without our content, or a content that is without our process, refuses the silencing of women by the masculinization of the feminist project, and the feminization of patriarchy by Dionysus and postmodernism. Only our autonomy can fundamentally avoid a thanatical and patriarchal consciousness and practice. We must remember what matters. A feminist sensibility proceeds from a different understanding of psyche, consciousness and value than sexist non-sense. An understanding of the integrity of being and knowing, sense and sensuality, recognizes that the mind cannot exist without the body, and our bodies cannot live without our minds. Being comes from being, bodies come from other bodies – women's bodies – and not from the void or the Master's word. To make sense, we have to make knowledge with our experience, and if, yes, forms matter, it is also true and significant for our worldly desires, that matter forms.

References

Abelard, Pierre. (1964). *The Story of Abelard's Adversities*. (Translated by J.T. Muckle.) Toronto: The Pontifical Institute of Medieval Studies.

Alcoff, Linda. (1988, Spring). Cultural Feminism Versus Post-Structuralism: The Identity Crisis in Feminist Theory. *Signs: Journal of Women in Culture and Society, 13* (3), 405-437.

Alexander, George. (1976). The Group TEL QUEL. *Working Papers in Sex, Science and Culture, 1* (2), 3-11.

Allen, Christine Garside. (1979). Nietzsche's Ambivalence about Women. In Lorenne M.G. Clark and Lynda Lange (Eds.) *The Sexism of Social and Political Theory, Women and Reproduction from Plato to Nietzsche*. Toronto: University of Toronto Press.

Allen, Jeffner and Iris Marion Young. (Eds.) (1989). *The Thinking Muse, Feminism and Modern French Philosophy*. Bloomington: Indiana University Press.

Allen, Sister Prudence. (1985). *The Concept of Woman, the Aristotelian revolution 750 BC - AD 1250*. Montreal: Eden Press.

Allen, Sally G. and Hubbs, Joanna. (1987). Outrunning Atalanta: Feminine Destiny in Alchemical Transmutation. In Sandra Harding and Jean F. O'Barr (Eds.) *Sex and Scientific Inquiry*. Chicago: The University of Chicago Press.

Allison, David B., Prado de Oliveira, Mark S. Roberts and Allen S. Weiss. (Eds.) (1988). *Psychosis and Sexual Identity: Toward a Post-Analytic View of the Schreber Case*. Albany, NY: State University of New York Press.

Althusser, Louis. (1984). *Essays on Ideology*. London: Verso Editions.

Arac, Jonathan. (Ed.) (1986). *Postmodernism and Politics*. Minneapolis: University of Minnesota Press.

Arditti, Rita, Renate Duelli Klein and Shelley Minden. (Eds.) (1984). *Test-Tube Women: What Future for Motherhood?* London: Pandora Press.

Ascher, Carol. (1979). On Encountering the I and the We in Simone de Beauvoir's Memoirs. In *The Second Sex - Thirty Years Later*. New York: New York Institute for the Humanities. (A Commemorative Conference on Feminist Theory, Sept. 27-29, 1979.)

Balbus, Isaac D. (1987). Disciplining Women, Michel Foucault and the Power of Feminist Discourse. In Seyla Benhabib and Drucilla Cornell (Eds.) *Feminism as Critique*. Minneapolis: University of Minnesota.

Bannet, Eve Tavor. (1989). *Structuralism and the Logic of Dissent, Barthes, Derrida, Foucault, Lacan*. Urbana: University of Illinois Press.

Barr, Marleen S. and Richard Feldstein. (Eds.) (1989). *Discontented Discourses, Feminism/ Textual Intervention/Psychoanalysis*. Urbana: University of Illinois Press.

Barry, Kathleen. (1989). Tootsie Syndrome, or "We have met the enemy and they are us". *Women's Studies International Forum, 12* (5), 487-493.

Barry, Kathleen. (1990, Winter). The New Historical Synthesis: Women's Biography. *Journal of Women's History, 1* (3), 74-105.

Barry, Kathleen. (Jan/Feb, 1991). Deconstructing Deconstructionism (or, Whatever Happened to Feminist Studies?). *Ms. 1* (4), 83-85.

Bartkowski, Frances. (1980). Feminism and Deconstruction: "a union forever deferred". *enclitic, 4* (2), 70-77.

Bartkowski, Frances. (1987). Speculations on the Flesh: Foucault and the French Feminists. In Judith Genova (Ed.) *Power, Gender, Values*. Edmonton, Alberta: Academic Printing and Publishing.

Battersby, Christine. (1989). Post-modernism and the Female Author. In *Gender and Genius, Towards a Feminist Aesthetics*. Bloomington: Indiana University Press.

Bauberg, Fay. (1988). *A Critique of Jungian Archetypal Theory in the Light of the Sumerian Goddess Inanna*. Unpublished Master's Thesis, York University.

Baudrillard, Jean. (1986). *Amérique*. [America] Éditions Grasset et Fasquelle.

Baudrillard, Jean. (1987). *Forget Foucault*. Foreign Agents Series. New York: Semiotext(e). (Originally published in 1977, *Oublier Foucault*.)

Beckett, Samuel. (1954). *Waiting for Godot*. New York: Grove Press.

Bellour, Raymond. (1971). Entretien avec Michel Foucault. [Interview with Michel Foucault] In *Le Livre des Autres*. Paris: Éditions de l'Herme.

Benjamin, Andrew. (Ed.) (1988). *Post-Structuralist Classics*. Warwick Studies in Philosophy and Literature. New York: Routledge.

Bennington, Geoff. (1989). Introduction: The Question of Postmodernism. In Lisa Appignanesi (Ed.) *Postmodernism, ICA Documents*. London: Free Association Books.

Benstock, Shari. (Ed.) (1987). *Feminist Issues in Literary Scholarship*. Bloomington: Indiana University Press.

Bernstein, Charles. (1987, November/December). Centering the Postmodern, In the Middle of Modernism in the Middle of Capitalism on the Outskirts of New York... *Socialist Review, 17* (6), 45-56.

Blaise, Suzanne. (1988). *Le Rapt des origines ou le meurtre de la mère, De la communication entre femmes*. [The Theft of Origins or the Murder of the Mother. On Communication Between Women.] Paris, self-published.

Bonnefoy, Claude. (1966, juin 15-20). L'homme est-il mort? Un entretien avec Michel Foucault. [Is Man Dead? An Interview with Michel Foucault.] *Arts-Loisirs*, (38), 8-9.

Boyne, Roy. (1986). The Domain of the Third: French Social Theory into the 1980s. *Theory, Culture and Society, 3* (3), 7-24.

Bradbury, Malcolm. (1991, February 24). "The Scholar Who Misread History". (Review of *Signs of the Times, Deconstruction and the Fall of Paul de Man*, by David Lehman, New York, Poseidon Press, 1991.) *The New York Times Book Review*, p. 9.

Braidotti, Rosi. (1991). *Patterns of Dissonance*. New York: Routledge.

Breen, Jonathan. (1982, Mai). Interview: The Dark Side of the Moon. (Interview with Jacques Testart and René Frydman.) *Types, Paroles d' hommes, 4*, 89-108.

Brennan, Teresa. (Ed.) (1989). *Between Feminism and Psychoanalysis*. London: Routledge.

Brodribb, Somer. (1988a). Winonah's: In the Spirit of the Place. In Sue Findlay and Melanie Randall (Eds.) *Feminist Perspectives on the Canadian State*, Special Issue of *Resources for Feminist Research/Documentation sur la recherche féministe, 17* (3), 49-55.

Brodribb, Somer. (1988b). *Women and Reproductive Technologies*. Draft research document prepared for The Status of Women in Canada. Available free of charge from: The Status of Women Canada, Ste. 1005, 151 Sparks Street, Ottawa, Ontario, Canada, K1A 1C3.

Brodribb, Somer. (1989a). Delivering Babies: Contracts and Contradictions. In Christine Overall (Ed.) *The Future of Human Reproduction*. Toronto: The Women's Press.

Brodribb, Somer. (1989b). A Politics of Resistance. In Yolande Cohen (Ed.) *Women and Counter-Power*. Montreal: Black Rose. (Originally published as Une politique anti-patriarcale, In *Femmes et Contre-Pouvoirs*. Montreal: Boréal, 1987.)

Brodribb, Somer. (1991). Discarnate Desires: Thoughts on Sexuality and Post-Structuralist Discourse. *Women's Studies International Forum, 14* (3), 135-142.

Broekman, Jan. (1977). *Structuralism*. Amsterdam: Reidel.

Brown, Laura S. (1990, Winter). What's addiction got to do with it: a feminist critique of codependence. *Psychology of Women, Newsletter of Division 35, American Psychological Association, 17* (1), 1, 3, 4.

Bunch, Charlotte. (1987). *Passionate Politics: Feminist Theory in Action*. New York: St Martin's Press.

Burdekin, Katharine. (1940). *Swastika Night*. (Pseudonym of author: Murray Constantine.) London: Victor Gollanz Ltd. (Reissued by The Feminist Press, New York, 1985, with an introduction by Daphne Patai.)

Burfoot, Annette. (1989, September). The Tenacity of the Alchemic Imagination. In Somer Brodribb (Ed.) *Feminist Theory: The Influence of Mary O'Brien*. Special Issue of *Resources for Feminist Research, 18* (3), 57-61.

Burke, Carolyn Greenstein. (1978, Summer). Report from Paris: Women's Writing and the Women's Movement. *Signs: Journal of Women in Culture and Society, 3* (4), 843-855.

Burke, Carolyn. (1981, Summer). Irigaray Through the Looking Glass. *Feminist Studies, 7* (2), 288-306.

Burke, Carolyn. (1989). Romancing the Philosophers: Luce Irigaray. In Dianne Hunter (Ed.) *Seduction and Theory, Readings of Gender, Representation, and Rhetoric*. Chicago: University of Illinois Press.

Butler, Judith. (1990). *Gender Trouble, Feminism and the Subversion of Identity*. New York: Routledge.

Callinicos, Alex. (1990a). *Against Postmodernism, A Marxist Critique*. New York: St. Martin's Press.

Callinicos, Alex. (1990b). Reactionary postmodernism? In R. Boyne and A. Rattansi (Eds.) *Postmodernism and Social Theory*. Houndmills: Macmillan.

Canguilhem, Georges. (1967, juillet). Mort de l'homme ou épuisement du cogito? [The death of man or the exhaustion of the cogito?] *Critique*, (242), 599-618.

Caplan, Paula J. and Margrit Eichler. (1990, Winter). Delusional Dominating Personality Disorder (DDPD). *Psychology of Women, Newsletter of Division 35, American Psychological Association, 17* (1), 5-6.

Caruso, Paolo. (1969). *Conversazione con Claude Lévi-Strauss, Michel Foucault, Jacques Lacan*. [Conversations with Claude Lévi-Strauss, Michel Foucault, Jacques Lacan.] Milan: Mursia.

Caws, Mary-Ann. (1973, Spring). Tel Quel: Text and Revolution. *Diacritics, 3* (i), 2-8.

Caws, Peter. (1968, Winter). What is Structuralism? *Partisan Review, 35* (1), 75-91.

Caws, Peter. (1990). *Structuralism: The Art of the Intelligible*. Atlantic Highlands, NJ: Humanities Press.

Chapsal, Madeleine. (1966, mai 16). Entretien: Michel Foucault. [Interview: Michel Foucault.] *La Quinzaine littéraire*, (5), 14-15.

Chiari, Joseph. (1975). Structuralism: Claude Lévi-Strauss, Michel Foucault, Louis Althusser. In *Twentieth Century French Thought: From Bergson to Lévi-Strauss*. London: Paul Elek.

Chodorow, Nancy J. (1989). *Feminism and Psychoanalytic Theory*. New Haven: Yale University Press.

Christian, Barbara. (1988). The race for theory. *Feminist Studies, 14* (1) 67-80.

Cixous, Hélène. (1976, Autumn). The Laugh of the Medusa. *Signs: Journal of Women in Culture and Society 1* (4), 875-893.

Cixous, Hélène. (1979). *Vivre l'Orange/To Live the Orange*. Paris: des femmes.

Cixous, Hélène and Catherine Clément. (1986). *The Newly Born Woman*. (Translated by Betsy Wing.) Minneapolis: University of Minnesota Press. (Originally published in 1975 as *La Jeune Née*, Union Générale d'Éditions.)

Clément, Catherine. (1983). *The Lives and Legends of Jacques Lacan*. (Translated by Arthur Goldhammer.) New York: Columbia University Press. (Originally published as *Vie et légendes de Jacques Lacan*, Grasset, 1981.)

Clément, Catherine. (1987). *The Weary Sons of Freud*. (Translated by Nicole Ball.) London: Verso. (Originally published as *Les fils de Freud sont fatigués*.)

Clément, Catherine. (1988). *Opera, or the Undoing of Women*. Foreword by Susan McClary. Minneapolis: University of Minnesota Press. (Originally published as *L'opéra ou la défaite des femmes*, Éditions Grasset and Fasquelle, 1979.)

Cocks, Joan. (1989). *The Oppositional Imagination, Feminism, Critique and Political Theory*. London: Routledge.

Collins, Margery and Pierce, Christine. (1976). Holes and Slime: Sexism in Sartre's Psychoanalysis. In Carol C. Gould and Marx W. Wartofsky (Eds.) *Women and Philosophy: Toward a theory of liberation.* New York: Perigee Books, G.P. Putnam's Sons.

Comte-Sponville, André. (1990, November 4). Stretched on the rack of Marxist thought. *Guardian Weekly*, p. 16ff.

Conley, Verena Andermatt. (1984). *Hélène Cixous: Writing the Feminine.* London: University of Nebraska Press.

Connor, Steven. (1989). *Postmodernist Culture, An Introduction to Theories of the Contemporary.* Oxford: Basil Blackwell.

Corea, Gena. (1985a). *The Mother Machine; Reproductive Technologies from Artificial Insemination to Artificial Wombs.* New York: Harper & Row.

Corea, Gena, et. al. (1985b). *Man-made Women.* London: Hutchinson.

Daly, Mary. (1978). *Gyn/Ecology, The Metaethics of Radical Feminism.* Boston: Beacon Press.

Dardigna, Anne Marie. (1981) *Les châteaux d'Éros ou les infortunes du sexe des femmes.* [The Castles of Eros or the misfortunes of women's sex.] Paris: Maspero.

Darwin, Charles. (1900). *The origin of species by means of natural selection: or, The preservation of favored races in the struggle for life and The descent of man and selection in relation to sex.* New York: The Modern Library.

Dean, Carolyn. (1986, Winter). Law and Sacrifice: Bataille, Lacan and the Critique of the Subject. *Representations, 13*, 42-62.

De Beauvoir, Simone. (1948). *The Ethics of Ambiguity.* Secaucus, N.J.: Citadel Press.

De Beauvoir, Simone. (1949, novembre). *Les structures élémentaires de la parenté par Lévi-Strauss.* [*The Elementary Structures of Kinship by Lévi-Strauss.*] *Les temps modernes*, (49), 943-949. (Review).

De Beauvoir, Simone. (1955). *Privilèges.* Paris: Gallimard. (Idées edition: *Faut-il brûler Sade?* [Must we Burn Sade?]).

De Beauvoir, Simone. (1968). *Force of Circumstance.* (Translated by Richard Howard.) Harmondsworth: Penguin. (Originally published as *La Force des choses*, Gallimard, 1963.)

De Beauvoir, Simone. (1974). *The Second Sex.* New York: Vintage Books. (Originally published in two volumes in 1949, *Le deuxième sexe*.)

De Koven, Marianne. (1989, Spring). Gendered Doubleness and the 'Origins' of Modernist Form. *Tulsa Studies in Women's Literature, 8* (1), 197-220.

De Lauretis, Teresa. (1985, Spring). The Violence of Rhetoric: Considerations on Representation and Gender. *Semiotica, 54* (1/2), 11-31.

De Lauretis, Teresa. (1989, Summer). The Essence of the Triangle or, Taking the Risk of Essentialism Seriously: Feminist Theory in Italy, the U.S. and Britain. *Differences: A Journal of Feminist Cultural Studies, 1* (2), 3-37.

Deleuze, Gilles and Félix Guattari. (1988). *A Thousand Plateaus, Volume II of Capitalism and Schizophrenia.* (Translated by Brian Massumi.) London: The Athlone Press. (Originally published as *Mille Plateaux*, 1980, Éditions de Minuit.)

Deleuze, Gilles. (1988). *Foucault.* (Translated and edited by Seán Hand.) Minneapolis: University of Minnesota Press.

de Man, Paul. (1988). La littérature française devant les événements, *Le Soir*, 20 January, 1942, 188-189. In Werner Hamacher, Neil Hertz and Thomas Keenan (Eds.) *Wartime Journalism, 1939-1943, By Paul de Man*, Lincoln: University of Nebraska Press.

Deming, Barbara. (1977, Summer). Remembering Who We Are: An Open Letter to Susan Saxe. *Quest, 4* (1), 52-74.

Derrida, Jacques. (1973). *Speech and Phenomena and Other Essays on Husserl's Theory of Signs*. (Translated by David B. Allison.) Evanston, Ill.: Northwestern University Press. (Originally published in 1967.)

Derrida, Jacques. (1976). *Of Grammatology*. (Translated by Gayatri Chakravorty Spivak, with a Translator's Preface.) Baltimore: John Hopkins University Press.

Derrida, Jacques. (1977). The Question of Style. In David B. Allison (Ed.) *The New Nietzsche*. New York: Dell Publishing Company.

Derrida, Jacques. (1978a). Becoming Woman. *Semiotext(e)*, (3), 128-137.

Derrida, Jacques. (1978b). Cogito and the History of Madness. In *Writing and Difference*. (Translated by Alan Bass.) Chicago: University of Chicago Press. (Originally published as *L'écriture et la différence*.)

Derrida, Jacques. (1978c). Force and signification. In *Writing and Difference*. Chicago: University of Chicago Press.

Derrida, Jacques. (1978d). Ellipsis. In *Writing and Difference*. (Translated by Alan Bass.) Chicago: University of Chicago Press.

Derrida, Jacques. (1980, Spring). The Law of Genre. *Glyph, 7*, 55-81.

Derrida, Jacques. (1981a). *Dissemination*. (Translated with an introduction and additional notes by Barbara Johnson.) Chicago: University of Chicago Press.

Derrida, Jacques. (1981b). *Spurs: Nietzsche's Styles*. (Translated by Barbara Harlow.) Chicago: University of Chicago Press.

Derrida, Jacques. (1982). The Ends of Man. In *Margins of Philosophy*. 109-136. (Translated by Alan Bass.) Chicago: University of Chicago Press. (Originally published in 1972, *Marges de la philosophie*.)

Derrida, Jacques. (1986). *Glas*. (Translated by J.P. Leavy and R. Rand.) Lincoln: University of Nebraska Press.

Derrida, Jacques. (1987a). The Political Theology of Language. Summer course at the Ninth International Institute for Semiotic and Structural Studies, University of Toronto.

Derrida, Jacques. (1987b). *The Post Card: From Socrates to Freud and Beyond*. (Translated by Alan Bass.) Chicago: University of Chicago Press. (Originally published as *La carte postale*, Paris: Aubier-Flammarion, 1980.)

Derrida, Jacques. (1988, Spring). Like the Sound of the Sea Deep Within A Shell: Paul de Man's War. *Critical Inquiry, 14* (3), 590-652.

Derrida, Jacques with Geoff Bennington. (1989a). On Colleges and Philosophy (Interview). In Lisa Appignanesi (Ed.) *Postmodernism, ICA Documents*. London: Free Association Books.

Derrida, Jacques. (1989b). *Of Spirit, Heidegger and the Question*. (Translated by Geoffrey Bennington and Rachel Bowlby.) Chicago: University of Chicago Press.

Descartes, René. (1958). *Descartes: Philosophical Writings*. (Selected and translated by Norman Kemp Smith.) New York: The Modern Library.

Descombes, Vincent. (1986). Introduction: Analytical versus Continental Philosophy. In *Objects of All Sorts, A Philosophical Grammar*. (Translated by Lorna Scott-Fox and Jeremy Harding.) Baltimore: Johns Hopkins University Press. (Originally published in 1983, *Grammaire d'objets en tous genres.*)

Descombes, Vincent. (1988). *Modern French Philosophy*. (Translated by L. Scott-Fox and J.M. Harding.) Cambridge: Cambridge University Press. (Originally published by Les Éditions de Minuit, 1979, *Le Même et L'Autre.*)

Descombes, Vincent. (1989). *Philosophie par gros temps*. [Philosophy in stormy weather.] Paris: Éditions de Minuit.

Dews, Peter. (1987). *Logics of Disintegration: Post-Structuralist Thought and the Claims of Critical Theory*. London: Verso.

Dews, Peter. (1989). From Post-Structuralism to Postmodernity. In Lisa Appignanesi (Ed.) *Postmodernism, ICA Documents*. London: Free Association Books.

Diamond, Irene and Lee Quinby. (Eds.) (1988). *Feminism and Foucault: Reflections on Resistance*. Boston: Northeastern University Press.

Dinnerstein, Dorothy. (1976). *The Mermaid and the Minotaur: Sexual Arrangements and Human Malaise*. New York: Harper & Row.

Di Stefano, Christine. (1983). Masculinity as Ideology in Political Theory: Hobbesian Man Considered. *Women's Studies International Forum, 6* (6), 633-644.

Domenach, Jean-Marie. (1967, mai). Le système et la personne. [The system and the person.] *Ésprit, 35* (360), 771-780.

Domenach, Jean-Marie. (1973, March). Le requiem structuraliste. [The Structuralist Requiem.] *Ésprit, 41* (430), 692-703.

Dreyfus, Hubert L. and Rabinow, Paul. (1986). *Michel Foucault, Beyond Structuralism and Hermeneutics*. Brighton: The Harvester Press.

duBois, Page. (1988). *Sowing the Body, Psychoanalysis and Ancient Representations of Women*. Chicago: University of Chicago Press.

Duchen, Claire. (1986). *Feminism in France, From May '68 to Mitterrand*. London: Routledge & Kegan Paul.

Duchen, Claire. (Ed.) (1987). *French Connections, Voices from the Women's Liberation Movement in France*. (Translated by Claire Duchen.) Amherst: University of Massachusetts Press.

DuPlessis, Rachel Blau. (1979). Romantic Thralldom in H.D. *Contemporary Literature, XX* (2), 178-203.

DuPlessis, Rachel Blau and Susan Stanford Friedman. (1981, Fall). "Woman is Perfect": H.D.'s Debate with Freud. *Feminist Studies, 7* (3), 417-430.

DuPlessis, Rachel Blau. (1986). *H.D. The Career of That Struggle*. Brighton: Harvester Press.

Dworkin, Andrea. (1981). *Pornography: Men Possessing Women*. New York: Perigee.

Ebert, Teresa L. (1991, January). Postmodernism's infinite variety. (Review of *Feminism/Postmodernism*, edited by Linda Nicholson.) *The Women's Review of Books, VIII* (4), 24-25.

Edwards, Anne. (1989, Summer). The Sex/Gender Distinction: Has it Outlived its Usefulness? *Australian Feminist Studies, 10*, 1 -12.

Ésprit, 35 (360). (1967, mai). Structuralismes: Idéologie et Méthode [Structuralisms: Ideology and Method.] (Special Issue).

Eagleton, Terry. (1989). The Emptying of a Former Self, Paul de Man. *Times Literary Supplement*, May 26-June 1, 573-574.

Eisenstein, Hester and Alice Jardine (Eds.) (1985). *The Future of Difference*. New Brunswick: Rutgers University Press.

Elliott, Gregory. (1991, Spring). The Lonely Hour of the Last Instance, Louis Pierre Althusser, 1918-1990. *Radical Philosophy, 57*, 28-30.

Eribon, Didier. (1989). *Michel Foucault (1926-1984)*. Paris: Flammarion, 1989.

Euripides. (1987). *The Bacchae and Other Plays*. (Translated by Philip Vellacott.) New York: Penguin.

Evans, Arthur. (1988). *The God of Ecstasy: Sex-Roles and the Madness of Dionysos*. New York: St. Martin's Press.

Falco, Maria J. (Ed.) (1987). *Feminism and Epistemology*: *Approaches to Research in Women and Politics*. New York: The Haworth Press.

Farias, Victor. (1989). *Heidegger and Nazism*. (Edited by Joseph Margolis and Tom Rockmore. Translated by Paul Burrell and Gabriel R. Ricci.) Philadelphia: Temple University Press.

Farrington, Benjamin. (1951). *Temporis Partus Masculus*: [The Masculine Birth of Time] An Untranslated Writing of Francis Bacon. *Centaurus, 1*, 193-205.

Feldstein, Richard and Judith Roof. (Eds.) (1989). *Feminism and Psychoanalysis*. Ithaca: Cornell University Press.

Felman, Shoshana. (1989). Paul de Man's Silence. *Critical Inquiry, 15* (4), 704-744.

Ferry, Luc & Alain Renaut. (1990). *French Philosophy of the Sixties, An Essay on Anti-humanism*. (Translated by Mary H.S. Cattani.) University of Massachusetts Press.

Ferry, Luc and Alain Renaut. (1990). *Heidegger and Modernity*. (Translated by Franklin Philip.) Chicago: University of Chicago Press. (Originally published as *Heidegger et les modernes*, Éditions Grasset & Fasquelle, 1988.)

Finn, Geraldine. (1981, September/October). Why Althusser Killed His Wife. *Canadian Forum*, 28-29.

Finn, Geraldine. (1989, September). Natural Woman, Cultural Man: the Anthropology of Male Hysteria and Father Right. In Somer Brodribb (Ed.) *Feminist Theory: The Influence of Mary O'Brien*. Special Issue of *Resources for Feminist Research/Documentation sur la recherche féministe, 18* (3), 24-28.

Flax, Jane. (1977/78, Winter). Do Feminists Need Marxism? *Isis, International Bulletin*, (6), 17-22.

Flax, Jane. (1986). Psychoanalysis as Deconstruction and Myth: On Gender, Narcissism and Modernity's Discontents. In Gunter H. Lenz, Kurt L. Shell (Eds.) *The Crisis of Modernity: Recent Critical Theories of Culture and Society in the United States and West Germany*. Boulder, CO: Westview Press.

Flax, Jane. (1990). *Thinking Fragments: Psychoanalysis, Feminism, and Postmodernism in the Contemporary West*. Berkeley: University of California Press.

Foreman, P. Gabrielle. (1991, September). The racism of postmodernism. *The Women's Review of Books, VIII* (12), pp. 12-13.

Forman, Frieda Johles with Caoron Sowton. (Eds.) (1989). *Taking Our Time: Feminist Perspectives on Temporality*. New York: Pergamon Press.

Foster, John Burt, Jr. (1981). *Heirs to Dionysus: A Nietzschean Current in Literary Modernism*. Princeton: Princeton University Press.

Foucault, Michel. (1973a). *Madness and Civilization*. (Translated by Richard Howard.) New York: Vintage Books. (Originally published in 1961, *Histoire de la Folie*.)

Foucault, Michel. (1973b). *The Order of Things: An Archaeology of the Human Sciences*. New York: Vintage Books. (Originally published in 1966, *Les Mots et Les Choses*.)

Foucault, Michel. (1974). *The Archaeology of Knowledge*. (Translated by A.M. Sheridan.) London: Tavistock Publications. (Originally published in 1969, *L'Archéologie du savoir*.)

Foucault, Michel. (1977a). *Language, Counter-Memory, Practice: Selected Essays and Interviews*. (Edited with an introduction by Donald F. Bouchard. Translated by Donald F. Bouchard and Sherry Simon.) Ithaca, New York: Cornell University Press.

Foucault, Michel. (1977b). Power and Sex: An Interview with Michel Foucault. Interviewed by Bernard-Henri Lévy. (Translated by David Parent.) *Telos, 32* (Summer), 152 -161. (Originally published in *Le Nouvel Observateur*, March 12, 1977.)

Foucault, Michel. (1978, 26 novembre). Il mitico capo della rivolta. *Corriere della Sera*. Milano.

Foucault, Michel. (1979, Autumn)."My Body, This Paper, This Fire," (Translated by Geoff Bennington.) *The Oxford Literary Review, 4* (1), 9-28. (Originally published in 1972, Mon corps, ce papier, ce feu. In *Histoire de la folie: l'âge classique*. 583-603 Paris: Gallimard.)

Foucault, Michel. (1980a). *The History of Sexuality*. (Translated by Robert Hurley.) New York: Vintage Books. (Originally published in 1976, *La Volonté de savoir*.)

Foucault, Michel. (1980b). *Michel Foucault, Power/Knowledge: Selected Interviews and Other Writings 1972-1977*. (Translated and edited by C. Gordon. L. Marshall, J. Mepham and K. Soper.) New York: Pantheon Books.

Foucault, Michel. (1984). Nietzsche, Genealogy, History. In Paul Rabinow (Ed.) *The Foucault Reader*. New York: Pantheon Books. (Originally published in 1971.)

Foucault, Michel. (1987). Questions of method: an interview with Michel Foucault. *Ideology and Consciousness*, (8), 3-14. (Previously published in a volume edited by Michelle Perrot, *L'impossible prison: Recherches sur le système penitentiaire au XIXe siècle*.)

Foucault, Michel. (1988). *Michel Foucault. Politics, philosophy, culture. Interviews and other writings, 1977-1984*. (Edited with an introduction by Lawrence D. Kritzman. Translated by Alan Sheridan and others.) New York: Routledge.

Fraser, Nancy. (1989). *Unruly Practices: Power, Discourse and Gender in Contemporary Social Theory*. Minneapolis: University of Minnesota Press.

Freeland, Cynthia A. (1986, Fall). Woman: Revealed or Reviled? *Hypatia, 1* (2), 49-70.

Freud, Sigmund. (1913). Totem and Taboo. *Standard Edition*, *3*, 1-161.

Freud, Sigmund. (1930). Civilization and Its Discontents, *Standard Edition*, *21*, 59-145.

Freud, Sigmund. (1939). Moses and Monotheism, *Standard Edition*, *23*, 3-137.

Friedman, Susan Stanford. (1981). *Psyche Reborn, The Emergence of H.D.* Bloomington: Indiana University Press.

Friedman, Susan Stanford. (1985, Fall). Palimpsest of Origins in H.D.'s Career. *Poesis, 6* (3/4), 56-73.

Friedman, Susan Stanford and Rachel Blau DuPlessis. (Eds.) (1990). *Signets, Reading H.D.* Madison: University of Wisconsin Press.

Froula, Christine. (1988, Fall). Rewriting Genesis: Gender and Culture in 20th Century Texts. *Tulsa Studies in Women's Literature, 7* (2), 197-220.

Frye, Marilyn. (1983). *The Politics of Reality: Essays in Feminist Theory.* Freedom, CA: The Crossing Press.

Fuss, Diana. (1989). *Essentially Speaking: Feminism, Nature and Difference.* New York: Routledge.

Gallop, Jane. (1982). *The Daughter's Seduction: Feminism and Psychoanalysis.* Ithaca, New York: Cornell.

Gallop, Jane. (1988). *Thinking Through the Body.* New York: Columbia University Press.

Garner, Shirley Nelson and Kanane, Claire and Sprengnether, Madelon. (Eds.) (1985). *The (M)other Tongue, Essays in Feminist Psychoanalytic Interpretation.* Ithaca and London: Cornell University Press.

Gatens, Moira. (1989, Summer). Woman and Her Double(s): Sex, Gender and Ethics. *Australian Feminist Studies, 10*, 33-47.

Gentis, Roger. (1986, décembre 1 au 15). L'après-Lacan, une ère nouvelle: Entretien avec Philippe Julien. [Post-Lacan, a new era. Interview with Philippe Julien.] *La Quinzaine Littéraire, 475* (20), 22.

Giddens, Anthony. (1987). Structuralism, Post-Structuralism and the Production of Culture. In Anthony Giddens and Jonathan H. Turner (Eds.) *Social Theory Today.* Stanford University Press.

Graybeal, Jean. (1990). *Language and "the feminine" in Nietzsche and Heidegger.* Bloomington: Indiana University Press.

Gross, Elizabeth. (1986). Philosophy, subjectivity and the body: Kristeva and Irigaray. In Carole Pateman & Elizabeth Gross (Eds.) *Feminist Challenges, Social and Political Theory.* Boston: Northeastern University Press.

Grosz, Elizabeth. (1989). *Sexual Subversions.* Sydney: Allen & Unwin.

Grosz, Elizabeth. (1990). *Jacques Lacan, a feminist introduction.* New York: Routledge.

Guattari, Félix and Gilles Deleuze. (1983). *Anti-Oedipus, Capitalism and Schizophrenia.* Volume 1. (Translated from the French by Robert Hurley, Mark Seem and Helen R. Lane. Preface by Michel Foucault.) London: The Athlone Press. (Originally published in 1972.)

Guthrie, W.K.C. (1955). *The Greeks and Their Gods.* Boston: Beacon Press.

H.D. (1956). *Tribute to Freud.* Boston: David R. Godine.

H.D. (1981, Fall). The Master. *Feminist Studies, 7* (3), 47-416.

Habermas, Jürgen. (1985). Neoconservative cultural criticism in the United States and West Germany: an intellectual movement in two political cultures. In Richard J. Bernstein (Ed.) *Habermas and Modernity*, Cambridge, MA: MIT Press.

Hamacher, Werner, Hertz, Neil and Keenan, Thomas. (Eds.) (1988). *Wartime Journalism: 1939-1943 By Paul de Man*. Lincoln: University of Nebraska Press.

Hamacher, Werner, Hertz, Neil and Keenan, Thomas. (Eds.) (1989). *Responses: On Paul de Man's Wartime Journalism*. Lincoln: University of Nebraska Press.

Harari, Josué V. (1979). *Textual Strategies: Perspectives in Post-Structuralist Criticism*. Ithaca, New York: Cornell University Press.

Harding, Sandra and Hintikka, Merrill B. (Eds.) (1983). *Discovering Reality: Feminist Perspectives on Epistemology, Metaphysics, Methodology and Philosophy of Science*. Boston: D. Reidel Publishing Co.

Harland, Richard. (1987). *Superstructuralism: The Philosophy of Structuralism and Post-Structuralism*. London: Methuen.

Hartman, Geoffrey. (1966). Structuralism: The Anglo-American Adventure. In Jacques Ehrmann (Ed.) *Structuralism*. 137-157. Garden City, NY: Anchor Books.

Hartsock, Nancy C.M. (1983). *Money, Sex and Power: Toward a Feminist Historical Materialism*. New York: Longman.

Hartsock, Nancy C.M. (1987, Winter). False Universalities and Real Differences: Reconstituting Marxism for the Eighties. *New Politics: A Journal of Socialist Thought, 1* (2), 83-96.

Hartsock, Nancy C.M. (1990). Foucault on Power: A Theory for Women. In Linda J. Nicholson (Ed.) (1990). *Feminism/Postmodernism*. New York: Routledge.

Hassan, Ihab. (1987). *The Postmodern Turn: Essays in Postmodern Theory and Culture*. Ohio State University Press.

Hawthorne, Susan and Renate Klein. (Eds.) (1991). *Angels of Power and other reproductive creations*. Melbourne: Spinifex Press.

Heidegger, Martin. (1962). *Being and Time*. (Translated by J. Macquarrie and E. Robinson.) New York: Harper & Row.

Hekman, Susan J. (1990). *Gender and Knowledge: Elements of a Postmodern Feminism*. Boston: Northeastern University Press.

Hermand, Jost. (1975). French Structuralism From a German Point of View. *Books Abroad, 49* (2), 212-221.

Hoagland, Sarah Lucia. (1988). *Lesbian Ethics: Toward New Value*. Palo Alto, CA: Institute of Lesbian Studies.

Holland, Peggy. (1978, Summer). Jean-Paul Sartre as a NO to Women. *Sinister Wisdom*, (6), 72-79.

Holloway, Wendy. (1984). Heterosexual Sex: Power and Desire for the Other. In Sue Cartledge and Joanna Ryan (Eds.) *Sex and Love, New Thoughts on Old Contradictions*. London: Women's Press.

hooks, bell. (1990). *Yearning, race, gender and cultural politics*. Boston: South End Press.

hooks, bell. (1991a, Spring). Essentialism and Experience. *American Literary History*. 3, 1, p. 180.

hooks, bell. (1991b). Sisterhood: Political Solidarity Between Women. In Sneja Gunew (Ed.) *A Reader in Feminist Knowledge*. New York: Routledge.

Horowitz, Gad. (1987). The Foucaultian Impasse: No Sex, No Self, No Revolution. *Political Theory, 15* (1), 61-80.

Hunter, Dianne. (1985). Hysteria, Psychoanalysis and Feminism: The Case of Anna O. In Shirley Nelson Garner et. al. (Eds.) *The (M)other Tongue*. Ithaca: Cornell University Press.

Hutcheon, Linda. (1988a). *The Canadian Postmodern: A Study of Contemporary English-Canadian Fiction*. Toronto: Oxford University Press.

Hutcheon, Linda. (1988b). *A Poetics of Postmodernism: History, Theory and Fiction*. New York: Routledge.

Hutcheon, Linda. (1989). *The Politics of Postmodernism*. New York: Routledge.

Huyssen, Andreas. (1984/1990). Mapping the Postmodern. In Linda Nicholson (Ed.) *Feminism/Postmodernism*. New York: Routledge.

Huyssen, Andreas. (1986). Mass Culture as Woman: Modernism's Other. In Tania Modleski (Ed.) *Studies in Entertainment, Critical Approaches to Mass Culture*. Bloomington: Indiana University Press.

Ingram, David. (1990). *Critical Theory and Philosophy*. New York: Paragon House.

Irigaray, Luce. (1969, automne). Le V(i)ol de la lettre. [The Theft/Rape of the Letter.] *Tel Quel*, (39), 64-77.

Irigarary, Luce. (1977, May). Women's exile, Interview with Luce Irigaray. *Ideology & Consciousness*, 57-76. (Translated by Couze Venn.)

Irigaray, Luce. (1980). *Amante marine de Friedrich Nietzsche*. [Marine Lover of Friedrich Nietzsche.] Paris: Les Éditions de Minuit. (Translated by Gillian Gill.) New York: Columbia University Press, 1991.

Irigaray, Luce. (1981, Autumn). And the One Doesn't Stir without the Other. (Translated by Hélène Vivienne Wenzel.) *Signs, 7* (1), 60-67.

Irigaray, Luce. (1983). An Interview with Luce Irigaray, by Kiki Amsberg and Aafke Steenhuis. (Translated by Robert van Krieken.) *Hecate, 9*, 192-202.

Irigaray, Luce. (1984). *Éthique de la différence sexuelle*. [The Ethics of Sexual Difference.] Paris: Les Éditions de Minuit. (Translation in preparation by Carolyn Burke for Cornell University Press.)

Irigaray, Luce. (1985a, mars). Femmes divines. [Divine women.] *Critique*, (454), 294-308. (Reprinted in *Sexes et parentés*.)

Irigaray, Luce. (1985b). *Parler n'est jamais neutre*. [To speak is never neutral/neutre.] Paris: Les Éditions de Minuit.

Irigaray, Luce. (1985c). *Speculum of the Other Woman*. (Translated by Gillian C. Gill.) Ithaca, New York: Cornell University Press. (Originally published in 1974, *Speculum, De l'autre femme*.)

Irigaray, Luce. (1985d). *This Sex Which Is Not One*. (Translated by Gillian C. Gill.) Ithaca, New York: Cornell University Press. (Originally published in 1977, *Ce sexe qui n'en est pas un*.)

Irigaray, Luce. (1986). The Fecundity of the Caress: A Reading of Levinas, "Totality and Infinity, section IV, B, 'The Phenomenology of Eros'". In Richard A. Cohen (Ed.) *Face to Face with Levinas*, New York: State University of New York Press. (Originally published in 1984, in *Éthique de la différence sexuelle*.)

Irigaray, Luce. (1987a, December). La Culture de la différence. [The Culture of Difference.] *Resources for Feminist Research/Documentation sur la recherche féministe, 16* (4), 7-8.

Irigaray, Luce. (1987b, mai). Égales à qui? [Equal to Whom?] *Critique*, (480), 420-437. Review of *En mémoire d'elle*. [In Memory of Her.]

Irigaray, Luce. (1987c). Is the Subject of Science Sexed? *Hypatia: a journal of feminist Philosophy, 2* (3), 65-87. (Translated by Carol Mastrangelo Bové.)

Irigaray, Luce. (1987d, mars). L'ordre sexuel du discourse in *Le sexe linguistique*. [The sexual order of discourse in *The linguistic sex*.] (Special Issue edited by Luce Irigaray.) *Langages*, (85), 81-121.

Irigaray, Luce. (1987e). *Sexes et parentés*. [Sex and Kinship.] Paris: Éditions de Minuit.

Irigaray, Luce. (1989, Winter). Sorcerer Love: A Reading of Plato's Symposium, Diotima's Speech. *Hypatia, 3* (3), 32-44. (Translated by Eleanor H. Kuykendall, this is a section of *Éthique de la différence sexuelle*, 1984.)

Jackson, Margaret. (1984a). Sexology and the social construction of male sexuality. In Lal Coveney, et. al. (Eds.) *The Sexuality Papers: Male sexuality and the social control of women*. London: Hutchinson.

Jackson, Margaret. (1984b). Sexology and the universalization of male sexuality (from Ellis to Kinsey, and Masters and Johnson.) In Lal Coveney, et. al. (Eds.) *The Sexuality Papers: Male sexuality and the social control of women*. London: Hutchinson.

Jameson, Fredric. (1972). *The Prison-House of Language: A Critical Account of Structuralism and Russian Formalism*. Princeton University Press.

Jameson, Fredric. (1984). Postmodernism, or the cultural logic of late capitalism. *New Left Review, 146*, 53-92.

Jameson, Fredric. (1990). *Postmodernism, or, The Cultural Logic of Late Capitalism*. Durham, North Carolina: Duke University Press.

Janssen-Jurreit, Marielouise. (1982). The Vaginal Death Threat. In Marielouise Janssen-Jurreit (Ed.) *Sexism: The Male Monopoly on History and Thought*. (Translated by Verne Moberg.) New York: Farrar Straus Giroux.

Jardine, Alice A. (1985). *Gynesis: Configurations of Woman and Modernity*. Ithaca, New York: Cornell University Press.

Jay, Nancy. (1985). Sacrifice as Remedy for Having Been Born of Woman. In Clarissa W. Atkinson, Constance H. Buchanan and Margaret R. Miles (Eds.) *Immaculate and Powerful: The Female in Sacred Image and Social Reality*. Boston: Beacon Press.

Jeffreys, Sheila. (1985). *The Spinster and her Enemies: Feminism and Sexuality (1880-1930)*. London: Pandora Press.

Jeffreys, Sheila. (1990). *Anticlimax: a Feminist Perspective on the Sexual Revolution*. London: The Women's Press.

Johnson, Miriam. (1987). Reproducing Male Dominance: Psychoanalysis and Social Structure. In Jerome Rabow, Gerald Platt and Marion Goldman (Eds.) *Advances in Psychoanalytic Sociology*. Malabar, Florida: Robert E. Krieger.

Jonas, Hans. (1967). *The Gnostic Religion: The Message of the Alien God and the Beginnings of Christianity*. Second edition. Boston: Beacon Press.

Jones, Ann Rosalind. (1981, Summer). Writing the Body: Toward an Understanding of *L'écriture féminine*. *Feminist Studies, 7* (2), 247-263.

Kahn, Robbie Pfeufer. (1989, September). Mother's Milk: The "Moment of Nurture" Revisited. In Somer Brodribb (Ed.) *Feminist Theory: The Influence of Mary O'Brien*. Special Issue of *Resources for Feminist Research, 18* (3), 29-37.

Kaplan, Marion A. (1979). *The Jewish Feminist Movement in Germany: The Campaigns of the Jüdischer Frauenbund, 1904-1938*. Westport, CT: Greenwood Press.

Kaufmann, Walter. (1974). *Nietzsche: Philosopher, Psychologist, Antichrist*. Princeton, New Jersey: Princeton University Press.

Keating, Thomas. (1983). *And the Word was Made Flesh*. New York: Crossroad Publishing.

Keller, Evelyn Fox. (1985). *Reflections on Gender and Science*. New Haven: Yale University Press.

Kellner, Douglas. (1989a). *Jean Baudrillard: From Marxism to Postmodernism and Beyond*. Stanford: Stanford University Press.

Kellner, Douglas. (1989b). Introduction: Jameson, Marxism and Postmodernism. In Douglas Kellner (Ed.) *Postmodernism/Jameson/Critique*. Washington: Maisonneuve Press.

Kennedy, Ellen. (1987). Nietzsche: Woman as Untermensch. In Ellen Kennedy and Susan Mendus (Eds.) *Women in Western Political Philosophy*. Brighton: Wheatsheaf Books.

Kintz, Linda. (1989). In-different Criticism, the Deconstructive "parole". In Jeffner Allen and Iris Young (Eds.) *The Thinking Muse: Feminism and Modern French Philosophy*. Bloomington: Indiana University Press.

Kirby, Vicki. (1991). *Corpus delicti*: the body at the scene of writing. In Rosalyn Diprose and Robyn Ferrell (Eds.) *Cartographies: Poststructuralism and the Mapping of Bodies and Spaces*. Sydney: Allen & Unwin.

Klein, Renate Duelli. (1983). The "Men-Problem" in Women's Studies: The Expert, the Ignoramus and the Poor Dear. *Women's Studies International Forum, 6* (4), 413-421.

Klein, Renate et al. (1991). *RU 486: Misconceptions, Myths and Morals*. Melbourne: Spinifex Press.

Kloepfer, Deborah Kelly. (1984, Spring). Flesh Made Word: Maternal Inscription in H.D. *Sagetrieb, 3* (1), 27-48.

Kofman, Sarah. (1979). *Nietzsche et la scène philosophique*. Paris: Inédit.

Kolodny, Annette. (1980). Dancing through the Minefield: Some Observations on the Theory, Practice, and Politics of Feminist Literary Criticism. *Feminist Studies, 6* (1), 1-25.

Kramarae, Cheris and Paula A. Treichler, with assistance from Ann Russo. (1985). *A Feminist Dictionary*. Boston: Pandora Press.

Krell, David Farrell. (1986). *Postponements, Woman, Sensuality and Death in Nietzsche*. Bloomington: Indiana University Press.

Krell, David Farrell. (1988). Consultations with the Paternal Shadow: Gasché, Derrida and Klossowski on Ecce Homo. In David Farrell Krell and David Wood (Eds.) *Exceedingly Nietzsche: Aspects of Contemporary Nietzsche Interpretation*. London: Routledge and Kegan Paul.

Kristeva, Julia. (1974/1981). La femme, ce n'est jamais [a Woman can never be defined], an interview by "psychoanalysis and politics" in *Tel Quel*, Autumn, 1974. Translated and quoted in Elaine Marks and Isabelle de Courtivron, *New French Feminisms: An Anthology*. New York: Schocken Books.

Kristeva, Julia. (1986). Stabat Mater. In Susan Rubin Suleiman (Ed.) *The Female Body in Western Culture*. Cambridge: Harvard University Press. (Originally published in 1983, as a section of *Histoires d'amour*.)

Kristeva, Julia. (1987). Talking About Polylogue. In Toril Moi (Ed.) *French Feminist Thought: A Reader*. New York: Basil Blackwell.

Kristeva Julia. (1987/1989). *Black Sun: Depression and Melancholia*. (Translated by Leon S. Roudiez.) New York: Columbia University Press. (Originally published in 1987 by Gallimard, *Soleil noir: dépression et melancolie*.)

Kroker, Arthur and David Cook. (1986). *The Postmodern Scene: Excremental Culture and Hyper-Aesthetics*. Montreal: New World Perspectives.

Kurzweil, Edith. (1980). *The Age of Structuralism: Lévi-Strauss to Foucault*. New York: Columbia University Press.

Kuykendall, Eleanor. (1989). Questions for Julia Kristeva's Ethics of Linguistics. In Jeffner Allan and Iris Marion Young (Eds.) *The Thinking Muse: Feminism and Modern French Philosophy*. Bloomington: Indiana University Press.

Lacan, Jacques. (1953). Some Reflections on the Ego. *International Journal of Psycho-Analysis. 34* (Part II), 11 -17.

Lacan, Jacques. (1966). *Écrits*. Paris: Éditions du Seuil. (Translated by Alan Sheridan. Published in English by W.W. Norton & Co., *Écrits: A Selection*.)

Lacan, Jacques. (1978). *The Four Fundamental Concepts of Psycho-analysis*. New York: W.W. Norton.

Lacan, Jacques. (1980). Dissolution. *Ornicar?* (20-21), 9-20.

Lacan, Jacques. (1985a). God and the *Jouissance* of *The* Woman. In Juliet Mitchell and Jacqueline Rose (Eds.) *Feminine Sexuality: Jacques Lacan and the école freudienne*. (Translated by Jacqueline Rose.) New York: W.W. Norton & Co. (Dieu et la jouissance de La femme. Livre XX. In *Le Séminaire de Jacques Lacan*, livre XX, Encore. Texte établi par Jacques-Alain Miller. Paris: Éditions du Seuil. Originally published 1975.)

Lacan, Jacques. (1985b). The Meaning of the Phallus. In Juliet Mitchell and Jacqueline Rose (Eds.) *Feminine Sexuality: Jacques Lacan and the école freudienne*. (Translated by Jacqueline Rose.) New York: W.W. Norton & Co. (Originally published in 1966.)

Lacan, Jacques. (1986). *Le Séminaire de Jacques Lacan, Livre VII, L'éthique de la psychanalyse*. [The Seminar of Jacques Lacan, Book VII, The ethics of psychoanalysis.] Paris: Éditions du Seuil. (Translation in preparation by W.W. Norton.)

Lacan, Jacques. (1989). Geneva Lecture on the Symptom. *Analysis, 1*, 7-26.

Lange, Lynda. (1983). Woman Is Not a Rational Animal: On Aristotle's Biology of Reproduction. In Sandra Harding and Merrill B. Hintikka (Eds.) *Discovering Reality: Feminist Perspectives on Epistemology, Metaphysics, Methodology, and Philosophy of Science*. Boston: D. Reidel Publishing Co.

Lash, Scott. (1984). Genealogy and the Body: Foucault/Deleuze/Nietzsche. *Theory, Culture and Society, 2* (2), 1-17.

Lash, Scott. (1990). *The Sociology of Postmodernism*. New York: Routledge.

Lazreg, Marnia (1988, Spring). Feminism and difference: the perils of writing as a woman on women in Algeria. *Feminist Studies, 14* (1), 81-107.

Leclerc, Annie. (1987). Parole de femme. In Toril Moi (Ed.) *French Feminist Thought: A Reader*. New York: Basil Blackwell. (An excerpt from the book *Parole de femme* originally published in 1974 by Éditions Bernard Grasset.)

Le Doeuff, Michèle. (1987). Women and Philosophy. In Toril Moi (Ed.) *French Feminist Thought: A Reader*. Oxford: Basil Blackwell. (Originally published in 1977.)

Le Doeuff, Michèle. (1989). *The Philosophical Imaginary*. (Translated by Colin Gordon.) Stanford University Press. (Originally published in 1980 as *L'Imaginaire philosophique*.)

Leidholdt, Dorchen and Janice Raymond. (Eds.) (1990). *The Sexual Liberals and the Attack on Feminism*. New York: Pergamon.

Lehman, David. (1991). *Signs of the Times: Deconstruction and the Fall of Paul de Man*. New York: Poseidon Press.

Lerner, Gerda. (1986). *The Creation of Patriarchy*. New York: Oxford University Press.

Lévi-Strauss, Claude. (1960). L'Analyse morphologique des contes russes. [A morphological analysis of Russian stories] *International Journal of Slavic Linguistics and Poetics*, III, 122-149.

Lévi-Strauss, Claude. (1966). *The Savage Mind*. London: Weidenfield and Nicolson. (Originally published in 1962, *La pensée sauvage*.)

Lévi-Strauss, Claude. (1969). *The Elementary Structures of Kinship*. Boston: Beacon Press. (Originally published in 1968, *Les structures élémentaires de la parenté*.)

Lévi-Strauss, Claude. (1975). *The Raw and the Cooked*. (Translated by John and Doreen Weightman.) New York: Harper and Colophon. (Originally published in 1965, *Le cru et le cuit*.)

Lévi-Strauss, Claude. (1981). *The Naked Man, Introduction to a Science of Mythology*. (Translated by John & Doreen Weightman.) New York: Harper & Row. (Also published in 1981, *L'homme nu*.)

Lévy, Bernard-Henri. (1977, Summer). Power and Sex: An Interview with Michel Foucault. *Telos*, (32), 152-161.

Lloyd, Geneviève. (1984). *The Man of Reason, "Male" and "Female" in Western Philosophy*. Minneapolis: University of Minnesota Press.

Lloyd, Geneviève. (1989, Summer). Woman as Other: Sex, Gender and Subjectivity. *Australian Feminist Studies, 10*, 13-22.

Lorde, Audre. (1981). The Master's Tools Will Never Dismantle the Master's House. In Cherríe Moraga and Gloria Anzaldúa (Eds.) *This Bridge Called My Back: Writings by Radical Women of Color*. New York: Kitchen Table Press.

Lorde, Audre. (1984). *Sister Outsider: Essays and Speeches by Audre Lorde.* Trumansburg, NY: The Crossing Press.

Lyotard, Jean-François. (1984). *The Postmodern Condition: A Report on Knowledge.* (Translated by Geoff Bennington and Brian Massumi.) Minneapolis: University of Minnesota Press. (Theory and History of Literature, Volume 10.) (Originally published in 1979.)

Lyotard, Jean-François and Élie Théofilakis. (1985). Les Petits Récits de Chrysalide [Short stories of Chrysalids.] Interview. In Élie Théofilakis (Ed.) *Modernes et après, Les Immatériaux.* Paris: Autrement.

Lyotard, Jean-François. (1989). Defining the Postmodern. In Lisa Appignanesi (Ed.) *Postmodernism, ICA Documents.* London: Free Assocation Books.

Macciocchi, Maria-Antonietta. (1983). *Deux Mille Ans de Bonheur.* [Two Thousand Years of Happiness.] (Translated from the Italian by Jean-Noël Schifano.) Paris: Grasset.

Major-Poetzl, Pamela. (1983). *Michel Foucault's Archaeology of Western Culture: Toward a New Science of History.* Chapel Hill: University of North Carolina Press.

Marcus, Jane. (1982, Spring). Storming the Toolshed. *Signs, 7* (3), 622-640.

Marks, Elaine. (1973). *Simone de Beauvoir: Encounters With Death.* New Brunswick: Rutgers University Press.

Marks, Elaine and de Courtivron, Isabelle. (Eds.) (1981). *New French Feminisms: An Anthology.* New York: Schocken Books.

Martin, Biddy. (1988). Feminism, Criticism, and Foucault. In Irene Diamond and Lee Quinby (Eds.) *Feminism and Foucault: Reflections on Resistance.* Boston: Northeastern University Press.

Mascia-Lees, Frances E., Sharpe, Patricia and Colleen Ballerino Cohen. (1989). The Postmodernist Turn in Anthropology: Cautions from a feminist perspective. *Signs, 15* (1), 7-33.

Matt, Daniel C. (1990). *Ayin*: The Concept of Nothingness in Jewish Mysticism. In Robert K. C. Forman (Ed.) *The Problem of Pure Consciousness, Mysticism and Philosophy.* New York: Oxford University Press.

McCaffery, Larry. (Ed.) (1986). *Postmodern Fiction: A Bio-Bibliographic Guide.* New York: Greenwood Press.

McDermott, Patrice. (1987, Fall). Post-Lacanian French Feminist Theory: Luce Irigaray. *Women and Politics, 7* (3), 47-64.

McGregor, Gaile. (1989, Autumn). The Mainstreaming of Postmodernism: A Status Report on the "New" Scholarship in Canada. *Journal of Canadian Studies/Revue d' études canadiennes, 24* (3), 146-173.

McNally, Sheila. (1984). The Maenad in Early Greek Art. In John Peradotto and J. P. Sullivan (Eds.) *Women in the Ancient World: The Arethusa Papers.* Albany: State University of New York Press.

Meese, Elizabeth A. (1986). *Crossing the Double-Cross: The Practice of Feminist Criticism.* University of North Carolina Press.

Meese, Elizabeth A. (1990). *(Ex)Tensions: Re-Figuring Feminist Criticism.* Urbana: University of Illinois Press.

Megill, Allan. (1985). *Prophets of Extremity: Nietzsche, Heidegger, Foucault, Derrida*. Berkeley: University of California Press.

Mellor, Anne K. (1988). Possessing Nature, The Female in *Frankenstein*. In Anne K. Mellor (Ed.) *Romanticism and Feminism*. Bloomington: Indiana University Press.

Merquior, J.G. (1989). Spider and Bee. In Lisa Appignanesi (Ed.) *Postmodernism, ICA Documents*. London: Free Association Books.

Milan Women's Bookstore Collective. (1990). *Sexual Difference: A Theory of Social-Symbolic Practice*. (Translated from the Italian by Patricia Cicogna and Teresa de Lauretis.) Bloomington: Indiana University Press.

Miles, Angela. (1993, forthcoming). *Transformative Feminisms: Integrative Global Perspectives*. New York: Routledge.

Millett, Kate. (1971). *Sexual Politics*. New York: Avon Books (Equinox).

Mills, Patricia Jagentowicz. (1987). *Woman, Nature and Psyche*. New Haven: Yale University Press.

Minh-ha, Trinh T. (1989). *Woman, Native, Other*. Bloomington: Indiana University Press.

Mitchell, Juliet. (1975). *Psychoanalysis and Feminism: Freud, Reich, Laing and Women*. New York: Vintage Books.

Modleski, Tania. (1982). *Loving with a Vengeance*. New York: Methuen.

Modleski, Tania. (1986). Femininity as Mas(s)querade: A Feminist Approach to Mass Culture. In Colin McCabe (Ed.) *High Theory, Low Culture*. Manchester: The University of Manchester Press.

Modleski, Tania. (1991). *Feminism without Women: Culture and Criticism in a "Postfeminist" Age*. New York: Routledge.

Moi, Toril. (1988, Spring). Feminism, Postmodernism and Style: Recent Feminist Criticism in the United States. *Cultural Critique*, 3-22.

Moore, Suzanne and Stephen Johnstone. (1989, January). Politics of Seduction (Interview with Jean Baudrillard). *Marxism Today*, 54-55.

Morgan, Robin. (1989). *The Demon Lover: On the Sexuality of Terrorism*. New York: W.W. Norton.

Morris, Meaghan. (1988). *The Pirate's Fiancée: Feminism Reading Postmodernism*. London: Verso.

Mussolini, Benito. (1952). The Doctrine of Fascism. (Translated by I.S. Munro.) In *Readings on Fascism and National Socialism*. Selected by Members of the Department of Philosophy, University of Colorado. Chicago: Swallows Press.

Neusner, Jacob. (1987). *What is Midrash?* Philadelphia: Fortress Press.

Newman, Amy. (1990, Summer). Aesthetics, Feminism, and the Dynamics of Reversal. *Hypatia, 5* (2), 20-32.

Newton, Judith. (1988, Spring). History as Usual?: Feminism and the "New Historicism". *Cultural Critique*, 87-121.

Nicholson, Linda J. (Ed.) (1990). *Feminism/Postmodernism*. New York: Routledge.

Nietzsche, Friedrich. (1954). *The Portable Nietzsche*. (Selected and translated by Walter Kaufmann.) New York: Viking Books.

Nietzsche, Friedrich. (1969). *Twilight of the Idols and The Anti-Christ.* (Translated with an introduction and commentary by R.J. Hollingdale.) Baltimore: Penguin Books. (Originally published in 1889 and 1895.)

Nietzsche, Friedrich. (1974). *The Gay Science.* (Translated with commentary by Walter Kaufmann.) New York: Vintage Books. (Originally published in 1882.)

Nietzsche, Friedrich. (1978). *The Will to Power.* (Translated by Walter Kaufmann and R.J. Hollingdale.) New York: Vintage Books. (Originally published 1901.)

Nietzsche, Friedrich. (1984). *Dithyrambs of Dionysus.* (Translated by R.J. Hollingdale.) Redding Ridge, CT: Black Swan Books Ltd.

Nietzsche, Friedrich. (1986a). *Thus Spoke Zarathustra, A Book for Everyone and No One.* (Translated with an introduction by R.J. Hollingsdale.) Harmondsworth: Penguin Books Ltd.

Nietzsche, Friedrich. (1986b). *Ecce Homo, How One Becomes What One Is.* (Translated with an introduction and notes by R.J. Hollingdale.) Harmondsworth: Penguin Books Ltd.

Nietzsche, Friedrich. (1987). *Beyond Good and Evil, Prelude to a Philosophy of the Future.* (Translated with an introduction and commentary by R.J. Hollingdale.) Harmondsworth: Penguin Books Ltd.

Norris, Christopher. (1987). *Derrida.* London: Fontana Press.

Norris, Christopher. (1988). *Paul de Man: Deconstruction and the critique of aesthetic ideology.* New York: Routledge.

Notar, Clea. (1986, Spring). The Omnipresent Language of the Patriarchy and the Boys of the Avant Garde. *Hejira: a journal for women's art, 3* (2), 29-32.

Nye, Andrea. (1989). *Feminist Theories and the Philosophies of Man.* New York: Routledge. (First published by Croom Helm, 1988.)

O'Brien, Mary. (1976). The Politics of Impotence. In William R. Shea and John King-Farlow (Eds.) *Contemporary Issues in Political Philosophy.* New York: Science History Publications.

O'Brien, Mary. (1981). *The Politics of Reproduction.* Boston: Routledge & Kegan Paul.

O'Brien, Mary. (1989a). Periods. In Frieda Johles Forman with Caoran Sowton (Eds.) *Taking Our Time, Feminist Perspectives on Temporality.* New York: Pergamon Press.

O'Brien, Mary. (1989b). *Reproducing the World, Essays in Feminist Theory.* Boulder: CO: Westview Press.

Oliver, Kelly. (1988, Spring). Nietzsche's Woman: The Poststructuralist Attempt To Do Away with Women. *Radical Philosophy, 48,* 25-29.

Owens, Craig. (1983). The Discourse of Others: Feminists and Postmodernism. In Hal Foster (Ed.) *The Anti- Aesthetic, Essays on Postmodern Culture.* Seattle: Bay Press.

Paglia, Camille. (1990). *Sexual Personae: Art and Decadence from Nefertiti to Emily Dickinson.* London: Yale University Press.

Parain-Vial, Jeanne. (1969). *Analyses structurales et idéologies structuralistes.* [Structural analyses and Structuralist ideologies.] Toulouse: Édouard Privat.

Parsons, Kathryn Pyne. (1974). Nietzsche and Moral Change. *Feminist Studies, 1* (2), 57-76.

Patai, Daphne. (1984a). Orwell's Despair, Burdekin's Hope: Gender and Power in Dystopia. *Women's Studies International Forum, 7* (2), 85-95.

Patai, Daphne. (1984b). *The Orwell Mystique: A Study in Male Ideology*. Amherst, MA: University of Massachusetts Press.

Pateman, Carol. (1989). *The Sexual Contract*. Stanford University Press.

Pavel, Thomas G. (1990). *The Feud of Language, A History of Structuralist Thought*. (Translated by Linda Jordan and Thomas Pavel.) Oxford: Basil Blackwell. (Originally published as *Le Mirage linguistique, Essai sur la modernisation intellectuelle*, Minuit, 1988.)

Penelope, Julia. (1990). *Speaking Freely: Unlearning the Lies of the Fathers' Tongues*. New York: Pergamon Press.

Piercy, Marge. (1982). *Circles on the Water: Selected poems of Marge Piercy*. New York: Alfred A. Knopf.

Pitkin, Hanna Fenichel. (1984). *Fortune Is a Woman: Gender and Politics in the Thought of Niccolò Machiavelli*. Berkeley: University of California Press.

Plato. (1956). *Plato's Symposium*. (Translated by Benjamin Jowett, with an introduction by Fulton H. Anderson.) Indianapolis: The Bobbs-Merrill Company, Inc.

Plaza, Monique. (1981, Summer). Our Damages and Their Compensation, Rape: The Will Not to Know of Michel Foucault. *Feminist Issues*, (3), 25-35.

Plaza, Monique. (1982, Spring). The Mother/The Same: Hatred of the Mother in Psychoanalysis. *Feminist Issues, 2* (1), 75-99. (Originally published in *Questions Féministes, 7* [February, 1980].)

Plaza, Monique. (1984a, Spring). Ideology Against Women. *Feminist Issues, 4* (1), 73-82.

Plaza, Monique. (1984b, Fall). Psychoanalysis: Subtleties and Other Obfuscations. *Feminist Issues, 4* (2), 51-58.

Poovey, Mary. (1988, Spring). Feminism and Deconstruction. *Feminist Studies 14* (1), 51-65.

Probyn, Elspeth. (1987). Bodies and Anti-Bodies: Feminism and the Postmodern. *Cultural Studies, 1* (3), 349-360.

Rabine, Leslie Wahl. (1988, Spring). A Feminist Politics of Non-Identity. *Feminist Studies, 14* (1), 11-31.

Ragland-Sullivan, Ellie. (1987). *Jacques Lacan and the Philosophy of Psychoanalysis*. Urbana: University of Illinois Press.

Ragland-Sullivan, Ellie. (1989). The Eternal Return of Jacques Lacan. In Joseph Natoli (Ed.) *Literary Theory's Future(s)*. Urbana: University of Chicago Press.

Rajchman, John. (1985). *Michel Foucault: The Freedom of Philosophy*. New York: Columbia University Press.

Rajchman, John. (1991). *Philosophical Events: Essays of the '80s*. New York: Columbia University Press.

Rassam, J. (1975). La déconstruction de la métaphysique selon M. Derrida, ou le retour au nominalisme le plus moyen-âgeux. [The deconstruction of metaphysics according to Derrida, or the return to the most Medieval nominalism.] *Revue de l'enseignement philosophique, 25* (2), 1-8.

Raulet, Gerard. (1983, Spring). Structuralism and Post-Structuralism: An interview with Michel Foucault. (Translated by Jeremy Harding.) *Telos, A Quarterly Journal of Critical Thought, 55,* 195-211.

Raymond, Janice. (1979). *The Transsexual Empire: The Making of the She-Male*. Boston: Beacon Press.

Raymond, Janice. (1986). *A Passion for Friends: Towards a Philosophy of Female Friendship*. London: The Women's Press.

Rhys, Jean. (1985). *Wide Sargasso Sea*. In *Jean Rhys, The Complete Novels*. New York: W.W. Norton.

Rich, Adrienne. (1979). *On Lies, Secrets and Silence: Selected Prose 1966-1978*. New York: W.W. Norton & Co.

Richlin, Amy. (1983). *The Garden of Priapus, Sexuality and Aggression in Roman Humor*. New Haven: Yale University Press.

Richlin, Amy. (1987). Ovid's Rape of Philomela. Presentation to the Third International Congress on Women, July, Dublin.

Riley, Denise. (1988). *"Am I That Name?" Feminism and the Category of "Women" in History*. Minneapolis: University of Minnesota Press.

Rooney, Ellen. (1989). *Seductive Reasoning: Pluralism as the Problematic of Contemporary Literary Theory*. Ithaca: Cornell University Press.

Rosen, Stanley. (1985, Fall). Post-Modernism and the End of Philosophy. *Canadian Journal of Political and Social Theory, IX* (3), 90-101.

Rosi. (1980, janvier). Le "comment-don". [The how-to-give; the Commander.] *Histoires d'elles, 19*, p. 10.

Ross, Andrew. (Ed.) (1989). *Universal Abandon? The Politics of Postmodernism*. Minneapolis: University of Minnesota Press.

Roudiez, Leon. (1975, Spring). With and Beyond Literary Structuralism. *Books Abroad, 49* (2), 204-212.

Rousseau, Jean-Jacques. (1979). *Emile: Or, On Education*. (Translated by Allan Bloom.) New York: Basic Books.

Rubin, Gayle. (1975). The Traffic in Women: Notes on the "Political Economy" of Sex. In Rayna R. Reiter (Ed.) *Toward an Anthropology of Women*. New York: Monthly Review Press.

Rubin, Gayle. (1979). Sexual Politics, the New Right, and the Sexual Fringe. In Samois (Ed.) *What Color is Your Handkerchief?: A Lesbian S/M Sexuality Reader*. Berkeley, CA: Samois.

Ruddick, Sara. (1989). *Maternal Thinking: Toward A Politics of Peace*. Boston: Beacon Press.

Rudolph, Kurt. (1983). *Gnosis*. (Translated and edited by Robert McLachlan Wilson.) San Francisco: Harper & Row.

Ruether, Rosemary Radford. (1975). *New Woman/New Earth: Sexist Ideologies and Human Liberation*. New York: Seabury.

Ruth, Sheila. (1980). *Issues in Feminism: A First Course in Women's Studies*. Boston: Houghton, Mifflin.

Ruth, Sheila. (1987, Winter). Bodies and Souls/Sex, Sin and the Senses in Patriarchy: A Study in Applied Dualism. *Hypatia, 2* (1), 149-163.

Sade, Donatien-Alphonse-François, Marquis de. (1965). *The Complete Justine: Philosophy of the Bedroom and other writings.* (Translated by Richard Seaver and Austryn Wainhouse.) New York: Grove Press. (Originally published in 1795, *La Philosophie dans le boudoir.)*

Sade, Donatien-Alphonse-François, Marquis de. (1968). *Juliette.* (Translated by Austryn Wainhouse.) New York: Grove Press. (Originally published in 1797, *Histoire de Juliette, ou les Prosperités du vice.)*

Sartre, Jean-Paul. (1968). *Search for a Method.* (Translated from the French with an introduction by Hazel E. Barnes.) New York: Vintage Books. (Originally published as Question de Méthode, the prefatory essay in *Critique de la raison dialectique, Volume I.)*

Sartre, Jean-Paul. (1971, Fall). Replies to structuralism: An interview with Jean-Paul Sartre. (Translated by Robert d'Amico.) *Telos,* (9), 110-116. (Originally published in *l'Arc,* 30.)

Sartre, Jean-Paul. (1976). *Critique of Dialectical Reason.* (Translated by Alan Sheridan-Smith.) London: New Left Books. (Originally published in 1960, *Critique de la raison dialectique.)*

Sartre, Jean-Paul. (1978). *Being and Nothingness.* (Translated by Hazel E. Barnes.) New York: Pocket Books. (Originally published in 1956, *L'Être et le néant.)*

Saxonhouse, Arlene. (1991). Aristotle: Defective Males, Hierarchy, and the Limits of Politics. In Mary Lyndon Shanley and Carole Pateman (Eds.) *Feminist Interpretations and Political Theory.* Pennsylvania State University Press.

Scheman, Naomi. (1982, March 18). *Truth and Honesty in Henry James and Adrienne Rich: Making it all up.* Paper presented at a meeting of the Ontario Institute for Studies in Education.

Schiesari, Julianna. *The Gendering of Melancholia: Feminism, Psychoanalysis, and the Symbolics of Loss in Renaissance Literature.* Unpublished manuscript.

Schreber, Daniel Paul. (1955). *Memoirs of My Nervous Illness.* (Translated, edited, with introduction, notes and discussion by Ida Macalpine and Richard Hunter.) London: William Dawson and Sons.

Scott, Joan W. (1988, Spring). Deconstructing Equality-versus-Difference: Or, The Uses of Poststructuralist Theory for Feminism. *Feminist Studies, 14* (1), 33-50.

Sebeok, Thomas A. (1986). *I Think I Am a Verb: More Contributions to the Doctrine of Signs.* New York: Plenum Press.

Segal, Charles. (1984). The Menace of Dionysus: Sex Roles and Reversals in Euripides' *Bacchae.* In John Peradotto and J. P. Sullivan (Eds.) *Women in the Ancient World: The Arethusa Papers.* Albany: State University of New York Press.

Shakespeare, William. (1964). *Macbeth* (The Arden Edition of the Works of William Shakespeare Ed.) London: Methuen & Co.

Shapiro, Gary. (1989). *Nietzschean Narratives.* Bloomington: Indiana University Press.

Simons, Margaret A. and Jessica Benjamin. (1979, Summer). Simone de Beauvoir: An Interview. *Feminist Studies, 5* (2), 330-345.

Simons, Margaret A., Ed. (1985). Beauvoir and Feminist Philosophy: Selected papers from the University of Pennsylvania International Conference, After The Second Sex: New Directions. Held in Philadelphia, April 5-8, 1984 (Special Issue). *Hypatia: A Journal of Feminist Philosophy, 8* (3).

Smith, Dorothy E. (1990). *Texts, Facts and Femininity: Exploring the Relations of Ruling.* London: Routledge.

Solanas, Valerie. (1983). *The SCUM Manifesto.* London: The Matriarchy Study Group, Publ.

Spelman, Elizabeth V. (1983). Aristotle and the Politicization of the Soul. In Sandra Harding and Merrill B. Hintikka (Eds.) *Discovering Reality: Feminist Perspectives on Epistemology, Metaphysics, Methodology, and Philosophy of Science.* Boston: D. Reidel Publishing Co.

Spender, Dale. (1983). *Women of Ideas and What Men Have Done to Them: From Aphra Behn to Adrienne Rich.* London: Ark Paperbacks. (First published in 1982.)

Spivak, Gayatri Chakravorty. (1983). Displacement and the Discourse of Woman. In Mark Krupnick (Ed.) *Displacement, Derrida and After.* Bloomington: Indiana University Press.

Spivak, Gayatri Chakravorty. (1987). *In Other Worlds: Essays in Cultural Politics.* New York: Methuen.

Spivak, Gayatri Chakravorty. (1989, Summer). In a Word. Interview [with Ellen Rooney]. "The Essential Difference, Another Look at Essentialism", Special Issue of *Differences: A Journal of Feminist Cultural Studies, 1* (2), 124-156.

Spivak, Gayatri Chakravorty. (1990). *The Post-Colonial Critic: Interview, Strategies, Dialogues.* (Edited by Sarah Harasym.) New York: Routledge.

Stanley, Liz. (1984). Whales and Minnows: Some sexual theorists and their followers and how they contribute to making feminism invisible. *Women's Studies International Forum, 7* (1), 53-62.

Stanley, Liz (1990). Recovering *Women* in History from feminist deconstruction. *Women's Studies International Forum, 13* (1/2), 151-157.

Stephens, Anthony. (1986). Nietzsche: the Resurrection of Parts. *Thesis Eleven,* (13), 94-109.

Stephanson, Anders and Daniela Salvioni. (1986/87, Winter). A Short Interview with Dario Fo. *Social Text, Theory/Culture/Ideology, 16,* 162-167.

Stephanson, Anders. (1989). Regarding Postmodernism – A Conversation with Fredric Jameson. In Douglas Kellner (Ed.) *Postmodernism/Jameson/Critique.* Washington: Maisonneuve Press.

Suleiman, Susan Rubin. (Ed.) (1985). *The Female Body in Western Culture: Contemporary Perspectives.* Cambridge, Massachusetts: Harvard University Press.

Thalmann, Rita. (1983, automne). Le national-socialisme: logique extrême du monopole culturel masculin. [National socialism: the ultimate logic of the masculine cultural monopoly.] *La revue d'en face, 14,* 45-55.

Théofilakis, Élie. *Modernes et après: Les Immatériaux.* Paris: Autrement.

Thiele, Bev. (1989 September). Dissolving Dualisms: O'Brien, Embodiment and Social Construction. In Somer Brodribb (Ed.) *Feminist Theory: The Influence of Mary O'Brien.* Special issue of *Resources for Feminist Research, 18* (3), 7-12.

Thompson, Denise. (1989, Summer). The "Sex/Gender" Distinction: A Reconsideration. *Australian Feminist Studies, 10,* 23-31.

Tucker, Robert. (Ed.) (1978). *The Marx-Engels Reader: Second edition.* New York: W.W. Norton & Co., Inc. (Originally published in 1867.)

Turkle, Sherry. (1978). *Psychoanalytic Politics: Freud's French Revolution*. New York: Basic Books.

Valadier, Paul. (1977). Dionysus versus The Crucified. In David B. Allison (Ed.) *The New Nietzsche*. New York: Delta Books, Dell Publ. Co., Inc.

Walker, Alice. (1983). *In Search of our Mothers' Gardens*. New York: Harcourt Brace Jovanovich.

Walker, Barbara G. (1983). *The Woman's Encyclopedia of Myths and Secrets*. San Francisco: Harper & Row.

Weed, Elizabeth. (Ed.) (1989). *Coming to Terms: Feminism, Theory, Politics*. New York: Routledge.

Weedon, Chris. (1987). *Feminist Practice and Poststructuralist Theory*. London: Basil Blackwell.

Weisstein, Naomi. (1971). Psychology Constructs the Female; or the Fantasy Life of the Male Psychologist – With Some Attention to the Fantasies of His Friends, the Male Biologist and the Male Anthropologist. *Social Education,* (April), 363-373.

Whitbeck, Caroline. (1989). A Different Reality: Feminist Ontology. In Ann Garry and Marilynn Pearsall (Eds.) *Women, Knowledge and Reality: Explorations in Feminist Philosophy*. London: Unwin Hyman, 1989.

Whitford, Margaret. (1988). Luce Irigaray's Critique of Rationality. In Morwenna Griffiths and Margaret Whitford (Eds.) *Feminist Perspectives in Philosophy*. Bloomington: Indiana University Press.

Whitford, Margaret. (1989). Rereading Irigaray. In Teresa Brennan (Ed.) *Between Feminism and Psychoanalysis*. New York: Routledge.

Wilson, E.O. (1975). *Sociobiology: The New Synthesis*. Cambridge: Harvard.

Wittig, Monique. (1971). *Les Guérillères*. (Translated by David Le Vay.) New York: Picador. (Originally published in 1969.)

Wittig, Monique. (1984, Fall). The Trojan Horse. *Feminist Issues, 4* (2), 45-49.

Woolf, Virginia. (1947). *Three Guineas*. London: The Hogarth Press.

Young, Robert. (1981). Post-Structuralism: An Introduction. In Robert Young (Ed.) *Untying the Text: A Poststructuralist Reader*. Boston: Routledge & Kegan Paul.

Zavala, Iris M. (1988). On the (Mis-)uses of the Post-modern: Hispanic Modernism Revisited. In Theo D'haen and Hans Bertens (Eds.) *Postmodern Fiction in Europe and the Americas*. Amsterdam: Rodopi.

Zavala, Iris M. (1989). The Social Imaginary: The Cultural Sign of Hispanic Modernism. *Cultural Studies, A Journal of Critical Theory, Literature and Culture, 1* (1), 23-41.

Permissions

Excerpt from *The Story of Abelard's Adversities*. Translated by J.T. Muckle. © 1964 Pontifical Institute of Studies. Reprinted by permission of the Pontifical Institute of Mediaeval Studies, Toronto.

Excerpt from *Juliette* by Marquis de Sade. Translated by Astryn Wainhouse. © 1968 Grove Press. Reprinted by permission of Grove Press, New York.

Excerpts from *The History of Sexuality vol. I: An Introduction* by Michel Foucault. Translated by Robert Hurley (Allen Lane, 1979). © 1976 by Editions Gallimard. Translation © 1978 Random House, Inc. Reprinted by permission of Georges Borchardt, Inc. and Penguin Books Ltd.

Excerpts from *The Order of Things* by Michel Foucault. © 1966 by Editions Gallimard. © 1970 by Random House, Inc. and © Tavistock Publications. Reprinted by permission of Georges Borchardt, Inc. and Tavistock Publications.

Excerpts from *Dissemination* by Jacques Derrida. © 1981 by The University of Chicago. © 1972 by Editions du Seuil. Reprinted by permission of The University of Chicago Press.

Excerpts from *The Politics of Reproduction* by Mary O'Brien. © 1981 Mary O'Brien. Reprinted by permission of HarperCollins Publishers.

Excerpts from *Feminist Theory and the Philosophies of Man* by Andrea Nye. © 1988 Andrea Nye. Reprinted by permission of Routledge, Chapman and Hall.

Excerpt from *The Naked Man* by Claude Lévi-Strauss. English translation © 1981 by Harper & Row, Publishers, Inc. and Jonathon Cape Ltd. Reprinted by permission of HarperCollins Publishers and Jonathon Cape Ltd.

Excerpts from *The Gay Science* by Friedrich Nietzsche. Translated by W. Kaufmann. © 1974 by Random House, Inc. Reprinted by permission of Random House, Inc.

Poem "In the Men's Room(s)", from *Circles on the Water* by Marge Piercy. © 1982 by Alfred A. Knopf. Reprinted by permission of Alfred A. Knopf and Wallace Literary Agency, Inc.

Translation of excerpt from Jacques Lacan, *L'éthique de la psychanalyse* with permission of W.W. Norton and Co. *The Seminar of Jacques Lacan, Book VII: The Ethics of Psychoanalysis*, 1959-60. Edited by Jacques-Alain Miller. Translated by Dennis Porter. New York: W.W. Norton, forthcoming.

Index